TO
BARCELONA

ANNELISE SORENSEN
RYAN CHANDLER

TRAVEL

G

Left **Interior, Casa Lleó Morera** Right **La Rambla**

LONDON, NEW YORK,
MELBOURNE, MUNICH AND DELHI
www.dk.com

Produced by Departure Lounge, London
Reproduced by Colourscan, Singapore
Printed and bound in China by Leo Paper Products Ltd
First American Edition, 2002
11 12 13 14 10 9 8 7 6 5 4 3 2 1
Published in the United States by DK Publishing,
375 Hudson Street New York, New York 10014

**Copyright 2002, 2011 © Dorling Kindersley
Limited, London
Reprinted with revisions 2004,
2005, 2006, 2008, 2009, 2010, 2011**

A catalog record for this book is available
from the Library of Congress.

ISSN 1479-344X
ISBN 978-0-75666-919-5

Within each Top 10 list in this book, no hierarchy of
quality or popularity is implied. All 10 are, in the editor's
opinion, of roughly equal merit.

Floors are referred to throughout in accordance
with British usage; ie the "first floor" is the
floor above ground level.

MIX
Paper from
responsible sources
FSC™ C018179
www.fsc.org

Contents

Barcelona's Top 10

The information in this DK Eyewitness Top 10 Travel Guide is checked regularly.
Every effort has been made to ensure that this book is as up-to-date as possible at the time of
going to press. Some details, however, such as telephone numbers, opening hours, prices,
gallery hanging arrangements and travel information are liable to change. The publishers
cannot accept responsibility for any consequences arising from the use of this book, nor for
any material on third party websites, and cannot guarantee that any website address in this
book will be a suitable source of travel information. We value the views and suggestions of
our readers very highly. Please write to: Publisher, DK Eyewitness Travel Guides,
Dorling Kindersley, 80 Strand, London, Great Britain WC2R 0RL or email travelguides@dk.com.

Cover: Front – **DK Images:** Alan Keehane clb; **SuperStock:** age fotostock main. Spine – **DK Images:**
Mike Dunning b. Back – **DK Images:** Max Alexander c; Naomi Peck cr; Paul Young cl.

Left **Jardins Mossèn Jacint Verdaguer** Centre **Bar, Pachito** Right **Terrace café, Barri Gòtic**

Left **Plaça de Sant Felip Neri, Barri Gòtic** Right **Stained-glass ceiling, Palau de la Música catalana**

Key to abbreviations
Adm *admission charge payable* **DA** *disabled access*

BARCELONA'S
TOP 10

BARCELONA'S TOP 10

🔟 Barcelona's Highlights

With warm, crystal-clear waters lapping its sandy shores and mountains nuzzling up to its northern edge, this glittering jewel in the Mediterranean is blessed with desirable geographical genes. From the buoyant, revamped port area to the atmospheric medieval streets of the Barri Gòtic and the beautiful Modernista *buildings of the Eixample, Barcelona has it all. A host of treasure-filled museums, architectural wonders, lively beaches and enchanting squares provide the icing on the cake.*

Sagrada Família
The enduring symbol of the city and its *Modernista* legacy is this church, Gaudí's other-worldly *pièce de résistance*. Piercing the Barcelona skyline are eight of the twelve planned spires *(above)* that have so far been built. *See pp8–10.*

La Rambla
Barcelona's centrepiece, this 1-km- (0.6-mile) long, thriving pedestrian thoroughfare *(above)* cuts a wide swathe through the old town, from Plaça de Catalunya to the glistening Mediterranean. *See pp12–13.*

Barcelona Cathedral
Dominating the heart of the old town is this magnificent Gothic Cathedral *(above)*, with a soaring, elaborate façade and a graceful, sun-dappled cloister containing palm trees and white geese. *See pp14–15.*

Parc de la Ciutadella
A verdant oasis in the city centre, Barcelona's largest park is criss-crossed with pleasant paths. It boasts a zoo, two museums and a lavish fountain *(right)*. *See pp16–17.*

5 Museu Nacional d'Art de Catalunya

The stately Palau Nacional *(right)* is home to the Museu Nacional d'Art de Catalunya (MNAC), which holds one of the most extensive collections of Romanesque art in the world. The works were rescued from churches around Catalonia in the 1920s. *See pp18–19.*

6 La Pedrera

Unmistakably Gaudí, this *Modernista* marvel *(below)* seems to grow from the very pavement itself. Fluid and eerily alive, its curving façade sprouts writhing wrought iron balconies. A cluster of mosaic chimneys keeps watch over the rooftop like shrewd-eyed knights. *See pp20–21.*

7 Fundació Joan Miró

An incomparable blend of art and architecture, this spacious museum, awash with natural light, showcases the work of Joan Miró, one of Catalonia's greatest 20th-century artists. Paintings, sculptures, drawings and textiles represent 60 prolific years. *See pp22–3.*

8 Museu Picasso

Housed in a medieval palace complex, this museum charts Picasso's rise to fame with an extensive collection of his early works, including numerous masterful portraits painted at the age of 13. *See pp24–5.*

9 Palau de la Música Catalana

No mere concert hall, the aptly named Palace of Catalan Music *(left)* is one of the finest, and most exemplary, *Modernista* buildings in Barcelona. *See pp26–7.*

10 Museu d'Art Contemporani & Centre de Cultura Contemporània

The city's gleaming contemporary art museum *(above)* and it's cutting-edge cultural centre have sparked an urban revival in the El Raval area. *See pp28–9.*

⑩ Sagrada Família

Nothing prepares you for the impact of the Sagrada Família. A tour de force of the imagination, Antoni Gaudí's church has provoked endless controversy. The church was only partially complete when Gaudí died in 1926 and, as a work in progress, it offers the unique chance to watch the eighth wonder of the world in the making. During the last 80 years and at incalculable cost, sculptors and architects have added their own touches to Gaudí's dream. Now financed by over a million visitors each year, it is estimated the project will be complete by 2026, the 100th anniversary of Gaudí's death.

Passion Façade

🍷 Try sitting in a terrace bar on nearby Avinguda Gaudí and drinking in the view of Gaudí's masterpiece illuminated at night.

📷 For the best photos, get to the temple before 8am: the light on the Nativity Façade is excellent and the tour buses haven't yet arrived.

Look out for the cryptogram on the Passion Façade, where all the numbers add up to the age of Christ at the time of his death.

• Entrances: C/Marina & C/Sardenya • Map G2 • 93 208 04 14 • Metro: Sagrada Família. • Open: Oct–Mar: 9am–6pm daily; Apr–Sep: 9am–8pm daily
• Adm: €12 or €16, including guided visit.
• Guided tours: May–Oct: 11am, 1pm, 3pm & 5pm daily; Nov–Apr: 11am & 1pm daily
• Limited DA

Top 10 Features

1. Nativity Façade
2. Passion Façade
3. Spiral Staircases
4. Spires
5. Hanging Model
6. Nave
7. Rosedoor Cloister
8. Crypt Museum
9. Apse
10. Unfinished Business

1 Nativity Façade
Gaudí's love of nature is visible in this façade *(above)*. Up to a hundred plant and animal species are sculpted into the stone, and the two main columns are supported by turtles.

2 Passion Façade
Started in 1978 and completed in 2002, this façade by Josep Subirachs represents the pain and sacrifice of Jesus. The difference between the Gothic feel of Subirachs' style and the intricacy of Gaudí's original work has not been without polemic.

3 Spiral Staircases
These helicoidal stone stairways, which wind up the bell towers, look like snail shells. They allow access to the towers.

4 Spires
For a close-up look at the gargoyles and mosaic tiling on the spires *(left)*, scale the bell tower stairs – or ride up in a lift. The views are equally spectacular *(see p55)*. Not for sufferers of vertigo.

For more churches in Barcelona See pp38–9

Hanging Model
This bizarre contraption in the crypt museum is testimony to Gaudí's ingenuity. Gaudí created his 3D construction – made of chains and small weighted sacks of sand – as a model for the arches and vaulted ceilings of the Colonia Güell crypt. No-one, in the history of architecture, had ever designed a building like this.

Sagrada Familia Floor Plan

Nave
The immense central body of the temple, now almost complete, is made up of leaning, tree-like columns with branches spreading out across the ceiling. Inspired by towering redwood trees, the overall effect is that of a stone forest.

Rosedoor Cloister
In the only cloister to be finished by Gaudí, the imagery is surprisingly modern. Thought to be inspired by the anarchist riots that began in 1909 (see pp30–31), the devil's temptation of man is represented by the sculpture of a serpent wound around a bomb-throwing rebel.

Crypt Museum
Gaudí now lies in the crypt (left) and his tomb is visible from the museum. Renovated to include audio-visual exhibits, the museum offers information about the temple's construction. The highlight is the maquette workshop, producing scale plaster and stone models for the ongoing work.

Apse
Adorned with lizards, serpents and two gigantic snails, the apse was the first section of the temple to be completed by Gaudí.

Unfinished Business
The church buzzes with activity: sculptors dangle from spires; stone masons carve huge slabs of stone; and cranes and scaffolding litter the site. Observing the construction in progress (left) enables visitors to grasp the monumental scale of the project.

Sight Guide
The entrances to the Sagrada Família are on C/Sardenya (along with the gift shop and one of the bell tower lifts) and C/Marina. On the C/Marina side, there are stairs (and another lift) to the other bell towers, and stairs to the museum below. If you don't want to pay the charge to use the lifts (€2), be warned – it's quite a climb.

Barcelona's Top 10

Left **Spiral staircase** Right **Detail of doorway, Passion Façade**

Key Sagrada Família Dates

1882
The first stone of the Sagrada Família is officially laid, with architect Francesc del Villar heading the project. Villar soon resigns after disagreements with the church's religious founders.

1883
The young, up-and-coming Antoni Gaudí is commissioned as the principal architect. He goes on to devote the next 40 years of his life to the project: by the end he even lives on the premises.

1889
The crypt is completed, ringed by a series of chapels, one of which is later to house the tomb of Gaudí.

1904
The final touches are made to the Nativity Façade, which depicts Jesus, Mary and Joseph amid a chorus of angels.

1925
The first of 18 bell towers, 100 m (328 ft) in height, is finished.

Stained-glass window

1926
On 10 June, Gaudí is killed by a tram while crossing the street near his beloved church. No-one recognizes the city's most famous architect.

1936
The advent of the Spanish Civil War brings construction of the Sagrada Família to a halt for some 20 years. During this time, Gaudí's studio and the crypt in the Sagrada Família are burned by revolutionaries, who despise the Catholic church for siding with the nationalists.

1987–1990
Artist Josep Maria Subirachs (b.1927) takes to living in the Sagrada Família just as his famous predecessor did. Subirachs completes the statuary of the Passion Façade. His angular, severe and striking sculptures draw both criticism and praise.

2000
On 31 December, the nave is at long last declared complete.

2010–2026
The vaults of the crossing and the apse have been renovated. The completion of the entire Sagrada Família is forecast for 2026, though this depends largely on funding. The building of the Sagrada Família – as Gaudí intended – relies on donations. With so many paying visitors pouring in daily, construction work is gaining momentum.

For more on Modernista *architecture* **See pp32–3**

Top 10 Gaudí Sights in Barcelona

1. Sagrada Familia
2. La Pedrera (1910)
   See pp20–21
3. Parc Güell (1900)
   See p112
4. Casa Batlló (1905)
   See p33
5. Palau Güell (1890)
   See p81
6. Bellesguard (1875)
7. Finca Güell (1887)
8. Casa Calvet (1899)
9. Colegio Teresiano (1890)
10. Casa Vicens (1885)

Antoni Gaudí

A flag bearer for the late 19th-century Modernista movement, Antoni Gaudí is Barcelona's most famous architect. A devout Catholic and a strong Catalan nationalist, he led an almost monastic existence, consumed by his architectural vision and living in virtual poverty for most of his life. In 2001, he was beatified and there are currently moves within the Catalan Catholic Church to declare him a saint.

Chimneypot, Casa Vicens

Gaudí's extraordinary legacy dominates the architectural map of Barcelona. His name itself comes from the Catalan verb gaudir, *"to enjoy", and an enormous sense of exuberance and playfulness pervades his work. As was characteristic of Modernisme, nature prevails, not only in the decorative motifs, but also in the very structure of Gaudí's buildings. His highly innovative style is also characterized by intricate wrought-iron gates and balconies and* trencadís *tiling.*

Antoni Gaudí (1852–1926)

Trencadís Tiling

Gaudí's revolutionary use of *trencadís* tiling, a decorative art form which consisted of smashing up ceramics and piecing them back together in mosaic patterns, is particularly prevalent at Parc Güell. Another fine example of this technique is the rooftop of La Pedrera where some of the chimneys were tiled using hundreds of broken *cava* bottles.

Trencadís-tiled lizard, Parc Güell

La Rambla

There may be no better place in the country to indulge in the Spanish ritual of the paseo (stroll) than on this wide, pedestrian street that is anything but pedestrian. An orgy of activity day and night, La Rambla is voyeuristic heaven. Spray-painted human statues stand motionless among the passing crowds; buskers croon crowd-pleasing classics; caricaturists deftly sketch faces; bustling stalls create an open-air market of bright bouquets and chattering parakeets; and round-the-clock kiosks sell everything from The Financial Times to adult videos.

Street performer

🟢 Kick back at the Cafè de l'Òpera at No. 74 *(see p42)* and soak up the Rambla ambience with a cool *granissat* (crushed ice drink) in hand.

⚫ Be warned: La Rambla is rife with pick-pockets.

• Map L2–L6 • Metro: Catalunya; Liceu; Drassanes • Gran Teatre del Liceu: open 11:30am–1pm daily (€4); guided tour of the main building: 10am (€8.70); guided backstage tour: 9:30am (€10); box office: open 1:30–8pm Mon–Fri, one hour before the performance Sat & Sun
• Mercat de La Boqueria: open 7am–8pm Mon–Sat • DA
• Palau de la Virreina: open 11am–2pm, 4–8pm Tue–Fri, 11am–8pm Sat & Sun; free; special exhibitions at Espai 2 €4.10
• DA • Arts Santa Mònica: open 11am–9pm Tue–Sun; free • Església de Betlem: open 8am–1:30pm & 5:30–8pm daily

Top 10 Attractions

1. Gran Teatre del Liceu
2. Monument a Colom
3. Mercat de La Boqueria
4. Flower & Bird Stalls
5. Font de Canaletes
6. Miró Mosaic
7. Palau de la Virreina
8. Arts Santa Mònica
9. Bruno Quadras Building
10. Església de Betlem

Gran Teatre del Liceu
The city's grand opera house *(above)*, founded in 1847, brought Catalan opera stars such as Montserrat Caballé to the world. Twice gutted by fire, it has been fully restored.

Monument a Colom
Pointing resolutely out to sea, this statue *(above right)* of Christopher Columbus (1888) commemorates his return to Spain after discovering the Americas. An elevator takes visitors to the top for sensational views *(see p54)*.

Mercat de La Boqueria
A cacophonous shrine to food, this cavernous market has it all, from stacks of fruit to suckling pigs and writhing lobsters.

For sights in the Barri Gòtic & La Ribera See pp70–73

Flower & Bird Stalls

Will the real Rambla please stand up? Amid the here-today-gone-tomorrow street performers and tourists, the true Rambla old-timers are the flower and bird stalls that flank the pedestrian walkway. Many of the stalls have been run by the same families for decades.

Font de Canaletes

Ensure your return to the city by drinking from this 19th-century fountain, inscribed with the legend that anyone who drinks from it "will fall in love with Barcelona and always return".

La Rambla

Miró Mosaic

Splashed on the walkway on La Rambla is a colourful pavement mosaic (above) by Catalan artist Joan Miró. His signature abstract shapes and primary colours unfold at your feet.

Palau de la Virreina

This Neo-Classical palace was built by the vicroy of Peru in 1778. The Palace of the Viceroy's Wife, as it translates, is split into Espai 2 for mixed media and Espai Miserachs for photography.

Arts Santa Mònica

Once the hallowed haunt of rosary beads and murmured prayers, this former 17th-century monastery was reborn in the 1980s. Thanks to a massive government-funded facelift, it is now a cutting-edge contemporary art centre. Temporary exhibitions run the gamut from large-scale video installations to sculpture and photography.

Bruno Quadras Building

Once an umbrella factory, this playful, late 19th-century building (left) is festooned with umbrellas.

Església de Betlem

A relic from a time when the Catholic Church was rolling in pesetas (and power), this hulking 17th-century church is a seminal reminder of when La Rambla was more religious than risqué.

For sights in El Raval **See pp80–83**

📷⁹ Barcelona Cathedral

From its Gothic cloister and Baroque chapels to its splendid, 19th-century façade, the Cathedral, dating from 1298, is an amalgam of architectural styles, each one paying homage to a period in Spain's religious history. Records show that an early Christian baptistry was established here in the 6th century, later replaced by a Romanesque basilica in the 11th century, which gave way to the current Gothic Cathedral. This living monument still functions as the Barri Gòtic's spiritual hub.

Main entrance

🍽 Bask in the Cathedral's Gothic glory at the outdoor terrace of Estruch café on Plaça de la Seu.

🎵 Organ and choral concerts are usually held monthly; enquire at the Pia Almoina. Watch *sardanes* – Catalonia's regional dance – in Plaça de la Seu (6pm Sat, noon Sun).

• Plaça de la Seu
• Map M3 • 93 342 82 60 • Metro: Liceu, Jaume I • Cathedral: 8am–12:45pm, 5:15–7pm Mon–Fri (until 6pm Sat & Sun); Church and cloister free access; lift to roof €2.50, choir €2; choir and museum €5 (1:30–4pm) • Casa de L'Ardiaca: open Sep–Jul: 9am–8:45pm Mon–Fri, 9am–1pm Sat; Aug: 9am–7:30pm Mon–Fri; free • Museu Diocesà: open Jun–Sep: daily; Oct–May: Tue–Sun (daily in Dec); €6 • DA

Top 10 Features

1. Main Façade
2. Choir Stalls
3. Cloister
4. Crypt of Santa Eulàlia
5. Capella del Santíssim Sacrament i Crist de Lepant
6. Capella de Sant Benet
7. Capella de Santa Llúcia
8. Nave & Organ
9. Pia Almoina & Museu Diocesà
10. Casa de L'Ardiaca

Main Façade
Flanking the entrance of the 19th-century façade *(right)* are twin towers, *Modernista* stained-glass windows and 100 carved angels. A seven-year restoration was completed in 2010.

Choir Stalls
The lavish choir stalls (1340), crowned with wooden spires, are decorated with colourful coats of arms *(left)* by artist Joan de Borgonya.

Cloister
Graced with a fountain, palm trees and roaming geese, the cloister dates back to the 14th century. The mossy fountain is presided over by a small, iron statue *(right)* of Sant Jordi (St George).

For more churches in Barcelona See pp38–9

Crypt of Santa Eulàlia

In the crypt's centre lies the graceful alabaster sarcophagus (1327) of Santa Eulàlia, Barcelona's first patron saint. Reliefs depict her martyrdom.

Capella del Santíssim Sacrament i Crist de Lepant

This 15th-century *capella* (chapel) features the Crist de Lepant, which, legend has it, guided the Christian fleet in its 16th-century battle against the Ottoman Turks.

Cathedral Floor Plan

Capella de Sant Benet

Honouring Sant Benet, the patron saint of Europe, this chapel showcases the 15th-century altarpiece *Transfiguration of the Lord (below)* by illustrious Catalan artist Bernat Martorell.

Capella de Santa Llúcia

This lovely Romanesque chapel is dedicated to Santa Llúcia, the patron saint of sight and vision. On her saint's day (13 December), the blind (*els cecs*) arrive in large numbers to pray at her chapel.

Nave & Organ

The immense nave *(below)* is supported by soaring Gothic buttresses, which arch over 16 chapels. The 16th-century organ looming over the interior fills the Cathedral with music during services.

Cathedral Guide

The most impressive entrance to the Cathedral is its main portal on Plaça de la Seu. As you enter, to the left lie a series of chapels, the organ and elevators that take you to the terrace for phenomenal views of the Barri Gòtic *(see p55)*. The Casa de L'Ardiaca lies to the right of the Cathedral's main entrance (at Carrer Santa Llúcia 1); the Museu Diocesà is to the left (at Avinguda de la Catedral 4).

Pia Almoina & Museu Diocesà

The 11th-century Pia Almoina, once a rest house for pilgrims and the poor, houses the Museu Diocesà, with Romanesque and Gothic works of art from around Catalonia.

Casa de L'Ardiaca

Originally built in the 12th century, the Archdeacon's House sits near what was once the Bishop's Gate in the city's Roman walls. Expanded over the centuries, it now includes a leafy patio with a fountain.

For more sights in the Barri Gòtic & La Ribera See pp70–73

Parc de la Ciutadella

Unfolding languidly just to the east of the old town, this green, tranquil oasis provides a welcome respite from the city centre. Built in the late 1860s on the site of a former military fortress (ciutadella), the park was artfully designed to offer Barcelona's citizens an experience of nature (shady corners, paths and greenhouses), recreation (rowing boats on the lake) and culture (two museums). The 1888 Universal Exhibition was held here and in preparation the city's great Modernista architects were brought in to work their magic. Lluís Domènech i Montaner created the Castell dels Tres Dragons (today the Natural Science Museum) and a young Antoni Gaudí helped design the flamboyant Cascade Fountain.

Statuary on the Cascade Fountain

Pick up a picnic at the bustling Santa Caterina food market (northwest of the park), or have a drink and a snack in the pretty outdoor café, El Drac, next to the Natural History Museum.

• Main entrance: Pg Pujades • Map R4
• Park: open 8am–sunset daily; free; • DA
• Zoo: open Nov–Feb: 10am–5pm daily; Mar–May & Oct: 10am–6pm daily; Jun–Sep: 10am–7pm daily; €16, children €9.60; • DA • Museu de Ciències Naturals (Castell dels Tres Dragons) & Museu de Ciències Naturals (Edifici Geologia): open 10am–6:30pm Tue–Sat, 10am–2:30pm Sun; €4 joint ticket (includes admission to Jardí Botànic); • DA

Top 10 Sights

1. Cascade Fountain
2. Arc de Triomf
3. Parc Zoològic
4. Llac
5. Antic Mercat del Born
6. Museu de Ciències Naturals (Castell dels Tres Dragons)
7. Museu de Ciències Naturals (Edifici Geologia)
8. Hivernacle & Umbracle
9. Parlament de Catalunya
10. *Homenatge a Picasso*

Cascade Fountain
One glimpse of this Baroque-style fountain *(right)* and you'll guess Gaudí had a hand in its creation. Winged horses with serpent tails rear over a waterfall and cherubs play amid jets of water.

Arc de Triomf
The grandest entrance to the park is the Arc de Triomf *(above)*, designed for the 1888 Exhibition by Josep Vilaseca i Casanoves. Topping the arch are angels tooting horns and offering wreaths.

Parc Zoològic
These colourful flamingos are just some of the stars at this child-friendly zoo, which also has pony rides, electric cars and a train *(see p62)*.

For sights in the Barri Gòtic & La Ribera See p70–73

Llac

Located in the centre of the park is a placid, man-made lake *(above)*, where it's possible to rent a boat for half an hour or more.

5 Antic Mercat del Born

The outline of Barcelona's medieval streets, houses, shops and palaces are revealed below this old market. The foundations date from 1714, the year Felipe V and his French allies entered the city.

Park Plan

6 Castell dels Tres Dragons

Domènech i Montaner's striking building is now part of the Natural Science Museum. The centrepiece is a huge whale skeleton, which hangs amid scores of stuffed animals, including a sabre-toothed tiger.

7 Edifici Geologia

Roam to your heart's content among 15,000 minerals, 14,000 rocks and over 100,000 palaeontological pieces, including a collection of Catalonian fossils.

8 Hivernacle & Umbracle

The late 19th-century Hivernacle and Umbracle greenhouses *(above)* are currently empty pending renovation work. The latter was designed by architect Josep Fontseré, the former by Josep Amargós.

9 Parlament de Catalunya

Housed in the lovely Palau de la Ciutadella *(below)*, 1891, is the Catalonian Parliament, where José Montilla (the President of Catalonia) and other political groups meet. In front is the Plaça d'Armes and a graceful water-lily pond with a sculpture (1907) by Josep Llimona.

10 Homenatge a Picasso

Antoni Tàpies toasts Picasso's cubist legacy with an abstract creation of his own. Tàpies' *Homage to Picasso* – a large glass cube filled with furnishings and abstract objects – requires some mental gymnastics to decipher its meaning.

Park Guide

Two metro stops provide access to the park: to approach through the grand Arc de Triomf, disembark at the metro station of the same name. If you're heading to the zoo, get off at Barceloneta metro stop, which is within easy walking distance.

For more of Barcelona's parks **See pp56–7**

17

🔟 Museu Nacional d'Art de Catalunya

Incorporating one of the most important medieval art collections in the world, the Museu Nacional d'Art de Catalunya (MNAC) is housed in the majestic Palau Nacional, built in 1929. The high point of the museum is the Romanesque art section, consisting of the painted interiors of churches from the Pyrenees dating from the 11th and 12th centuries. There is also the Thyssen-Bornemisza Collection, with works from the Gothic period to the Rococo; the Cambó Bequest, with works by the likes of Goya and Zurbarán; and a collection of works by Catalan artists from the early 19th century to the 1940s.

Palau Nacional façade

🍽 On the first floor there is a top-notch restaurant in impressively elegant surroundings. There's also a great café in the Oval Room.

📷 There are spectacular city views from the patio by the main entrance. There's a summer café here, too.

• Palau Nacional, Parc de Montjuïc
• Map B4
• Metro: Espanya
• 93 622 03 76
• www.mnac.cat
• Open 10am–7pm Tue–Sat, 10am–2:30pm Sun
• Adm: €8.50; con €6 (valid for two days within one month; free first Sun of the month; includes audioguide, available in several languages)
• Guided tours by appointment • DA

Top 10 Exhibits

1. Murals: Santa Maria de Taüll
2. Frescoes: Sant Climent de Taüll
3. Crucifix of Batlló Majesty
4. The Madonna of the Councillors
5. Cambó Bequest
6. Thyssen-Bornemisza Collection
7. *Ramon Casas and Pere Romeu on a Tandem* (1897)
8. *Confidant from the Batlló House* (1907)
9. *Woman with Hat and Fur Collar* (1937)
10. Numismatics

Murals: Santa Maria de Taüll

The well-preserved interior of Santa Maria de Taüll (c.1123) gives an idea of how incredibly colourful the Romanesque churches must have been. The symbolism concentrates on Jesus's early life, with scenes of the Wise Men and John the Baptist.

First Floor

Key

■ Romanesque Art Gallery

■ Modern Art; Drawings, Prints and Posters

■ Gothic Art Gallery

■ Renaissance and Baroque Art

■ Library

Frescoes: Sant Climent de Taüll

The Taüll interior *(left)*, is a melange of Byzantine, French and Italian influences. The apse is dominated by *Christ in Majesty* and the symbols of the four Evangelists and the Virgin, with the apostles beneath.

For more sights in Montjuïc **See pp88–91**

Crucifix of Batlló Majesty

This splendid, mid-12th-century wooden carving *(right)* depicts Christ on the cross with open eyes and no signs of suffering, as he has defeated death.

The Madonna of the Councillors
Commissioned by the city council in 1443, this work *(left)* by Lluis Dalmau is rich in political symbolism. It reveals the head councillors, supported by saints and martyrs, kneeling before an enthroned Virgin.

Cambó Bequest
Catalan politician Franscesc Cambó (1876–1974) bequeathed his enormous art collection to Catalunya; two large galleries contain artworks from the 16th to early 19th centuries, including Titian's *Girl Before A Mirror* (c. 1515).

Thyssen-Bornemisza Collection
A small but fine selection of Baron Thyssen-Bornemisza's vast collection. Among the magnificent paintings are Fra Angelico's sublime *Madonna of Humility* (1433–5) and a charmingly domestic *Madonna and Child* (c.1618) by Rubens.

Ramon Casas and Pere Romeu on a Tandem
This painting *(above)* depicts the painter Casas and his friend Romeu, with whom he began the bohemian tavern Els Quatre Gats (see pp44–5)

Confidant from the Batlló House
Among the fine *Modernista* furnishings are some exquisite pieces by Antoni Gaudí, including this undulating wooden chair *(left)* designed for confidences between friends.

Toilets
Café
Book Shop
Gift shop
Ticket office
Cloakroom
Stairs down to temporary exhibitions
Main Entrance
Toilets
Ground Floor

Woman with Hat and Fur Collar
Picasso's extraordinary depiction of his lover Maria-Thérèse Walter shows him moving beyond Cubism and Surrealism into a new personal language, which would simply become known as the "Picasso style".

Numismatics
The public numismatic collection dates back to the 6th century BC and features medals, coins (including those from the Greek colony of Empúries, which had its own mint from the 5th century BC), paper money and 15th-century Italian bills.

Gallery Guide
The Cambó Bequest and the Thyssen-Bornemisza Collections are on the main floor, off the Oval floor. On the first floor are the Modern art galleries, the photography collections and numismatics collections.

For information on the Font Màgica, located at the bottom of the steps that lead up to the Palau Nacional See p89

TOP 10 La Pedrera

Completed in 1910, this fantastic, undulating apartment block, with its out-of-this-world roof and delicate wrought ironwork, is one of the most emblematic of all Gaudí's works. La Pedrera (the Stone Quarry), also known as Casa Milà, was Gaudí's last great civic work before he dedicated the rest of his life to the Sagrada Família (see pp8–10). Restored to its former glory during the 1980s, La Pedrera now contains a museum dedicated to the architect, the exhibition centre of the Caixa de Catalunya, a furnished museum apartment, as well as private residences. What makes La Pedrera so magical is that every last detail, from door knobs to light fittings, bears the hallmark of Gaudí's visionary genius.

Façade, La Pedrera

⭐ During the summer months, a terrace bar on the roof (9pm–midnight Fri & Sat) allows visitors to enjoy a drink and live music amid the spectacular surroundings. Reservations essential *(see p47).*

🕐 For more information on temporary exhibitions held here, check the website of the Caixa de Catalunya (http://obrasocial. caixacatalunya.es)

• Pg de Gracia 92
• Map E2
• 90 240 09 73
• Metro: Diagonal
• Open: 9am–8pm daily (Nov–Feb: 9am–6:30pm; mid-Jun–late Jul: 9am–midnight Fri & Sat with reservation – 902 400 973)
• Adm: €10; con €6; Audioguides €3; Free admission to the temporary exhibition space.

Top 10 Features

1. Façade & Balconies
2. Roof
3. Espai Gaudí
4. El Pis de La Pedrera
5. Interior Courtyard: C/Provença
6. Gates
7. Temporary Exhibition Room
8. Interior Courtyard: Pg de Gràcia
9. Auditorium
10. La Pedrera Shop

1 Façade & Balconies
Defying the laws of gravity, La Pedrera's irreverent curved walls are held in place by undulating horizontal beams attached to invisible girders. Intricate wrought-iron balconies *(above)* are a perfect example of the artisan skill so integral to *Modernisme.*

2 Roof
The strikingly surreal rooftop sculpture park *(above)* has chimneys resembling medieval warriors and huge ventilator ducts twisted into bizarre organic forms *(below);* not to mention good views over the Eixample.

3 Espai Gaudí
A series of drawings, photos, maquettes and multimedia displays helps visitors grasp Gaudí's architectural wizardry. The museum is housed in the breathtaking, vaulted attic with its 270 brick arches forming skeletal corridors.

For more on Modernista *architecture* **See pp32–3**

El Pis de La Pedrera

This furnished *Modernista* flat *(right)*, decorated with period furniture, is a reconstruction of a typical bourgeois flat of late 19th-century Barcelona. It provides an engaging contrast between the staid middle-class conservatism of the era and the undeniable wackiness of the outer building itself.

Interior Courtyard: C/Provença

A brigade of guides takes a multitude of visitors through here each day. A closer inspection of this first courtyard reveals its beautiful mosaics and wall paintings lining a swirling, fairytale staircase.

Gates

The mastery involved in these huge, wrought-iron gates reveals the influence of Gaudí's predecessors – four generations of artisan metalworkers. The use of iron is integral to many of Gaudí's buildings.

Temporary Exhibition Room

This gallery space, run by the Caixa de Catalunya, holds regular free art exhibitions. It has shown work by Marc Chagall, Salvador Dalí, Francis Bacon and others. The ceiling *(above)* looks as if it has been coated with whisked egg whites.

Interior Courtyard: Pg de Gràcia

Like the first courtyard, here, too, is a grand, ornate staircase (left). This one is adorned with a stunning, floral ceiling painting.

Auditorium

The auditorium, housed in the basement, hosts regular events such as conferences and concerts. The adjacent garden offers visitors a pleasant glimpse of greenery.

La Pedrera Shop

A wide range of Gaudí-related memorabilia includes replicas of the warrior chimneys in ceramic and bronze.

Sight Guide

The Espai Gaudí (attic), El Pis (fourth floor) and the rooftop are all accessible by lift. The Temporary Exhibition Room is located upstairs from the Pg de Gràcia courtyard. The courtyards, staircases and shops are accessible from the entrance on the corner of Pg de Gràcia and C/Provença.

For more on Antoni Gaudí **See p11**

Fundació Joan Miró

This superb tribute to a man whose legacy as an artist and as a Catalan is visible city-wide was founded in 1975 by Joan Miró himself, who wanted it to be a contemporary arts centre. The museum holds more than 11,000 examples of the artist's colourful paintings, sketches and sculptures. The 400 or so on display trace Miró's development from an innovative Surrealist phase in the 1920s to his place as one of the world's most challenging masters in the 1960s.

Façade, Fundació Joan Miró

🍴 The restaurant-café here is one of the best dining options in the area *(see p93)*.

🎵 In summer, live experimental music is showcased in the Fundació auditorium, usually on Thursday nights.

The gift shop has an original range of Miróesque curiosities, from tablecloths to champagne glasses.

• Av Miramar, Parc de Montjuïc
• Map B4
• 93 443 94 70
• www.fundaciomiro-bcn.org
• Metro to Paral·lel, then funicular; or metro to Pl. Espanya, then bus 61 or PM (also called 193); or buses 50 or 55 from the city centre
• Open: 10am–7pm Tue, Wed, Fri & Sat (until 8pm Jul–Sep) 10am–9:30pm Thu, 10am–2:30pm Sun
• Adm: €8.50 (complete collection), con €6; €4 (temp exhibitions) • DA

Top 10 Works of Art

1 *Tapis de la Fundació* (1979)
2 *L'Estel Matinal* (1940)
3 *Pagès Català al Cla de Lluna* (1968)
4 *Home i Dona Davant un Munt d'Excrement* (1935)
5 *Sèrie Barcelona* (1944)
6 *Font de Mercuri* (1937)
7 Sculpture Room
8 Terrace Garden
9 Visiting Exhibitions
10 Espai 13

Tapis de la Fundació
This immense, richly-coloured tapestry *(right)* represents the culmination of Miró's work with textiles, which began in the 1970s.

L'Estel Matinal
This is one of 23 paintings on paper known as the *Constellation Series.* The *Morning Star's* introspective quality reflects Miró's state of mind at the outbreak of World War II, when he was hiding in Normandy. Spindly shapes of birds, women and heavenly bodies are suspended in an empty space.

Pagès Català al Cla de Lluna
The figurative painting *Catalan Peasant by Moonlight (left)* dates from the late 1960s and depicts two of Miró's favourite themes: earth and night. The figure of the peasant, a simple collage of colour, is barely decipherable, as the crescent moon merges with his sickle and the night sky takes on the rich green tones of earth.

For more on contemporary Catalan art, visit MACBA See pp28–9

4 Home i Dona Davant un Munt d'Excrement

Tortured, misshapen and lurid semi-abstract figures attempt to embrace against a black sky. Miró's pessimism at the time of *Man and Woman in Front of a Pile of Excrement (right)* would soon be confirmed by the outbreak of Spain's Civil War.

5 Sèrie Barcelona

The Fundació holds the only complete set of prints of this series of more than 50 black-and-white lithographs. This important collection is only occasionally on display.

6 Font de Mercuri

Alexander Calder donated the *Mercury Fountain* to the Fundació as a mark of his friendship with Miró. The work was an anti-fascist tribute, conceived in memory of the attack on the town of Almadén.

7 Sculpture Room

This room *(above)* focuses on Miró's sculptures from the mid-1940s to the late 1950s when he experimented first with ceramic, then bronze and finally with painted media and found objects. Outstanding works include *Sun Bird* (1946–9) and *Moon Bird* (1946–9).

8 Terrace Garden

More of Miró's vibrantly colourful and playful sculptures are randomly scattered on a spacious terrace *(right)*, from which you can appreciate city views and the rationalist architecture of Josep Lluis Sert's geometric building. The 3-m (10-ft) tall *Caress of a Bird* (1967) dominates the terrace.

10 Espai 13

This space showcases the experimental work of new artists from around the world. The exhibitions, which are based on a single theme each year, are usually radical and often make full use of new technologies.

9 Visiting Exhibitions

Over the years, these temporary exhibitions (usually held in the west wing) have included retrospectives of high-profile artists such as Rothko, Warhol and Magritte.

The New Gallery Extension

The Fundació celebrated its 25th anniversary in 2001 by opening an extension (known as Sala K) to house 25 Miró paintings on long-term loan from a private collection.

The Fundació's collection is vast; only a portion of it is on show at any one time.

Museu Picasso

Pay homage to the 20th-century's most acclaimed artist at this treasure-filled museum. Highlighting Pablo Picasso's (1881–1973) formative years, the museum boasts the world's largest collection of the artist's early works. At the tender age of 10, Picasso was already revealing remarkable artistic tendencies. In 1895, aged 14, he and his family moved from the town of La Coruña to Barcelona, where Picasso blossomed as an artist. From precocious schoolbook sketches and powerful family portraits to selected works from his Blue and Rose periods, the Museu Picasso offers visitors the rare chance to discover the artist as he was discovering himself.

Entrance, Carrer Montcada

○ The museum has a café with outdoor tables in summer. It offers a changing menu of daily specials at lunchtimes.

✪ The Museu Picasso is housed in a Gothic palace complex, replete with leafy court-yards, all of which can be explored.

• C/Montcada 15–23
• Map P4 • 93 256 30 00
• www.museupicasso. bcn.cat • Metro: Jaumel
• Open 10am–8pm Tue–Sun • Guided tours: noon Sat & Sun (Catalan), 6pm Tue & Thu (Spanish), 4pm Tue & Thu (English); (reservations essential, email museupicasso_ reserves@bcn.cat)
• Adm: €9 (guided tour); €5.80 (temporary shows); free first Sun of month (permanent collection) and every Sun 3–8pm; carnet for unlimited adm all year €10; €15 (for families) • DA

Top 10 Exhibits

1. *Hombre con boina* (1895)
2. *Autoretrato con peluca* (1896)
3. *Ciencia y Caridad* (1897)
4. Menu de Els Quatre Gats (1899–1900)
5. *Margot* & *La Nana* (1901)
6. *El Loco* (1904)
7. *Arlequín* (1917)
8. *Caballo corneado* (1917)
9. *Hombre sentado* (1917)
10. *Las Meninas* Series (1957)

Hombre con boina

This insightful portrait *(below)* reveals brush strokes – and a subject matter – that are far beyond a child who has just turned 13. No puppies or racing cars for the young Picasso; instead, he searched for the oldest men in the village and painted their portraits. The artist signed this portrait P Ruiz, because at this time he was still using his father's last name.

Autoretrato con peluca

At 14, Picasso painted a series of self-portraits, including *Self-portrait with Wig*, a whimsical depiction of how he might have looked during the time of his artistic hero, Velázquez.

Ciencia y Caridad

One of Picasso's first publicly exhibited paintings was *Science and Charity*. Picasso's father posed as the doctor.

For more museums See pp40–41

4 Menu de Els Quatre Gats
Picasso's premier Barcelona exhibition was in 1900, held at the Barri Gòtic café, Els Quatre Gats *(see p45)*. The artist's first commission was the pen-and-ink drawing of himself and a group of artist friends in top hats, which graced the menu of this bohemian hang-out.

5 Margot & La Nana

Picasso's *Margot (centre)* is an evocative painting depicting a call-girl as she waits for her next customer, while *La Nana* captures the defiant expression and stance of a heavily rouged female dwarf dancer.

6 El Loco
The Madman (left) is a fine example of Picasso's Blue period. This artistic phase, which lasted from 1901 to 1904, was characterized by melancholic themes and sombre colours.

7 Arlequín
A lifting of spirits led to Picasso's Neo-Classical period, typified by paintings like *Arlequín*, celebrating the light-hearted liberty of circus performers.

8 Caballo corneado
The anguished horse in this painting later appears in *Guernica*, which reveals the horrors of war. This work gives viewers the chance to observe the process that went into the creation of Picasso's most famous painting.

9 Hombre sentado
Works such as *Man Sitting (right)* confirmed Picasso's status as the greatest Analytic Cubist painter of the 20th century.

10 Las Meninas Series
Picasso's reverence for Velázquez culminated in this remarkable series of paintings *(below)*, based on the Velázquez painting *Las Meninas*.

Gallery Guide
The museum is made up of five inter-connected medieval palaces. The permanent collection is arranged chronologically on the first and second floors of the first three palaces. Temporary exhibitions – usually showcasing one modern artist – are housed on the first and second floors of the last two palaces.

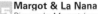

Barcelona's Top 10

For more sights in the Barri Gòtic & La Ribera **See pp70–73**

🔟 Palau de la Música Catalana

Barcelona's Modernista movement reached its aesthetic culmination in this magnificent concert hall (1905–8), designed by renowned architect Lluís Domènech i Montaner. The lavish façade, ringed by mosaic pillars and brick arches, just hints at what awaits within. Domènech's "garden of music" (as he called it) unfolds beyond the front doors, with each surface of the ornate foyer, from pillars to banisters, emblazoned with a flower motif. The concert hall – designed so that its height is the same as its breadth – is a celebration of natural light and forms, climaxing in a stained-glass, golden orb skylight that showers the hall with sunlight.

Façade, Palau de la Música Catalana

🍸 For a pre-concert, cocktail, settle in at the *Modernista* stained-glass bar just beyond the foyer.

🎵 Look out for *Els Diumenges Al Palau*, well-priced concerts on Sunday evenings. There are four cycles during the year, so check in advance.

Buy tickets for the shows and guided tours from the box office round the corner at C/Sant Francesc de Paula 2: (90 244 28 82), open 10am–9pm daily.

• Sant Pere Més Alt
• Map N2 • 90 244 28 82 • www.palaumusica.org • Metro: Urquinaona
• Guided tours every half hour: Sep–Jul: 10am–3:30pm; Aug & Easter: 10am–6pm (no advance booking)
• Adm: €10 • Limited DA

Top 10 Features

1. Stained-Glass Ceiling
2. Stage
3. Stained-Glass Windows
4. Busts
5. Horse Sculptures
6. Chamber Music Room
7. Lluís Millet Hall
8. Foyer & Bar
9. Façade
10. Concert & Dance Series

Stained-Glass Ceiling

Topping the concert hall is a breathtaking, stained-glass inverted dome ceiling *(right)*, surrounded by 40 angels. By day, light streams through the fiery red and orange stained glass, illuminating the hall.

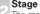

Stage

The main, semicircular stage *(above)* swarms with activity – even when no-one's performing. Eighteen mosaic and terracotta muses spring from the backdrop, playing everything from the harp to the castanets.

Stained-Glass Windows

Blurring the boundaries between the outdoors and the interior, Domènech encircled the concert hall with vast stained-glass windows to let in sunlight and reveal the changing times of day.

 For more on Modernista *architecture* **See pp32–3**

Horse Sculptures
Charging forth from the ceiling are winged horses (by the sculptor Eusebi Arnau), infusing the concert hall with movement and verve. Also depicted is a representation of Wagner's chariot ride of the Valkyries, led by galloping horses that leap toward the stage.

Busts
A bust of Catalan composer Josep Anselm Clavé (1824–74) celebrates the Palau's commitment to Catalan music. Facing him across the concert hall, a stern-faced, unruly-haired Beethoven *(above)* represents the hall's classical and international repertoire.

Chamber Music Room
Designed as a rehearsal space, the semicircular, accoustically-sound Chamber Music Room is a smaller version of the massive concert hall one floor above. In its centre is an inlaid foundation stone commemorating the construction of the Palau.

Lluís Millet Hall
Named after Catalan composer Lluís Millet, this immaculately preserved lounge boasts gorgeous stained-glass windows. On the main balcony outside are rows of stunning mosaic pillars *(right)*.

Foyer & Bar
Modernista architects worked with ceramic, stone, wood, marble and glass, all of which Domènech used liberally, most notably in the opulent foyer and bar.

Façade
The towering façade *(below)* reveals *Modernista* delights on every level. An elaborate mosaic represents the Orfeó Català choral society, founded in 1891.

Concert & Dance Series
Over 300 concerts and dance shows are staged each year, and seeing a show here is an experience not to be missed. For traditional Catalan dance and choral singing, look out for the *Cobla, Cor, i Dansa* series (usually begins February).

Orfeó Català
Perhaps the most famous choral group to perform here is the Orfeó Català, for whom the concert hall was originally built. This 90-person chorus performs regularly and holds a concert on 26 December every year. Book in advance.

For more sights in the Barri Gòtic & La Ribera **See pp70–73**

Museu d'Art Contemporani & Centre de Cultura Contemporània

Barcelona's sleek contemporary art museum looms in bold contrast to the surrounding area. Together with the nearby Centre de Cultura Contemporània (CCCB), the Museu d'Art Contemporani (MACBA) has provided a focal point for modern Barcelona since its opening in 1995, and has played an integral part in the rejuvenation of El Raval. MACBA's permanent collection includes a slew of big-name Spanish and international contemporary artists, while excellent temporary exhibits feature everything from painting to video installations. The CCCB serves as a crossroads of contemporary culture with cutting-edge art exhibits, lectures and film screenings.

Gallery space, MACBA

🍴 Snack at the nearby restaurant Pla dels Àngels (on Carrer Ferlandina), which offers budget-priced nouvelle/Catalan food to a hip crowd.

- *MACBA*
- *Plaça dels Àngels*
- *Map K2*
- *Metro: Catalunya*
- *93 412 08 10*
- *www.macba.cat*
- *Open late Sep–late Jun: 11am–7:30pm Mon & Wed–Fri, 10am–8pm Sat, 10am–3pm Sun; Jul–Sep: 11am–8pm Mon, Wed & Fri, 11am–midnight Thu, 10am–8pm Sat, 10am–3pm Sun*
- *Adm: €7.50 (all floors); €6 (temporary exhibitions); €3.50 (all floors) Wed • DA*

- *CCCB*
- *Montalegre 5 • Map K1 • Metro: Catalunya*
- *93 306 41 00 • www.cccb.org • Open: 11am–8pm Tue–Sun (to 10pm Thu) • Adm: €4.50; free first Wed of month, 8–10pm Thu and 3–8pm Sun*

Top 10 Features

1. Interior Corridors
2. Visiting Artist's Space
3. Revolving Permanent Collection
4. Façade
5. Capella MACBA
6. *A Sudden Awakening*
7. Thinking & Reading Spaces
8. El Pati de les Dones/CCCB
9. Temporary Exhibitions/CCCB
10. Plaça Joan Coromines

1 Interior Corridors
Space and light are omni-present in the walkways between floors. Look through the glass panels onto the Plaça dels Àngels for myriad images before you even enter the gallery spaces.

3 Revolving Permanent Collection
The permanent collection comprises over 2000 – mostly European – modern artworks, 10 per cent of which are on show at any one time. All major contemporary artistic trends are represented. This work *(right)* by Eduardo Arranz Bravo is titled *Homea* (1974).

2 Visiting Artist's Space
The *raison d'etre* of MACBA is this flexible area showing the best in contemporary art. Past exhibitions have included Zush and acclaimed painter Dieter Roth.

For more museums See pp40–41

4 Façade
American architect Richard Meier's stark, white, geometrical façade makes a startling impression against the backdrop of this dilapidated working-class neighbourhood. Hundreds of panes of glass reflect the skateboarders who gather here daily.

5 Capella MACBA
One of the few surviving Renaissance chapels in the city has been converted for use as MACBA's temporary exhibition space. It is located in a former convent across the Plaça dels Àngels.

6 A Sudden Awakening
One of the only pieces of art on permanent display is Antoni Tàpies' deconstructed bed (1992–3), with its bedding flung across the wall in disarray *(above)*. Its presence to the right of the main entrance underlines Tàpies' importance as a key player in the world of Catalan modern art.

7 Thinking & Reading Spaces
Pleasant and unusual features of MACBA are the white leather sofas between the galleries. Usually next to a shelf of relevant books and a set of headphones, these spaces provide the perfect resting spot to contemplate – and learn more about – the art.

8 El Pati de les Dones/CCCB
This courtyard *(left)* off Carrer Montalegre forms part of the neighbouring CCCB. An ultra-modern prismatic screen provides a mirror reflecting the 18th-century patio – a magical juxtaposition of different architectural styles.

9 Temporary Exhibitions/CCCB
Unlike MACBA, exhibitions at the CCCB tend to be more theme based than artist specific. Home to both a festival of cinema shorts (Sep) and the Sònar techno festival (Jun), the CCCB always manages to be at the forefront of the latest cultural trend.

10 Plaça Joan Coromines
The contrast between the modern MACBA, the University building, the Tuscan-style CCCB and the 19th-century mock-Romanesque church make this square one of the most enchanting in the city. It is home to the terrace restaurants of MACBA and CCCB.

Sights Guide
The MACBA and CCCB have separate entrances, though they share the Plaça Joan Coromines courtyard. The CCCB is accessible from C/Montalegre and MACBA from the Plaça dels Àngels. Both multi-level galleries have flexible display spaces.

For more sights in El Raval **See pp80–83**

Left **La Setmana Tràgica, 1909** Right **Olympic Games, 1992**

Stages in Barcelona's History

BC: The Founding of a City
Barcino, as the city was first known, was founded in the 3rd century BC by Carthaginian Hamilcar Barca. It was taken by the Romans in 218 BC, but played second fiddle in the region to the provincial capital of Tarragona.

4th–11th Centuries: Early Invasions
As the Roman Empire began to fall apart in the 5th century, the Visigoths took over the city, followed by the Moors in the 8th century. Around AD 800, Charlemagne conquered the area with the help of the Pyrenean counts.

EXPOSICION INTERNACIONAL DE BARCELONA 1929 EL ARTE EN ESPAÑA

Poster, 1929 International Exhibition

12th–16th Centuries: The Middle Ages
During this period, Barcelona was the capital of a Catalan empire that included much of modern Spain and parts of the Mediterranean. The city's fortune was built on commerce, but as neighbouring Castile expanded into the New World, trading patterns shifted and the Catalan dynasty faltered. Barcelona fell into decline and came under Castilian domination.

1638–1652: Catalan Revolt
In reaction to the oppressive policies set out in Madrid, now ruled by the Austrian Habsburgs, various local factions, known as *Els Segadors*, revolted. Fighting began in 1640 and dragged on until 1652, when the Catalans and their French allies were defeated.

19th Century: Industry & Prosperity
Booming industry and trade with the Americas brought activity to the city. Immigrants poured in from the countryside, laying the foundations of prosperity but also the seeds of unrest. The old city walls came down, broad Eixample avenues were laid out and workers crowded the old city neighbourhoods left behind by the middle classes.

1888–1929: The Renaixença
This new wealth, showcased in the International Exhibitions of 1888 and 1929, sparked a Catalan renaissance. *Modernista* mansions sprouted up, and the nationalist bourgeoisie sparked a revival of Catalan culture, particularly of literature, theatre and art.

1909–1931: The Revolutionary Years
But discontent brewed among workers, Catalan nationalists, communists, Spanish fascists, royalists, anarchists and

Share your travel recommendations on traveldk.com

republicans. In 1909, protests against the Moroccan war sparked a brutal riot, the *Setmana Tràgica* (Tragic Week). Lurching towards Civil War, Catalonia passed under a dictatorship before being declared a Republic in 1931.

1936–1975: Civil War & Franco

At the outbreak of war in 1936, Barcelona's workers and militants managed to fend off Franco's troops for a while. The city was taken by Fascist forces in 1939, prompting a wave of repression, particularly of the Catalan language which was banned in schools.

1975–1980s: Transition to Democracy

Franco's death in 1975 paved the way for democracy. The Catalan language was rehabilitated and, following the introduction of a new democratic constitution in Spain, Catalonia was granted regional autonomy. The first Catalan government was elected in 1980.

1992–Present Day: The Olympics & Beyond

Barcelona was catapulted onto the world stage in 1992 with the highly successful Olympics. Today, the city remains socialist in politics and ready to perceive itself as both Spanish and Catalan.

Civil War, 1936

Top 10 Historical Figures

1 Guifré the Hairy
The first Count of Barcelona (d. 897) is regarded as the founding father of Catalonia.

2 Ramon Berenguer IV
He united Catalonia and joined it with Aragon by marrying Princess Petronila in 1137.

3 Jaume I the Conqueror
This 13th-century warrior-king (d. 1276) conquered the Balearics and Valencia, laying the foundations for the empire.

4 Ramon Llull
Mallorcan philosopher and missionary, Llull (d. 1316) is the greatest figure in medieval Catalan literature.

5 Ferdinand the Catholic
King of Aragon and Catalonia (d.1516), he married Isabel of Castile, paving the way for the Kingdom of Spain's formation and the end of Catalan independence.

6 Idlefons Cerdà
19th-century urban planner who designed the Eixample.

7 Antoni Gaudí
An idiosyncratic and devout *Modernista* architect, Gaudí was responsible for Barcelona's most famous monuments.

8 Francesc Macià
This socialist nationalist politician proclaimed the birth of the Catalan Republic (1931) and Catalan autonomy (1932).

9 Lluís Companys
Catalan president during the Civil War. Exiled in France, he was arrested by the Gestapo in 1940 and returned to Franco, who had him executed.

10 Jordi Pujol
A centre-right regionalist politician, Pujol's Convergència i Unió coalition ruled Catalonia from 1980 to 2003.

Stained-glass windows, Casa Lleò Morera

Modernista Buildings

1 Sagrada Família
Dizzying spires and intricate sculptures adorn Gaudí's magical masterpiece. Construction began at the height of *Modernisme*, but is still in progress more than a century later. *See pp8–10.*

2 La Pedrera
This amazing apartment block, with its curving façade and bizarre rooftop, has all of Gaudí's architectural trademarks. Especially characteristic are the wrought-iron balconies and the ceramic mosaics decorating the entrance halls. *See pp20–21.*

3 Palau de la Música Catalana
Domènech i Montaner's magnificent concert hall is a joyous celebration of Catalan music. Ablaze with mosaic friezes, stained glass, ceramics and sculptures, it displays the full glory of the *Modernista* style. The work of Miquel Blay on the façade is rated as one of the best examples of *Modernista* sculpture in Barcelona. *See pp26–7.*

4 Hospital de la Santa Creu i de Sant Pau
In defiant contrast to the Eixample's symmetrical grid-like pattern, this ambitious project was planned around two avenues running at 45-degree angles to the Eixample streets. Started by Domènech i Montaner in 1905 and later completed by his son in 1930, the hospital pavilions are lavishly embellished with mosaics, stained glass and sculptures by Eusebi Arnau. The octagonal columns with floral capitals are inspired by those in the Monestir de Santes Creus *(see p124)*, to the south of Barcelona. *See p103.*

5 Fundació Tàpies
With a rationally plain façade alleviated only by its *Mudéjar*-style brick work, this austere building, dating to 1886, was originally home to the publishing house Montaner i Simon. It bears the distinction of being the first *Modernista* work to be designed by Domènech i Montaner, which explains why it has so few of the ornate decorative touches that distinguish his later works. Home to the Fundació Tàpies, it is now dominated by an enormous sculpture by the contemporary Catalan artist, Antoni Tàpies. *See p104.*

Chimneys and rooftop, Casa Batlló

A ticket for La Ruta Modernista *includes discounted entry to many* Modernista *buildings and a map/guide* **See p133**

Casa Batllò
6 Illustrating Gaudí's nationalist sentiments, Casa Batllò, on La Mansana de la Discòrdia *(see p103)*, represents an allegory of the legend of Sant Jordi *(see p39)*. The roof is the dragon's back and the balconies, sculpted in the form of carnival masks, are the skulls of the dragon's victims. The polychrome façade reveals Gaudí's remarkable use of colour and texture.
◈ Pg de Gràcia 43 • Map E2 • Open 9am–8pm daily • 93 216 03 06 • Adm €16.50 • DA

Casa Amatller
7 The top of Casa Amatller's façade bursts into a brilliant display of blue, cream and pink ceramics with burgundy florets. Architect Puig i Cadafalch's exaggerated decorative use of ceramics is typical of *Modernisme*. Tours include the *Modernista* apartment, a slide show in Amatller's former photography studio and describe the neo-medieval vestibule. ◈ Pg de Gràcia 41 • Map E2 • Tours & temporary exhibition: 10am–8pm Mon–Sat, 10am–3pm Sun; tours noon Mon–Fri • 93 487 72 17 • www.amatller.org • Adm €10 • DA

Palau Güell
8 This is a fine example of Gaudí's experiments with structure, especially the use of parabolic arches to orchestrate space. He also used unusual building materials, such as ebony and rare South American woods. *See p81.*

Casa de les Punxes (Casa Terrades)
9 Taking *Modernisme's* Gothic and medieval obsessions to extremes

that others seldom dared, Puig i Cadafalch created this imposing, castle-like structure between 1903 and 1905. Nicknamed the "House of Spines" because of its sharp, needle-like spires rising up from conical turrets, its true name is Casa Terrades. The flamboyant spires contrast with a façade that is, by *Modernista* standards, sparsely decorated.
◈ Diagonal 416 • Map F2 • Closed to public

Casa de les Punxes

Casa Lleò Morera
10 Ironwork, ceramics, sculpture and stained glass come together here in a synthesis of the decorative and fine arts. The interior of this house, by Domènech i Montaner, has some superb sculptures by Eusebi Arnau and some of the finest *Modernista* furniture in existence. ◈ Pg de Gràcia 35 • Map E3 • Closed to public

Following pages **Rooftop, La Pedrera**

Left **Plaça de Catalunya** Right **Plaça Reial, Barri Gòtic**

🔟 Perfect Squares

1 Plaça Reial

The arcaded Plaça Reial, in the heart of the Barri Gòtic, is unique among Barcelona's squares, with its old-world charm, gritty urbanization and Neo-Classical flair. It is home to majestic, mid-19th-century buildings, Gaudí lampposts, a slew of happening bars and clubs, and an entertaining and colourful crowd of inner-city denizens. *See p72.*

2 Plaça de Catalunya

Barcelona's nerve centre is the huge Plaça de Catalunya, a lively hub from which all the city's activity seems to radiate. This square is most visitors first real glimpse of Barcelona. The airport bus stops here, as do RENFE trains and countless metro and bus lines. The square's commercial swagger is evident all around, headed by Spain's omnipresent department store, El Corte Inglés *(see p139)*. Pigeons flutter chaotically in the square's centre, lively Peruvian

bands play to booming sound systems and hordes of travellers – from backpackers to tour groups – meander about. To add to the melting pot, the square is allegedly home to 25 people (mostly homeless immigrants). 🔊 *Map M1*

3 Plaça del Rei

One of the city's best preserved medieval squares, the Barri Gòtic's Plaça del Rei is ringed by grand buildings. Among them is the 14th-century Palau Reial *(see p71)*, which houses the Saló del Tinell, a spacious Catalan Gothic throne room and banqueting hall. 🔊 *Map N4*

4 Plaça de Sant Jaume

Weighty with power and history, this is the administrative heart of modern-day Barcelona. The *plaça* is flanked by the city's two key government buildings, the stately Palau de la Generalitat and the 15th-century Ajuntament. *See p71.*

Café, Plaça Sant Josep Oriol, Barri Gòtic

Sign up for DK's email newsletter on traveldk.com

5 Plaça de Rius i Taulet
The progressive, bohemian area of Gràcia, a former village annexed by Barcelona in 1897, still exudes a small-town ambience, where socializing with the neighbours means heading for the nearest *plaça*. Topping the list is this atmospheric square, with an impressive clock tower rising out of its centre. Bustling outdoor cafés draw buskers and a sociable crowd. ◈ Map F1

Façade, Plaça del Pi

6 Plaça de Sant Josep Oriol & Plaça del Pi
Old-world charm meets café culture in the Barri Gòtic's leafy Plaça de Sant Josep Oriol and Plaça del Pi, named after the pine trees (*pi*, in Catalan) that shade its nooks and crannies. The lovely Gothic church of Santa Maria del Pi *(see p38)* rises between the two squares. ◈ Map M3 & M4

7 Plaça Comercial
The buzzy Passeig del Born culminates in Plaça Comercial, an inviting square dotted with cafés and bars. It faces the 19th-century Born Market *(see p72)*, which is being transformed into a cultural centre and exhibition space. ◈ Map P4

8 Plaça del Sol
Tucked within the cosy grid of Gràcia, this square is surrounded by handsome 19th-century buildings. As evening descends, it becomes one of the most lively spots to start your night-time festivities, along with all the *Barcelonins* who mingle on the outdoor terraces. ◈ Map F1

9 Plaça de Santa Maria
The magnificent Església de Santa Maria del Mar *(see p76)* imbues its namesake *plaça*, in the El Born district, with a certain spiritual calm. Bask in its Gothic ambience, people watch, and soak up the sun at one of the outdoor terrace cafés. ◈ Map N5

10 Plaça de la Vila de Madrid
Mere steps from La Rambla *(see pp12–13)* is this spacious *plaça*, graced with the remains of a Roman necropolis. A remnant of Roman Barcino, the square sat just beyond the boundaries of the walled Roman city. A row of unadorned 2nd–4th-century AD tombs were discovered here in 1957. The complete remains are open to the public. ◈ Map M2

For parks & beaches See pp56–7

Left **Església del Betlem** Right **Temple Expiatori del Sagrat Cor**

Charming Churches & Chapels

1 Barcelona Cathedral
Barcelona's magnificent Gothic cathedral boasts an eye-catching façade and a peaceful cloister. *See pp14–15.*

2 Església de Santa Maria del Mar
The elegant church of Santa Maria del Mar (1329–83) is one of the finest examples of Catalan Gothic, a style characterized by measured simplicity. A spectacular stained-glass rose window illuminates the lofty interior. *See p76.*

3 Capella de Sant Miquel & Església al Monestir de Pedralbes
Inside the Monestir de Pedralbes *(see p111)* is a Gothic cloister and the Capella de Sant Miquel, decorated with murals by Catalan artist Ferrer Bassa in 1346. The adjoining Gothic church contains the alabaster tomb of Queen Elisenda, the monastery's founder. ✆ *C/Baixada del Monestir 14 • Map A1 • Open Oct–Mar: 10am–2pm Tue–Sat, 10am–3pm Sun; Apr–Sep: 10am–5pm Tue–Sat, 10am–3pm Sun (church also open 7–8:30pm)*

4 Església de Sant Pau del Camp
Founded as a Benedictine monastery in the 9th century by Guifre II, a count of Barcelona, this church was rebuilt the following century. Its sculpted façade

Santa Eulàlia, Barcelona Cathedral

and intimate cloister with rounded arches bear all the trademarks of the Romanesque style. *See p83.*

5 Església de Sant Pere de les Puelles
Built in 801 as a chapel for troops stationed in Barcelona, this *església* later became a spiritual retreat for young noble women. The church was rebuilt in the 1100s and is notable today for its Romanesque central cupola and a series of capitals topped with carved leaves. Look out for two stone tablets depicting a Greek cross, which are from the original chapel. ✆ *Pl de Sant Pere • Map P2 • Open 8:45am–1pm, 5–7:30pm Mon–Fri; 8:45am–1pm, 4:30–6:30pm Sat; 10am–2pm Sun*

6 Església de Santa Maria del Pi
This lovely Gothic church with its ornate stained-glass windows graces Plaça del Pi *(see p37).* ✆ *Pl del Pi • Map L3 • Open 9am–1:30pm, 4:30–9pm daily • DA*

7 Capella de Santa Àgata
Within the Palau Reial *(see p71)* is the medieval Capella de Santa Àgata, with its 15th-century altarpiece. The chapel can only be visited as part of the Museu d'Història de Barcelona *(see p40).* ✆ *Pl del Rei • Map N3 • Open 10am–8pm Tue–Sat (Oct–May: 10am–2pm, 4–7pm Tue–Sat), 10am–3pm Sun • Adm*

Temple Expiatori del Sagrat Cor

Mount Tibidabo is an appropriate perch for this huge, over-the-top Neo-Gothic church, topped with a gold Christ with outstretched arms. The name Tibidabo takes its meaning from the words, "I shall give you" (*tibi dabo*), uttered by the Devil in his temptation of Christ. Zealously serving the devoted, the priest here performs the Eucharist throughout the day. ◈ *Tibidabo • Map B1 • Open 10:30am–7:30pm daily*

Capella de Sant Jordi

Inside the Palau de la Generalitat *(see p71)* is this fine 15th-century chapel, dedicated to Catalonia's patron saint. ◈ *Pl Sant Jaume • Map M4 • Guided tours 10:30am–1:30pm 2nd & 4th Sun of month*

Església de Betlem

La Rambla was once dotted with religious buildings, most built in the 17th and 18th centuries when the Catholic Church was flush with money. This *església* remains one of the most important functioning churches from this period. ◈ *C/ Xuclà 2 • Map L3 • Open 8am–1:30pm & 5:30–8pm daily • DA*

Gothic nave, Capella de Santa Àgata

Top 10 Catalan Saints & Virgins

1 Sant Jordi
Catalonia's patron saint is Saint George, whose dragon-slaying prowess is depicted all over the city.

2 Virgin Mercè
She became the female patron saint of Barcelona in 1637. The most raucous festival in town is the Festes de La Mercè *(see p64)*.

3 Virgin of Montserrat
Catalonia's famous "Black Virgin" is the city's patron virgin.

4 Santa Eulàlia
Santa Eulàlia, Barcelona's first female patron saint, was martyred by the Romans when they took the city.

5 Santa Elena
Legend has it that Saint Helena converted to Christianity after discovering Christ's cross in Jerusalem in 346 AD.

6 Santa Llúcia
The saint of eyes and vision is celebrated on 13 December, when the blind come to worship at the Santa Llúcia chapel in the cathedral *(see pp14–15)*.

7 Sant Cristòfol
Though officially stripped of his sainthood as there was little evidence he existed, Saint Christopher was once the patron saint of travellers.

8 Sant Antoni de Padua
On 13 June, those seeking a husband or wife pray to the patron saint of love.

9 Santa Rita
Deliverer of the impossible, Santa Rita is prayed for by those searching for miracles.

10 Sant Joan
The night of Saint John *(see p64)* is celebrated with giant bonfires and fireworks.

Left **Frank Gehry's** *Peix* *Right* **Camp Nou Stadium**

TOP 10 Museums

1 Museu Nacional d'Art de Catalunya

Discover Catalonia's Romanesque and Gothic heritage at this impressive museum, housed in the 1929 Palau Nacional. Striking medieval frescoes and a collection of *Modernista* furnishings and artworks are highlights. *See pp18–19*.

2 Fundació Joan Miró

The airy, high-ceilinged galleries of this splendid museum are a fitting resting place for the bold, abstract works of Joan Miró, one of Catalonia's most acclaimed 20th-century artists. *See pp22–3*.

3 Museu Picasso

Witness the budding – and meteoric rise – of Picasso's artistic genius at this unique museum. One of the world's largest collections of the painter's early works. *See pp24–5*.

4 Museu d'Art Contemporani & Centre de Cultura Contemporània

Inaugurated in 1995, MACBA is Barcelona's centre for modern art. Combined with the neighbouring CCCB, the two buildings form an artistic and cultural hub in the heart of El Raval. Both regularly host temporary exhibitions: the MACBA showcases contemporary artists; the CCCB is more theme-based. *See pp28–9*.

5 Fundació Tàpies

Works by Catalan artist Antoni Tàpies are showcased in this graceful *Modernista* building. Venture inside to discover Tàpies' rich repertoire, from early collage works to large, abstract paintings, many alluding to political and social themes. *See p104*.

Terrace, Fundació Tàpies

6 Museu d'Història de Barcelona (MUHBA)

Explore the medieval Palau Reial and wander among the splendid remains of Barcelona's Roman walls and waterways at the city's history museum. The museum is partly housed in the 15th-century Casa Padellàs on the impressive medieval Plaça del Rei. *See p71*.

Badge, FC Barcelona

7 Museu del FC Barcelona

This shrine to the city's football club draws a mind-boggling number of fans paying homage to their team. Trophies, posters and other memorabilia celebrate the club's 100-year history. Also visit the adjacent Camp Nou Stadium. *See p111*.

8 Museu Marítim

Barcelona's formidable sea-faring history is showcased in the cavernous, 13th-century Drassanes Reials (Royal Ship-yards). The collection, which spans from the Middle Ages to the 19th century, includes a full-scale replica of the *Real*, the flagship galley of Don Juan of Austria, who led the Christians to victory against the Turks during the Battle of Lepanto in 1571. Also on display are model ships, maps and navigational instruments. *See p81.*

9 Museu Frederic Marès

Catalan sculptor Frederic Marès (1893–1991) was a passionate and eclectic collector. Housed here, under one roof,

are many remarkable finds amassed during his travels. Among the vast array of historical objects on display are Romanesque and Gothic religious art and sculptures, plus everything from dolls and fans to pipes and walking sticks. *See p72.*

Virgin, Museu Frederic Marès

10 CosmoCaixa Museu de la Ciència

Exhibits covering the whole history of science, from the Big Bang to the computer age, are housed in this modern museum. Highlights include an interactive tour of the geological history of our planet, an area of real Amazonian rain forest, and a planetarium. ◈ *Teodor Roviralta 47–51*
• *Map B1* • *Open 10am–8pm Tue–Sun*
• *Adm (free first Sun of month)*
• *DA* • *www.cosmocaixa.com*

Top 10 Quirky Museums/Monuments

1 Museu de Carrosses Fúnebres
Late 19th-century hearses reveal how *Barcelonins* of the past met their maker.
◈ *C/Sancho d'Àvila 2 • Map G3*

2 Centre d'Interpretació del Call
Artifacts from Barcelona's medieval Jewish community.
◈ *Pl de Manuel Ribé • Map M4*

3 Museu de la Màgia
A museum devoted to magic, with a collection dating from the 18th century.
◈ *Carrer Oli 6 • Map N4*

4 Museu dels Autòmates
A colourful museum of human and animal automatons. ◈ *Parc d'Atraccions del Tibidabo • Map B1*

5 Museu de la Xocolata
A celebration of chocolate, with interactive exhibits, edible city models and tastings.
◈ *Pl Pons i Clerch • Map P4*

6 Museu de Cera
Over 350 wax figures, from Marilyn Monroe to Franco and Gaudí. ◈ *Ptge de la Banca 7 • Map L5*

7 Museu del Calçat
Footwear from all ages, including shoes worn by famous folks. ◈ *Pl de Sant Felip Neri 5 • Map M3*

8 Museu del Perfum
Hundreds of perfume bottles from Roman times to the present. ◈ *Pg de Gràcia 39 • Map E2*

9 Cap de Barcelona
Pop artist, Roy Lichtenstein's "Barcelona Head" (1992).
◈ *Pg de Colom • Map N5*

10 Peix
Frank Gehry's huge shimmering fish sculpture (1992).
◈ *Port Olímpic • Map G5*

Many museums are free one day a month **See p140**

Barcelona's Top 10

Left **Cafè de l'Òpera, La Rambla** Right **Waterside dining, Port Vell**

Cafés & Light Bites

1 Café Bliss

Hidden down a tiny side street, in one of the loveliest Gothic squares in the old city, is this delightful café. There is a bright terrace, comfy sofas and a range of international magazines and newspapers to browse through. It is perfect for coffee, cakes, light meals or a romantic drink in the evening. *See p78.*

2 Café de l'Òpera

Kick back at this elegant, late 19th-century café while being tended to by vested *cambrers* (waiters). This former *xocolateria* (confectionary café) – named after the Liceu opera house opposite – still serves fine gooey delights such as *xurros amb xocolata* (strips of fried dough with thick chocolate). It's perfect for people-watching on La Rambla. ✪ *La Rambla 74* • *Map L4*

Bar Lobo

3 Drac Café

This tiny outdoor café is located next to the Castell dels Tres Dracs (now the Natural History Museum). It has cushioned wicker chairs, huge fans and a menu of fresh sandwiches, tapas and light meals. ✪ *Parc de la Ciutadella* • *Map Q4* • *Closed Dec–Feb*

4 Bar Lobo

This chic café is a popular brunch spot during the day, but it really comes alive in the evenings. From Thursday to Saturday, the second floor becomes a hip club, with guest DJs and a chill-out space. ✪ *Pintor Fortuny, 3* • *Map Q4* • *93 481 53 46* • *Closed Sun eve and for occasional events* • *DA*

5 Madame Jasmine

This relaxed, arty café is furnished with flea market finds, and the mismatched tables and chairs give it a boho-chic feel. There are delicious croissants at breakfast, huge salads at lunch-time and killer cocktails in the evenings. ✪ *Rambla de Raval 22* • *Map K4* • *60 788 04 43*

6 Bar Kasparo

This laid-back, outdoor café serves a sprightly menu of fresh, international fare with an Asiatic twist, including chicken curry and Greek salad. After the sun dips beneath the horizon, a bar-like vibe takes over, fuelled by beer and cider. ✪ *Pl Vicenç Martorell 4* • *Map L2* • *Closed Jan*

 All food and drink names are given in Catalan, but in many cases the Castilian variant is used just as commonly.

Cafè Salambó

7 Stylish evidence of Gràcia's intellectual and literary character, this airy, lofty café draws arty locals. While away the afternoon over a steaming *cafè amb llet* or munching on fresh salads and *entrepans* (sandwiches). *See p115.*

Cafè Salambó

Laie Llibreria Cafè

8 Tuck into a generous buffet of rice, pasta, greens, chicken and more at this charming, long-running Eixample café-bookshop. You can also opt for the well-priced vegetarian menu, including soup, salad and a main dish. *See p108.*

Granja Dulcinea

9 The *xocolateries* and *granjes* along Carrer Petritxol *(see p74)* have been satiating sugar cravings for decades. Among them is this old-fashioned café with to-die-for delights, from *xurros amb xocolata* to strawberries and whipped cream. In the summer, delicious *orxates* and *granissats* are on the menu. ◈ *C/ Potritxol 2 • Map L3 • Closes at 9pm*

El Jardí

10 This outdoor café-bar occupies a corner of the Gothic courtyard in front of the medieval hospital of Santa Creu. It is a great spot for a quiet drink, and there is live jazz in the summer. During the winter gas heaters are brought outside. *See p87.*

Top 10 Café Drinks

Cafè amb llet
1 Traditionally enjoyed in the morning, *cafè amb llet* is an ample cup of milky coffee.

Tallat & Cafè Sol
2 Need a fortifying caffeine fix? Try a *tallat*, a small cup of coffee with a dash of milk. A *cafè sol* is just plain coffee. In the summer, opt for either one *amb gel* (with ice).

Cigaló
3 For coffee with a bite, try a *cigaló (carajillo)*, which has a shot of alcohol, usually *conyac* (cognac), *whisky* or *ron* (rum).

Orxata
4 This sweet, milky-white drink made from a tuber (tiger nut) is a summertime favourite.

Granissat
5 Slake your thirst with a cool *granissat*, a crushed-ice drink, usually lemon flavoured.

Aigua
6 Stay hydrated with *aigua mineral* (mineral water) – *amb gas* is sparkling, *sense gas*, still.

Cacaolat
7 Chocolate lovers swoon over this chocolate-milk concoction, one of Spain's most popular sweet drink exports.

Una Canya & Una Clara
8 *Una canya* is roughly a quarter of a litre of *cervesa de barril* (draft beer). *Una clara* is the same, but with fizzy lemonade mixed in.

Cava
9 Catalonia's answer to champagne is its home-grown *cava*, of which Freixenet and Codorníu are the most famous brands.

Sangría
10 This ever-popular concoction of red wine, fruit juices, and liquors is ordered at cafés throughout the city.

For tips on dining and standard opening hours **See p138 & p140**

Left **Cinc Sentits** Right **Comerç 24**

Best Restaurants & Tapas Bars

1 Cal Pep
The line-up at this traditional, boisterous tapas bar includes top-notch cured hams and sausages, *truita de patates* (potato omelette), fresh *mariscs* (shellfish) and an array of daily tapas specials. *See p79.*

Wall tile advertising Barcelona restaurant

2 Noti
In a city where style often triumphs over substance, Noti stands out as a glorious exception. The decor is as stylish and glamorous as the crowd, but doesn't draw focus away from the main event – the exceptional Mediterranean and French cuisine, prepared with flair and originality. *See p109.*

3 El Asador d'Aranda
This palatial restaurant, perched high above the city on Tibidabo, dishes up the best in Castilian cuisine. Sizeable starters include *pica pica*, a tasty array of sausages, peppers and hams. The signature main dish is *lechazo* (young lamb) roasted in a wood-fired oven. *See p117.*

Paella

4 Kaiku
This unassuming, beachfront restaurant makes possibly the best paella in the city. It is on the menu as *arròs del xef*, and is prepared with smoked rice and succulent shellfish. The desserts are great too. In the summer book a table on the terrace and enjoy the views and sea breeze. *See p101.*

5 Inopia
It may be off the beaten track, but this bar is a must for dedicated foodies. The menu has gone back to basics, offering classic tapas such as *croquetas* and *patatas bravas,* prepared with the finest local ingredients. The tuna and tomato salad and anchovy-wrapped artichoke are both excellent. *See p109.*

6 Bar Ra
A funky, flower-filled oasis in El Raval, this juice-bar-café-restaurant is the place for organic, multi-cultural cuisine. Start your day with muesli or muffins and a fresh papaya or pear juice. The lunch and dinner menu might include Japanese tofu, Peruvian *ceviche* (raw seafood marinated in lemon) or a Cuban chicken and mango chutney dish. *See p87.*

7 Cinc Sentits
This elegant restaurant is known for its innovative cuisine. The tasting menu, created by

All food and drink names are given in Catalan, but in many cases the Castilian variant is used just as commonly.

chef Jordi Aretal, can be paired with specially chosen wines. The set-price lunch menu, available from Monday to Friday, is a bargain. *See p109.*

Casa Leopoldo
This comfortable, family-run restaurant serves some of the finest Catalan cuisine in the city. Fresh seafood is the highlight, with innovative platters of *bacallà* (salt cod), *llenguado* (sole) and *gambes* (prawns). *See p87.*

Bar-Restaurante Can Tomàs
A cheap, no-nonsense tapas bar in the uptown area of Sarrià. Every tapas-lover knows that the city's best *patates braves* and *patates amb alioli* are found here. Ask for the *doble mixta* to sample both. *See p117.*

Outdoor terrace, Bar Ra

Comerç 24
Perhaps one of the most adventurous restaurants in the city, Comerç 24 has an innovative head chef, Carles Abellan. The constantly changing menu consists of a series of *platillos* (small dishes), which fuse an extraordinary variety of flavours and textures. Try the quail lollipops, sea urchins with foie gras ice cream, or gold-wrapped macadamia nuts. *See p79.*

Top 10 Tapas

1 Patates Braves
This traditional tapas favourite consists of fried potatoes topped with a spicy sauce. Equally tasty are *patates* heaped with *alioli* (garlic mayonnaise).

2 Calamars
A savoury seafood option is *calamars* (squid) *a la romana* (deep-fried in batter) or *a la planxa* (grilled).

3 Pa amb Tomàquet
A key part of any tapas spread is this bread topped with tomato and olive oil.

4 Croquetes
A perennial favourite are croquettes; tasty fried morsels of bechamel, usually with ham, chicken or tuna.

5 Musclos o Escopinyes
Sample Barcelona's fruits of the sea with tapas of tasty mussels or cockles.

6 Truita de Patates
The most common tapas dish is this thick potato omelette, often topped with *alioli*.

7 Ensaladilla Russa
This "Russian salad" includes potatoes, onions, tuna (and often peas, carrots and other vegetables), all generously enveloped in mayonnaise.

8 Gambes al'allet
An appetizing dish of fried prawns (shrimp) coated in garlic and olive oil.

9 Pernil Serrà
Cured ham is a Spanish obsession. The best, and most expensive, is Extremadura's speciality, Jabugo.

10 Fuet
Embotits (Catalan sausages) include the ever-popular *fuet*, a dry, flavourful variety, most famously produced in the Catalonian town of Vic.

Elephant

Barcelona's Top 10

Night-time Hot Spots

1 Elephant
Housed in a *Modernista* villa, filled with candles and Moroccan lamps, this swish nightclub attracts a fashionable young crowd. But the real highlight is the garden, where lounge beds with diaphanous white drapes, fountains and giant elephant statues add an exotic touch. In winter, the outdoor dance floor is transformed into a spectacular tent. *See p116.*

Decoration, Elephant Club

2 Marsella
Founded in 1820, this atmospheric throwback, run by the fifth generation of the Lamiel family, sits in the heart of the Barri Xinès *(see p82)*. Marsella is one of the few places in town where you can enjoy the potent drink absinthe (*absenta*). Settle in at one of the wrought-iron *Modernista* tables, surrounded by ancient mirrors and old religious statues, and test your mettle with the potent yellow liquor that is specially bottled for the bar. *See p86.*

Sala BeCool

3 Otto Zutz
A swanky Barcelona nightlife institution, this three-storey disco is on the itinerary for well-heeled media types. The music verges on the mainstream, with big-name DJs spinning everything from techno to contemporary favourites. *See p116.*

4 CDLC
This trendy restaurant turns into a lively club as the evening goes on. It has a great location right on the beach and features guest DJs. Serves a range of cocktails. *See p100.*

5 Arena Madre
This gay disco, located in a basement, has an unpretentious atmosphere. Well-known for its dark room, Arena Madre also hosts leather shows, stripteases and comic performances. Music is mainly handbag house and Latin, while Sunday is 80s night.
🅢 Balmes, 32 • 93 487 83 42
• Open 12:30pm–5:30am daily • DA

6 La Terrrazza
Located inside the Poble Espanyol *(see p91)*, La Terrrazza is one of the most popular summer nightclubs in Barcelona. The patio becomes the dance-floor, the porches are bars and the garden provides a refreshing chill-out area. 🅢 Poble Espanyol, Av Marquès de Comillas • Map A3 • Open Thu–Sun (May–Sep) • Adm

For tips on drinking and standard opening hours **See p138 & p140**

Sala BeCool
This stylish club has become a staple on Barcelona's busy party scene. Situated in the chic, uptown Sant Gervasi neighbourhood, the multi-functional space has everything from live music, to club nights and theme parties. Downstairs there are hugely popular DJ sessions offering electro, techno and minimal music from Friday to Saturday; upstairs plays the latest indie hits. The website has a complete listing of the full weekly programme. *See p116.*

Inside Razzmatazz

La Pedrera de Nit
If Gaudí's undulating Pedrera rooftop *(see pp20–21)* looks surreal by day, experience it at night for full effect. On Friday and Saturday evenings between mid-June and late July, La Pedrera opens up its magical rooftop for a night of live music and *cava* drinking. Wander among Gaudí's mosaic chimneys, illuminated against the night sky, while enjoying jazz, flamenco fusion or tango. ◈ *C/Provença 261–265 • Map E2 • Reservations essential: call 90 210 12 12 • Adm • DA*

Jamboree
Venture underground – quite literally – to this popular, hopping jazz club-cum-nightclub in a vaulted space beneath Plaça Reial. Nightly live jazz sessions kick off around 11pm. DJs take over later with dance-inducing sounds. *See p77.*

Jamboree

Razzmatazz
This is nothing less than the city's best all-round nightlife venue. Music bands from around the world have played at Razzmatazz, and concerts have included Antony and the Johnsons, the Arctic Monkeys and Róisín Murphy. On Friday and Saturday nights (1am–6am), the venue is divided into five clubs, each with its own distinct individual theme. The club regularly hosts international guest DJs, including big names such as Jarvis Cocker, Shaun Rider and Peter Smith among others. *See p100.*

For more bars & clubs in the old town **See pp76–7 & p86**

Left **Club scene, Sitges** Right **Restaurante Castro**

🔟 Gay & Lesbian Hang-outs

1 Antinous Llibreria-Cafè

Antinous is a popular, gay meeting point just off the southern end of La Rambla. The café incorporates a spacious shop, stocking gifts, books and videos, and has a small bar area with exhibitions. Pick up a copy of *Nois*, a free magazine available in most gay venues, which gives the lowdown on the gay scene. ® C/Josep Anselm Clavé 6 • Map L6 • Closed Sun • DA

Party-goers at a club

2 Dietrich Gay Teatro Café

A gay venue with a mixed door policy, Dietrich is a trendy club with attractive golden walls and an internal garden. As well as playing house and garage music, it features performances by drag artists, dancers and acrobats. ® Consell de Cent 255 • Map D3

3 Restaurante Castro

This ultra-chic restaurant offers hefty portions of Mediterranean cuisine with an exotic twist. The heavy duty decor of industrial-style black chains and metal is toned down by soft lighting and relaxing music. Make a reservation, as this is one of the most popular gay restaurants in town. ® C/Casanova 85 • Map D2 • 93 323 67 84 • Closed Sun lunch • €€€€ • DA

4 Sauna Casanova

This gay sauna (for men only) is ultra-clean, and includes Turkish baths, Jacuzzis and saunas, as well as a handy bar and internet service. There are also private cabins, some with video players. ® C/Casanova 57 • Map D3 • Adm

5 Zeltas

One of the hottest club-bars in town, Zeltas has trendy decor, in the style of a loft apartment, and really pulls in the crowds. A heady mix of testosterone, potent drinks and pumping house makes this a prime spot to mingle with some of Barcelona's beauties. ® C/Casanova 75 • Map D3

Books, Antinous Llibería-Cafè

b-guided (see p134) *is available from selected stores and venues; it gives more information on gay-friendly restaurants, bars and shops.*

6 Martin's

This exclusively gay club (men only on Saturday nights) is at the top of the Passeig de Gràcia. Spread over three floors, there is a big dance floor, several bars, a pool area and a dark room. The atmosphere is hardcore without being sleazy.
⊗ *Passeig de Gràcia 130 • Map E1 • Adm*

7 Metro

Metro has two dance floors, one playing house, while the other has a free-and-easy music policy and a pool table. The club only livens up around 2am. You can sometimes pick up free tickets at nearby Dietrich restaurant, another gay haunt. ⊗ *C/Sepúlveda 185 • Map J1 • Adm • DA*

8 Loft

A huge music bar with dance floor, this is a perennial favourite to start the night in the Gaixample. Great cocktails, minimalist decor and DJs who know how to work a crowd mean it's always packed. ⊗ *C/Casanovas 75 • Map D3*

9 Punto BCN

This relaxed, friendly bar has stayed in vogue for many years on a fickle gay scene. It gets impossibly busy around midnight at weekends and the music is loud, but it's a good place to get fired up for a night out and get the latest on what else is happening in town. ⊗ *C/Muntaner 63 • Map D3 • DA*

10 Beaches

In summer, gay men gather for some sun, fun and plenty of posing in front of the Club de Natació Barcelona on Barceloneta beach near Plaça del Mar; the Marbella beach is also popular. ⊗ *Map E6*

Top 10 Gay Hot Spots in Sitges

1 XXL
Popular with the in-crowd, with nice decor, a good drinks selection and techno music.
⊗ *C/Joan Tarrida 7*

2 Parrots
A classic Sitges meeting point, this bar has drag queen waiters and a lovely outdoor terrace. ⊗ *Plaça Industrial 2*

3 El Mediterráneo
This multi-space bar with its original design is open in summer only.
⊗ *C/St Bonaventura 6*

4 Trailer
Sitges' oldest gay disco is always packed with friendly faces. ⊗ *C/Àngel Vidal 36 • Adm*

5 Organic
Organic is a hot disco on the gay scene, frequented by a fashion-industry crowd.
⊗ *C/Bonaire 15 • Adm*

6 Beaches
The beach in front of the Hotel Calípolis in Sitges' centre is a gay magnet, as is the nudist one on the way to the town of Vilanova.

7 Night-time Cruising
The pier just past Hotel Calípolis is one of the busiest cruising spots. Prime time is between 3am and dawn.

8 L'Atlantida
Shuttle buses take party-goers to this hugely popular, summer only, beach front club. ⊗ *Platja les coves*

9 Privilege
One of the best gay music bars in town, Privilege has a different theme every night.
⊗ *Carrer de Bonaire 24*

10 El Hotel Romàntic
A simple, gay-friendly hotel, with a pretty garden. ⊗ *C/St Isidre 33 • 93 894 83 75*

→ *The "Gaixample" around the intersection of C/Casanova and C/Diputació, is the heart of Barcelona's gay scene.*

Left **Handbags, Avinguda Diagonal** Right **Shop front, Passeig de Gràcia**

🔟 Best Shopping Areas

1 Passeig de Gràcia
Barcelona's grand avenue of lavish *Modernista* buildings is fittingly home to the city's premier fashion and design stores. From the international big league (Chanel, Gucci, Swatch) to Spain's heavy hitters (Loewe, Camper, Zara, Mango; *see p139*), it's all here. And topping the interior design list is the perennially popular Vinçon *(see p106)*. Side streets reveal more sublime shopping, notably Carrer Consell de Cent, which is dotted with art galleries, and carrers Mallorca, València and Roselló. 🚫 *Map E3*

2 Bulevard Rosa & Bulevard dels Antiquaris
Opened in 1978, Barcelona's first fashion mall, Bulevard Rosa, is still one of its classiest, with over 100 shops showcasing clothes, shoes and accessories by Spanish and international designers. The adjoining Bulevard dels Antiquaris is a spacious mall, with over 60 antiques and arts shops. 🚫 *Bulevard Rosa: Pg de Gràcia 53 • Map E2 • Open 10:30am–9pm Mon–Sat* 🚫 *Bulevard dels Antiquaris: Pg de Gràcia 55–57 • Map E2 • Open 10am–8:30pm Mon–Sat*

3 Plaça de Catalunya & Carrer Pelai
The city's booming centrepiece is also its commercial crossroads, flanked by the department store El Corte Inglés and the shopping mall El Triangle, which includes FNAC (books, CDs, videos) and Séphora (perfumes and cosmetics). Lined with shoe and clothing shops, the nearby Carrer Pelai is said to have more pedestrian traffic than any other shopping street in Spain. 🚫 *El Corte Inglés: Pl de Catalunya 14 • Map M1 • Open 10am–10pm Mon–Sat* 🚫 *El Triangle: C/Pelai 39 • Map L1 • Open 10am–10pm Mon–Sat*

4 Portal de l'Àngel
Once a Roman thoroughfare leading into the walled city of Barcino, today the pedestrian street of Portal de l'Àngel is traversed by hordes of shoppers toting bulging bags. The street is chock-full of shoe, clothing, jewellery and accessory shops. 🚫 *Map M2*

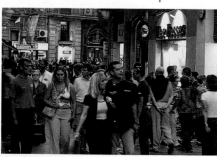

Shopping crowds, Portal de l'Àngel

5 Rambla de Catalunya
The genteel, classier extension of La Rambla, this well-maintained

Sign up for DK's email newsletter on traveldk.com

street offers a refreshing change from its cousin's more down-at-heel carnival atmosphere. Chic shops and cafés, as well as their moneyed customers, pepper the street's length, from Plaça de Catalunya to Diagonal. You'll find everything from fine footwear and leather bags to linens and lamps. ⊗ *Map E2*

Storefront, Carrer Portaferrisa

Avinguda Diagonal
Big and brash, traffic-choked Diagonal is hard to miss, a cacophonous avenue that cuts, yes, diagonally across the entire city. It is a premier shopping street, particularly west of Passeig de Gràcia to its culmination in L'Illa mall and the large El Corte Inglés department store near Plaça Maria Cristina. Lining this long stretch is a host of high-end clothing and shoe stores (Armani, Loewe and Hugo Boss among them), interior design shops, jewellery and watch purveyors, and more. ⊗ *Map D1*

Carrer Portaferrissa
From zebra platform shoes to bellybutton rings and pastel baby T-shirts, this street's other name could well be Carrer "Trendy". Along this strip you'll find El Mercadillo *(see p75)* mini-mall, crammed with hip little shops selling spiked belts, frameless sunglasses, surf wear and the like. Just off this street is Galeries Maldà, Barcelona's first shopping gallery, with a range of shops and a cinema showing original-version independent and Bollywood films *(see p67)*.
⊗ *Galeries Maldà: Pl del Pi 1 • Map M3 • Open 10am–1:30pm & 4–8pm Mon–Sat*

Gràcia
Old bookstores, family-run *botigues de comestibles* (grocery stores) and bohemian shops selling Indian clothing and accessories cluster along Carrer Astúries (and its side streets) and along Travessera de Gràcia. A string of contemporary clothing and shoe shops also lines Gran de Gràcia. ⊗ *Map F1*

El Born
Amid El Born's web of streets are all sorts of art and design shops. Passeig del Born and Carrer Rec are dotted with innovative little galleries (from sculpture to interior design), plus clothing and shoe boutiques. This area is by far the best for original fashion and accessories. ⊗ *Map P4*

Maremagnum
This modern shopping and entertainment centre on the water's edge is open every day of the year, including Sundays. All the main clothing chains can be found, along with cafés and restaurants. ⊗ *Muelle de España 5 • Map N5 • Open 10am–10pm daily*

➤ *For tips on shopping and standard opening hours See p139*

Produce, Mercat de Santa Caterina

Most Fascinating Markets

Mercat de La Boqueria

Barcelona's most famous food market is conveniently located on La Rambla *(see pp12–13)*. Freshness reigns supreme and shoppers are spoiled for choice, with hundreds of stalls selling everything from vine-ripened tomatoes to haunches of beef and moist wedges of Manchego cheese. The city's seaside status is in full evidence at the fish stalls. ✪ *La Rambla 91 • Map L3 • Open 7am–8pm Mon–Sat*

Els Encants

Barcelona's best flea market, Els Encants (east of the city) is where you'll find everything from second-hand clothes, electrical appliances and toys to home-made pottery and used books. Discerning browsers can fit out an entire kitchen from an array of pots and pans. Bargain-hunters should come early. The market is due to relocate nearby in 2011. ✪ *Pl de les Glòries Catalanes • Map H3 • Open 7am–5:30pm Mon, Wed, Fri & Sat • www.encantsbcn.com*

Fira de Santa Llúcia

The Christmas season is officially under way when local artisans set up shop outside the Cathedral for the annual Christmas fair. Well worth a visit if only to peruse the row upon row of *caganers*, miniature figures squatting to *fer caca* (take a poop). Uniquely Catalan, the *caganers* are usually hidden in the back of nativity scenes. This unusual celebration of the scatological also appears in other Christmas traditions. ✪ *Pl de la Seu • Map N3 • Open 1–23 Dec: 10am–8pm (times may vary) daily*

Book & Coin Market at Mercat de Sant Antoni

For book lovers, there's no better way to spend Sunday morning than browsing at this market (west of the city). You'll find a mind-boggling assortment of weathered paperbacks, ancient tomes, stacks of old magazines, comics, postcards and lots more, from coins to videos. ✪ *C/Comte d'Urgell • Map D2 • Open 8am–3pm Sun*

Fira de Santa Llúcia, Plaça de la Seu

5 Fira Artesana, Plaça del Pi

The Plaça del Pi (see p37) brims with natural and organic foods during the Fira Artesana, when producers bring their goods to this corner of the Barri Gòtic. The market specializes in home-made cheeses

Cheeses, Fira Artesana, Plaça del Pi

and honey – from clear clover honey from the Pyrenees to nutty concoctions from Morella. ◎ Pl del Pi • Map M3 • Open 10am–2pm & 5–9pm 1st & 3rd Fri, Sat & Sun of month

6 Fira de Filatelia i Numismàtica

Spread out in the elegant Plaça Reial (see p72), this popular stamp and coin market draws avid collectors from all over the city. The newest collectors' items are phone cards and old xapes de cava (cava bottle cork foils). When the market ends (and the local police go to lunch), a makeshift flea market takes over. Old folks from the barrio and immigrants haul out their belongings – old lamps, clothing, junk – and lay it all out on cloths on the ground. ◎ Pl Reial • Map L4 • Open 9:30am–2:30pm Sun

7 Mercat de Barceloneta

The striking Barceloneta covered market overlooks an expansive square. As well as produce stalls, there are a couple of excellent restaurants including the Michelin-starred Lluçanès. ◎ Pl Font 1, Barceloneta • Map F6 • Open 7am–3pm Mon & Sat (& 5pm–8:30pm Tue–Thu), 7am–8:30pm Fri

8 Mercat de Santa Caterina

Each barri has its own food market with tempting displays but this one boasts a spectacular setting. The building was designed by Catalan architect Enric Miralles (1955–2000). ◎ Av Francesc Cambó 16 • Map N3 • Open 8am–2pm Mon, 8am–3:30pm Tue, Wed & Sat, 8am–8:30pm Thu & Fri

9 Mercat del Art de la Plaça de Sant Josep Oriol

At weekends, local artists flock to this Barri Gòtic square to sell their art and set up their easels. You'll find everything from watercolours of Catalan landscapes to oil paintings of churches and castles. ◎ Pl de Sant Josep Oriol • Map M4 • Open 11am–8:30pm Sat, 10am–2pm Sun

10 Mercat dels Antiquaris

Antiques aficionados and collectors contentedly rummage through jewellery, watches, candelabras, silver trays, embroidery and assorted bric-a-brac at this long-running antiques market in front of the Cathedral. ◎ Pl de la Seu • Map N3 • Open 10am–9pm Thu

For more on shopping See pp50–51

Left **City vista, Mirador de Colom** Right **Gargoyles and view, Sagrada Família**

City Views

1 Tibidabo

The mountain of Tibidabo is the best vantage point for a bird's-eye view of Barcelona. Thrill-seekers opt for a spin on the Tibidabo fairground attraction *(see p111)* called La Atalaya, a rickety basket attached to an ancient crane-like contraption which gives a 360-degree view of Barcelona, the sea and the Pyrenees. A less giddy option is the Torre de Collserola *(see p111)* with its transparent lift rising up 288 m (945 ft). And for those who wish to keep their feet firmly on solid ground – cocktail in hand – settle in at the Mirablau bar. *See p116.*

2 Castell de Montjuïc

Montjuïc offers myriad viewpoints. The best is from the castle and gardens with their superb panoramas over the port and the city. Take the cable car up to the castle and walk down through ever-changing vistas to the Font del Gat café to enjoy a cool drink in its romantic gardens. *See p89.*

Barcelona from Castell de Montjuïc

3 Les Golondrines & Orsom Catamaran

The sea offers a less vertiginous view of the cityscape. Glide out of the harbour on the pleasure boats known as *golondrines* or try the exhilarating trip under sail on an enormous catamaran. Both trips offer ample views of the city and of the Port Olímpic area *(see p133)*. ⊗ *Les Golondrines, Portal de la Pau • Map L6 • Call 93 442 31 06 for times • www.lasgolondrinas.com* ⊗ *Orsom Catamaran, Portal de la Pau • Map L6 • Call 93 441 05 37 for times • www.barcelona-orsom.com*

4 Cable Cars

The swaying cable cars that glide slowly between the Port and Montjuïc are something of a Barcelona landmark. To those not afraid of heights, they reveal hidden aspects of the city and provide a pleasurable way to get to Montjuïc *(see p133)*. ⊗ *Miramar, Montjuïc/Port de Barcelona • Map C5, D6 & E6 • Open daily Apr, May & Oct: 10am–7pm; Jun–Sep: 10am–9pm; Nov–Mar: 10am–6pm • Adm*

5 Mirador de Colom

At the end of La Rambla, the statue of Christopher Columbus offers a good vantage point for viewing the city. The column, rising 80 m (262 ft), was built in 1888. The elevator that whisks visitors to the top has, fortunately, been renovated since then! ⊗ *La Rambla/Drassanes • Map L6 • Open May–Oct: 9am–8:30pm daily; Nov–Apr: 10am–6:30pm daily • Adm*

6 Sagrada Família

When work first began, Gaudí's magical church lay on the outskirts of the city and Barcelona would have been just a shadow in the distance. Almost a hundred years on, the church is located in the heart of the Eixample and the bell towers offer dizzying vistas of the

View of the city and Casa-Museu Gaudí, Parc Güell

entire city. An added bonus are the wonderful close-ups of the extraordinary Sagrada Família itself. *See pp8–11.*

7 El Corte Inglés

The top floor of this department store has a glass-fronted cafeteria and restaurant – an excellent place to lunch or just have a coffee. From here there are views of the nearby Plaça de Catalunya, the old town and the Eixample. The enormous store below stocks just about anything you might need to buy. ® *Pl de Catalunya 14 • Map M1 • Free • DA*

8 Parc Güell

In the north of the city, Gaudí's monumental *Modernista* park presents spectacular views across Barcelona and out to the Mediterranean from its various terraced levels. Trees and patches of woodland act as welcome shade from the fierce summer sun. *See p112.*

9 Barcelona Cathedral

From the heart of the Barri Gòtic, the Cathedral rooftop offers one of the least changed vistas in the city. Look out over the ramshackle rooftops – some dating to the 12th century – and the narrow alleys that spill out in all directions. There is a small charge for the elevator to the top. *See pp14–15.*

10 Helicopter Rides

For a bird's-eye view of Barcelona, consider a helicopter ride over the city. Cat Helicopters run tours of between five and 35 minutes over the city and as far as Montserrat. The five-minute tour over the port area costs €45 per person (maximum five people for each journey). ® *Moll Adossat s/n • Map D6 • Call 93 224 07 10 or check www.cathelicopters.com for more information • Adm*

Left **Barceloneta beach** Right **Parc de Joan Miró**

10 Parks & Beaches

1 Parc de la Ciutadella
Barcelona's largest land-scaped park offers a serene antidote to city life. Once the location of the 18th-century military citadel, this lovely 19th-century park is now home to the zoo, the Catalan parliament, two museums and a boating lake. There is an attractive outdoor café next to the Castell dels Tres Dracs (in the south-western corner). *See pp16–17.*

2 Parc Güell
Originally conceived as a suburban estate to the north of the city, Parc Güell is like a sur-real, Asian terraced farm. Twisting pathways and avenues of col-umned arches blend in with the hillside, playfully fusing nature and fantasy. The esplanade, with its stunning, curved, mosaic bench, is the park's centrepiece. From here

Cascade Fountain, Parc de la Ciutadella

there are spectacular views *(see p55)* of the entire city and of the fairy-tale gatehouses below. Gaudí's former home is now the Casa-Museu Gaudí. *See p112.*

3 Jardins del Laberint d'Horta
These enchanting Neo-Classical gardens date back to 1791, making this elegant park one of the oldest in the city. Situated up above the city, where the air is cooler and cleaner, the park includes themed gardens, waterfalls and a small canal. The highlight is the enor-mous maze, which has a statue of Eros at its centre. *See p113.*

4 Parc de Cervantes
Built in 1964 to celebrate 25 years of Franco rule, this beautiful park on the outskirts of town would have been more appropriately named Park of the Roses. There are over 11,000 rose bushes of 245 varieties; when in bloom, their aroma pervades the park. People pour in at weekends, but the park is blissfully deserted during the week. ✪ *Av Diagonal • Off map*

5 Jardins de Pedralbes
These picturesque gardens lie just in front of the former Palau Reial (royal palace) of Pedralbes – now home to the Museu de Ceràmica and Museu de les Arts Decoratives *(see p112)*. Under the shade of an enormous eucalyptus tree and near a small bamboo forest is a fountain by Gaudí,

All the city parks are officially open from around 10am until dusk.

which was only discovered in 1983.
◈ Av Diagonal 686
• Off map

6 Parc de Joan Miró

Also know as Parc de l'Escorxador, this park was built on the site of a 19th-century slaughter-house (excorxador). Dominating the paved upper level of the park is Miró's striking 22-m (72-ft) sculpture, Dona i Ocell (Woman and Bird; 1983). Elsewhere there are three children's play areas and a couple of kiosk cafés.
◈ C/Tarragona • Map B2

Parc de l'Espanya Industrial

7 Parc de l'Espanya Industrial

Built on the site of a former textiles factory, this modern park, by Basque architect Luis Peña Ganchegui, has emerged from an expensive restoration project. It's a very appealing space, with ten strange light-house-style towers that line the boating lake and an enormous cast-iron dragon, which doubles as a slide. There's a good terrace bar with a playground for the kids. ◈ Pl de Joan Peiró • Off map

8 City Beaches

The beaches of Barcelona were once insalubrious areas to be avoided. With the 1992 Olympics they underwent a radical face-lift and today the stretches of Barceloneta and the Port Olímpic are a major people magnet. Just a short hop on the metro from the city centre, they provide the perfect opportunity for a refreshing Mediterranean dip. The beaches are regularly cleaned and the many facilities in-clude showers, toilets, childrens' play areas, volleyball nets and an open-air gym. There are boats and surfboards for rent. Be warned: bag snatching is endemic. See p97.

9 Castelldefels

Just 20 km (12 miles) south of Barcelona are 5 km (3 miles) of wide, sandy beaches with shallow waters. Beach bars entice week-end sun worshippers out of the afternoon sun for long, lazy sea-food lunches and jugs of sangria aplenty. Windsurfers and pedalos are for hire. ◈ Off map • Train to Platja de Castelldefels from Estació de Sants or Passeig de Gràcia

10 Premià/El Masnou

Arguably the best beaches within easy reach of Barcelona, just 20 km (12 miles) to the north, these two adjoining beaches lure locals with gorgeous golden sand and clear, blue waters. ◈ Train to Premià or El Masnou from Plaça de Catalunya or Estació de Sants

Explore Barcelona's parks by bike
For details on bicycle hire See p131 & p133

57

Left **La Rambla** Right **Cyclist, Passeig Marítim**

TOP 10 Walks & Bike Rides

1 La Rambla & The Port

From Plaça de Catalunya, stroll the length of Barcelona's most famous street, La Rambla *(see pp12–13)*, stopping en route to enjoy the street performances. Turn left at the port and admire the luxury yachts as you follow the water round to Barceloneta. Continue along Pg Joan de Borbó and turn left down any of the side streets that lead to the sand and sea. ◈ *Map M1*

2 Barri Gòtic

Wandering this network of atmospheric, ancient streets is the best way to experience the old town. Take a short stretch of the busy C/Portaferrisa *(see p51)* from La Rambla and turn right down tiny C/Petritxol *(see p74)*, with its confectionery shops and jewellers, to the Església de Santa Maria del Pi. Continue down C/Rauric, left onto C/Ferran and up to Plaça de Sant Jaume *(see p71)*. Turn left onto C/Bisbe leading to Plaça de la Seu and the Cathedral *(see pp14–15)*. ◈ *Map L3*

3 Eixample

For some of the city's most breathtaking *Modernista* gems, walk the length of Pg de Gràcia south to north, past the Mansana de la Discòrdia *(see p103)* and La Pedrera *(see pp20–21)*. Turn right onto C/Mallorca, which leads to Gaudí's Sagrada Família *(see pp 8–11)*. Take a left along C/Marina, past the church's awe-inspiring Nativity Façade, and head up Av Gaudí to Hospital de la Santa Creu i de Sant Pau *(see p103)*. ◈ *Map E3*

4 Tibidabo

Get high above the city by following the gently climbing Av del Tibidabo from the FGC station. Then follow signposts to the right through the steep wooded park, Font del Racó, and continue until you arrive at Plaça Doctor Andreu with its terrace bars and panoramic city views. ◈ *Map B1*

5 Montjuïc

Take in the city's green scene with an amble around Montjuïc's verdant slopes. The initial climb

Parc de Collserola

➤ The CCCB *(see pp28–9)* offers occasional guided walks in English during the year. For more on walking tours **See p133.**

to the grandiose Palau Nacional *(see pp18–19)* from Plaça d'Espanya is eased by a series of escalators. From the palace, veer left and continue along the main road, stopping off at Jardí Mossèn Jacint Verdaguer *(see p94)* before continuing round to Miramar for a spectacular view. ◉ *Map B3*

Backstreet, Barri Gòtic

Parc de Collserola

It's difficult to believe that this serene nature reserve lies just 10 minutes drive from the metropolis. Explore its delightful hiking, biking and nature trails on foot or by mountain bike. Take the funicular train to the top of Tibidabo and head towards the Torre de Collserola *(see p111)*, turning off on any one of the colour-coded woodland paths. A tourist information point provides maps and further information. ◉ *Tourist Info. Carretera de Vallvidrera a Sant Cugat, km 4.7 • Map E3 • Open 9:30am–3pm daily*

Coastal Bike Ride

Breeze along the city's coastal cycle path and take in seaside Barcelona. Pick up the path from the bottom of La Rambla and follow it north to Barceloneta, where it runs along the beachfront, past the shiny Port Olímpic as far as the Platja Levant. ◉ *Map B3*

Diagonal Bike Ride

From Pedralbes to the sea, this route along the city's most elegant boulevard gives you a clear idea of Barcelona's size. The tree-lined cycle path follows Diagonal; start at the top (Zona Universitària) and continuing through the new city of Diagonal Mar until you arrive on the other side of the city just a stone's throw from the Besòs River. ◉ *Map A1*

Les Planes

Just a 15-minute *ferrocarril* ride from Plaça de Catalunya (in the direction of Sant Cugat) is the picturesque spot of Baixador de Valvidrera. Perfect for an out-of-town stroll, there is a steep path through the woods, which opens up into a beautiful, green valley. In summer, there are barbecue facilities where you can throw on your own steaks. ◉ *4 km N of Barcelona*

Costa Brava Coastal Path

At the end of the Platja de Sant Pol in Sant Feliu de Guíxols is the start of a beautiful, coastal path that winds north through shady tamarind trees with views of rocky coves and the Mediterranean. Around the headland and down a stairway, you will find the fabulous beach of Sa Conca, voted the sixth best in Spain. ◉ *75 km NE of Barcelona*

Bike rental is available from Barcelona Bici, Mirador de Colom (tel: 93 285 38 32). For more on bike rental **See p131 & p133**.

Left **Bernat Picornell outdoor pool** Right **Sunbathers, Platja de la Barceloneta**

Activities in Barcelona

1 Sunbathing & Swimming

Head to the city beaches *(see p57)* to cool down and escape the stifling heat. Barcelona boasts a wide range of fabulous beaches, from Barceloneta, lined with bars and restaurants, to the reclaimed beaches of Vila Olímpica, Bogatell and Mar Bella. ⬡ *Map F6–H6*

2 Watersports

A wide variety of activities is on offer in the jet-set surroundings of Port Olímpic and neighbouring beaches, including dinghy sailing and windsurfing. For the experienced, boats are available for hire from the Escola Municipal de Vela; for the beginner, there are classes. ⬡ *Escola Municipal de vela • Moll de Gregal • Map G6 • 93 225 79 40 • Open 9:30am–8pm daily*

3 Swimming

Set in the green environs of Montjuïc, the outstanding outdoor pool of Bernat Picornell is surprisingly uncrowded, especially in summer. Renovated for the Olympics, it has sun loungers, an ice-cream stall and a huge electronic timer with which swimmers in training or fitness enthusiasts can time their sprints. ⬡ *Av del Estadi • Map A4 • Open 7am–midnight Mon–Fri, 7am–9pm Sat, 7am–8:30pm (to 4pm winter) Sun • Adm • DA*

Volleyball, Platja de Nova Icària

4 Pitch-&-Putt Golf

The Costa Brava is emerging as one of Spain's top golf destinations but if you're looking to tee off in town, your best bets are the nearby pitch-and-putt courses in Badalona and Castelldefells. ⬡ *Castell de Godmar, Badalona, 5km NE Barcelona • 93 395 27 79 • Open 8:30am–dusk daily* ⬡ *Canal Olímpic • Castelldefels, 20 km S Barcelona • 93 636 28 96 • Open 9am–9pm Tue–Sat (to 8pm Sun)*

5 Beach Volleyball

On weekend mornings year-round you can pick up a volleyball game at Platja de la Nova Icària. It is best to go with enough people to form a team, but you are usually welcome to join in an ongoing game. ⬡ *Map H5*

6 Horse Riding

The municipal riding school, *Escola Municipal d'Hipica La Fuixarda*, in Montjuïc offers classes for riders of all levels. An hour-long session is €15 for adults and €12 for children. There are also Shetland ponies for small children. Take the Metro Espanya and then bus number 50. It is based in La Fuixarda, which is also a popular climbing venue. ⬡ *Av Montanyans 1, Montjuïc • Map B4 • 93 426 10 66 • Open 5:30–6pm Mon–Fri, 9am–1:30pm, 5–7pm Sat & Sun*

For more on Barcelona's parks & beaches See pp56–7

7 Biking
Hire a city bike from Barcelona Biking and breeze around Barcelona. Mountain bikes are also available for rent here. ⊗ *Barcelona Biking • Baixada de Sant Miquel, 6 • 65 635 63 00*

8 Pool & Billiards
Shoot some pool at Gràcia's lovely Cafè Salambó, where there are pool and billiard tables for rent upstairs, not to mention good drinks, tasty food, a friendly ambience and a lively, arty crowd *(see p115)*.

9 Sardanes
These traditional Catalan dances *(see p65)* take place regularly all over the city and at most local festas. Far from being exclusive, they often involve up to 200 people and there's no reason why you can't be one of them. The tourist office *(see p134)* can provide information on these events.

10 Frontó
Egalitarian tennis or poor man's squash, all you need is a tennis racket and ball to beat against the wall to enjoy this popular pastime. The city's parks are full of free *frontó* courts; one of the most central can be found on La Rambla. It is called Frontó Colom and is at La Rambla 18.

Biking in Barcelona

Top 10 Spectator Sports & Events

1 FC Barcelona Football
Tickets to see this side are rare; book online or by phone. ⊗ *Sep–Jun • 93 496 36 00/902 189 900 • www.fcbarcelona.com*

2 RCD Espanyol
It's easier to get tickets for this first-division football side; they play at Estadi del RCD Espanyol. *(see p90).* ⊗ *Sep–Jun • 90 266 69 02*

3 FC Barcelona Basketball
The team of the city's second favourite sport play at the Palau Blaugrana. ⊗ *Sep–May • 90 218 99 00/93 496 30 00*

4 Barcelona Marató
The marathon takes in the whole city before culminating at the Plaza d'España. ⊗ *Early March • 90 243 17 63*

5 Barcelona Open
This tennis tournament attracts some big names. ⊗ *mid–late Apr • 93 203 78 52*

6 Cursa El Corte Inglés
A 11-km (7-mile) run with thousands of participants. ⊗ *May or Jun • 90 112 21 22*

7 La Volta Ciclista de Catalunya
Cyclists warm up for the more serious European events with this testing route. ⊗ *late May–Jun • 93 431 82 98*

8 Montmeló
Motor racing, including Formula 1, regularly comes to this circuit. ⊗ *Apr–May • 93 571 97 71 • www.circuitcat.com*

9 Cursa La Mercè
A 10-km (6-mile) run through Barcelona's centre. ⊗ *Late Sep • 010*

10 Catalunya Rally
Top-class rally-driving in spectacular surroundings. ⊗ *Oct • ww.rallyracc.com*

For walks & bike rides in and around Barcelona See pp58–9

Left **Children at play, Port Olímpic beach** Right **Penguins, Parc Zoològic**

Attractions for Children

1 Parc d'Atraccions del Tibidabo

With its old-fashioned rides, the only surviving funfair in the city is a delight. The attractions include a rollercoaster, a House of Horrors, bumper cars, a ferris wheel and the Museu dels Autòmates *(see p41)*, with animatronics of all shapes and sizes. There's also a puppet show, picnic areas, playgrounds and plenty of bars and restaurants. See *p111*.

2 Parc Zoològic

The zoo has an enormous adventure playground where children can run wild. There are also dolphin shows in one of the aquariums. Other activities for children include guided tours and workshops. The "farm" area has goats and rabbits that younger children can stroke. See *p16*.

3 Museu Marítim

Ancient maps showing monster-filled seas, restored fishing boats and a collection of ships' figureheads give a taste of Barcelona's maritime history. Well worth a look is the full-size Spanish galleon complete with sound and light effects. Set in the vast former medieval shipyards, the Drassanes, this is an absolute must for any budding sea captain. See *p81*.

4 L'Aquàrium

One of Europe's biggest aquariums, this underwater kingdom is made up of 21 enormous tanks brimming with nearly 400 marine species. The highlight of a visit is the Oceanari, where a walk-through glass tunnel will bring you face to face with three huge grey sharks – named Drake, Morgan and Maverick – lurking in 4.5 million litres (990,000 gallons) of water. See *p97*.

5 Jardins del Laberint d'Horta

The main feature of this exceptional park is the huge, hedged maze where children can live

Children, Parc Zoològic

out their *Alice in Wonderland* fantasies. Unfulfilled expectations of mad hatters are made up for by an enormous play area with a bar and terrace. The park is particularly busy on Sundays. *See p113.*

6 Montjuïc Cable Cars

Unlike the nerve-jangling cable-car ride across the port, these smaller, lower-altitude cable car trips are a better option if you have children with you. The ride to the Montjuïc summit also has the added appeal of the castle *(see p89)* at the top, with cannons for the kids to clamber on. ✈ *Parc de Montjuïc • Map C5 • Open Nov–Mar: 10am–6pm daily; Apr, May, Oct: 10am–7pm daily; Jun–Sep: 10am–9pm daily • Adm*

Human statue, La Rambla

7 La Rambla

Your shoulders will be aching from carrying the kids high above the crowds by the time you reach the end of Barcelona's main boulevard. Fire eaters, buskers, human statues decked out as Greek goddesses – you name it and it's likely to be keeping the hordes entertained on La Rambla. Put a coin in the human statue's hat and be rewarded with a sudden move, or, if you're a child, the gift of a tiny lollipop. *See pp12–13.*

8 City Beaches

For kids, there's more to going to the beach in Barcelona than just splashing in warm waters and

frolicking in the sand. The Port Vell and Port Olímpic *platges* (beaches) offer a good choice of well-equipped play areas to keep the little ones entertained. Numerous bars and restaurants make finding refreshment easy, too. *See p97.*

9 Boat Trips

Barcelona's *golondrines (see p133)* make regular trips out of the port, providing a fun excursion for older children. Younger kids, however, will probably prefer paddling around in a rowing boat on the lake at the Parc de la Ciutadella. *See pp16–17.*

10 Museu d'Història de Catalunya

This child-friendly museum traces Catalonia's history through a range of dynamic, interactive exhibits. The best of these allows visitors to get dressed up as medieval knights and gallop around on wooden horses. Very popular with Catalan school groups, it's equally enjoyable for visitors. Every Saturday, the museum hosts a story hour when Catalan legends are re-enacted for children as well as other children's activities. *See p97.*

Festes de la Mercè

Catalan Folk Festivals & Traditions

1 Festes de la Mercè
Barcelona's main festival is a riotous week-long celebration in honour of La Mercè *(see p39)*. The night sky lights up with fireworks, outdoor concerts are held, and there's barely a bottle of *cava* left in the city by the festival's end. Processions and parades feature *gegants* (giant wooden figures operated by people). ✆ *Week of 23 Sep*

Gegants, Festes de la Mercè

2 El Dia de Sant Jordi
On this spring day, Barcelona is transformed into a vibrant, open-air book and flower market. Men and women exchange presents of roses, to celebrate Sant Jordi *(see p39)* and books, in tribute to Cervantes and Shakespeare, who both died on 23 April 1616. ✆ *23 Apr*

3 La Revetlla de Sant Joan
In celebration of Saint John, and the start of summer, this is Catalonians' night to play with fire and play they do, with gusto. Fireworks streak through the night sky and bonfires are set ablaze on beaches and in towns throughout the region. ✆ *23 Jun*

4 Festa Major de Gràcia
During this week-long *festa*, (the largest party of the summer), revellers congregate in Gràcia's decorated streets. Parades, open-air concerts, fireworks and plenty of beer and cava fuel the infectious merriment. ✆ *Mid- to late Aug*

5 Carnaval in Sitges
The buzzing beach town of Sitges *(see p121)* explodes during Carnaval, celebrated in flamboyant fashion. Over-the-top floats parade among drag queens, lip-synching contests and a fresh-off-the-beach crowd warmed by sun and plenty of beer. ✆ *3–4 days Feb*

6 Festa de la Patum
The village of Berga (90 km/ 60 miles north of Barcelona) hosts one of Catalonia's liveliest festivals. The event gets its name from the folks who used to chant *patum* (the sound of a drum). Streets spill over with merrymakers as fireworks crackle and dwarfs, devils and dragons dance atop parade floats. ✆ *Corpus Christi (May)*

7 Festes de Sant Medir
A 10th-century hermitage is the focus of a very picturesque pilgrimage featuring carriages and costumed attendants on horseback. Sweets are thrown from the carriages, which is a treat for the kids. ✆ *Around 3 Mar*

The English-language website www.spain.info has a section dedicated to Spanish festivals.

Castells

Castells is one of Catalonia's most spectacular folk traditions. Trained *castellers* stand on each other's shoulders to create a human castle – the highest tower takes the prize. The crowning moment is when a child scales the human mass to make the sign of the cross. *Castells* are often performed in Plaça Sant Jaume. ✪ *Jun*

Sardanes

"The magnificent, moving ring" is how Catalan poet Joan Maragall described the *sardana*, Catalonia's regional dance. Subdued yet intricate, it is performed to the tunes of the *cobla*, a traditional brass and woodwind band. *Sardanes* can be seen in Plaça de la Seu and Plaça Sant Jaume year round *(see p14)*.

Catalan Christmas & Cavalcada de Reis

The *Nadal* (Christmas) season begins on 1 December with the arrival of the festive artisan fairs. On 5 January is the Cavalcada de Reis, the spectacular Three Kings Parade. In Barcelona, the kings arrive by sea and are welcomed by city officials in front of transfixed children.

Castells

Top 10 Music, Theatre & Art Festivals

1 Festival del Grec
Barcelona's largest music, theatre and dance festival. ✪ *Late Jun–Jul* • 93 316 11 11 or 80 711 77 00

2 Festival del Sónar
This electronic music and multimedia festival has technology fairs and musical events. ✪ *Mid-Jun* • www.sonar.es

3 Festival Internacional de Jazz
Big-name and experimental live jazz. ✪ *Oct–Dec* • 93 481 70 40 • www.theproject.es

4 Sitges International Film Festival
The best fantasy film festival in the world. ✪ *Early Oct* • www.sitgesfilmfestival.com

5 Festival de Música Antiga
Concerts of early music in the Barri Gòtic and L'Auditori. ✪ *Apr & May* • www.auditori.org

6 Clàssica als Parcs
Classical music concerts are held in the city's parks. ✪ *Jul*

7 Festival de Guitarra
International guitar festival. ✪ *Mar–Jun* • 93 481 70 40 • www.theproject.es

8 Festival de Músiques del Món
Ethnic and world music at L'Auditori. ✪ *Oct* • www.auditori.org

9 Festival de Flamenco
A week of outstanding flamenco music at the CCCB in the Raval. ✪ *Late May* • 93 443 43 46

10 Concerts de L'Estiu
The Poble Espanyol hosts live outdoor concerts during July. Past performers have included George Benson and Jeff Buck. ✪ *Jul* • www.theproject.es

Tickets for Festival del Grec & Festival Internacional de Jazz are available from the Caixa de Catalunya ticket line: 90 210 12 12.

Left **Teatre Grec** Right **Gran Teatre del Liceu**

Performing Arts & Music Venues

1 Gran Teatre del Liceu
Phoenix-like, the Liceu has risen from the ashes of two devastating fires since its inauguration in 1847. Now one of the greatest opera houses in Europe, it has an innovative programme and is famed for performances by home-grown talent, including one of the "three tenors" José Carreras, as well as Montserrat Caballé. *La Rambla • Map L4 • 93 485 99 14 • Guided tours 10am daily • Adm • DA*

2 Palau Sant Jordi
The star of the Olympic buildings, this stadium is normally home to Barcelona's basketball team *(see p61)*. It doubles up as the city's main arena for macro-concerts, which have included Madonna and U2. *See p90. • Box office: 93 426 20 89 • Open for visits 10am–6pm (8pm Jul & Aug) Sat & Sun • Free • DA*

3 Teatre Grec
The most magical and enigmatic of all Barcelona's venues,
this open-air amphitheatre, set in thick, verdant forest, makes an incredible setting for ballet, music or theatre. Only used for shows during the summer arts Festival del Grec, the gardens are open all year to visitors. *See p90. • Tickets: 90 210 12 12 • Open for visits 10am–dusk daily • Free*

4 Palau de la Música Catalana
Domenèch i Montaner's epic *Modernista* gem regularly serves up the best in jazz and classical music. It has lost some of its prestige to the Auditori, but it still hosts some performances for the annual guitar festival and attracts many visiting world music artists. *See pp26–7.*

5 Auditori de Barcelona
Located near the Teatre Nacional, this large auditorium is home to the Orquestra Simfònica de Barcelona. Acoustics and visibility are excellent and, in addition to classical music, it hosts regular jazz concerts. *C/Lepant 150 • Map G1 • 93 247 93 00 • DA*

6 Harlem Jazz Club
This is one of the longest surviving clubs for jazz and blues. Admission usually includes a drink, and some shows are free. *See p77. • 93 310 07 55*

Concert, Palau de la Música Catalana

For Catalan speakers, the Teatre Nacional de Catalunya (93 306 57 00) is a fine showcase for Catalan drama.

Mercat de les Flors

7 The venue of choice for dance and performance theatre groups, such as La Fura dels Baus and Comediants, whose incredible mixture of circus and drama is easily accessible to non-Catalan speakers. ◈ C/Lleida 59 • Map B4 • 93 426 18 75 • www.mercatflors.org

Club Apolo

8 An old dance hall, with velvet covered balconies and panelled bars, this place has reinvented itself as one of the city's leading nightclubs. It attracts the latest in live techno and dance music. ◈ C/Nou de la Rambla 113 • Map K4 • 93 441 40 01 • www.sala-apolo.com

Harlem Jazz Club

JazzSí Club – Taller de Musics

9 Conceived as a multi-functional space, the JazzSí Club offers music workshops, lessons and daily concerts in the auditorium. The jazz, Cuban, flamenco or rock performances start between 7:30 and 9pm, and dinner is available from Monday to Friday. ◈ Requesens, 2 • Map J2 • 93 329 00 20 • www.tallerdemusics.com/jazzsi-club/ • Adm

Razzmatazz

10 This is one of the city's most famous venues. Hosting concerts several nights a week, the club's five areas offer a wide range of musical styles. *See p100.*

Top 10 Versión Original Cinemas

1 Verdi
One of the original VO cinemas, with five different screens. ◈ C/Verdi 32 • Map B2 • 93 238 79 90

2 Icària Yelmo Cineplex
An incredible 15 screens all showing original version films. ◈ C/Salvador Espriu 61 • Map H5 • 90 222 09 22

3 Casablanca
An old style, two-screen, cinema, which has retained its character. ◈ Pg de Gràcia 115 • Map E2 • 93 218 43 45

4 Boliche
A four-screen cinema showing mainly European films. ◈ Av Diagonal 508 • Map E1 • 93 451 00 51

5 Méliès Cinemes
Two-screened repertory cinema. ◈ C/Villarroel 102 • Map J1 • 93 451 00 51

6 Renoir-Les Corts
Multi-screened cinema with lots of Spanish and English films. ◈ C/Eugeni d'Ors 12 • Map A2 • 93 490 55 10

7 Verdi Park
Four-screen version of the original Verdi. ◈ C/Torrijos 49 • Map F1 • 93 238 79 90

8 Renoir Floridablanca
A multiplex that shows films from around the world. ◈ Floridablanca 135 • Map C3 • 90 222 16 22

9 Maldà
A small cinema showing independent and Bollywood movies. ◈ C/del Pi 5 • Map M3 • 93 317 85 29

10 Filmoteca
The Catalan government's repertory cinema runs three VO shows daily. ◈ Av Sarrià 31–33 • Map D1 • 93 410 75 90 • Closed Aug

→ *Barcelona's many versió original (original version) cinemas provide plenty of options for non-Catalan-speaking film aficionados.*

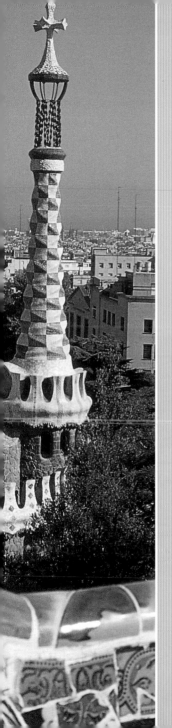

AROUND
TOWN

BARCELONA'S TOP 10

Left **Museu d'Història de la Ciutat** Right **Saló de Cent, Ajuntament**

Barri Gòtic & La Ribera

THOUGH HARD TO IMAGINE TODAY, *there was a time when Barcelona wa just a small Roman village (named Barcino) encircled by protective stone walls. Over the centuries, the village grew, culminating in a building boom in the 14th and 15th centuries. The Barri Gòtic (Gothic Quarter), a beautifully preserved neighbourhood of Gothic buildings, medieval places (squares) and atmospheric alleys, exists today as a splendid reminder of Barcelona's medieval heyday. The web of ancient, treasure-filled streets in this compact area is best explored by aimless wandering. The barri's centrepiece – and its religious and social heart – is the 13th-century Cathedral and surrounding complex of period buildings. Nearby, the stately Plaça del Rei (see p36) is ringed by some of the best preserved medieval buildings in the area. Extending*

east of the Barri Gòtic is the ancient barri of La Ribera, which includes El Born (see p72). Here, the lovely Carrer Montcada is lined with medieval palaces – five of which house the must-see Museu Picasso.

Roman Arch, Carrer Paradis

Sights

1. Barcelona Cathedral
2. Museu Picasso
3. Palau de la Música Catalana
4. Plaça de Sant Jaume
5. Conjunt Monumental de la Plaça del Rei
6. Plaça Reial
7. Museu Frederic Marès
8. Església de Santa Maria del Mar
9. Disseny Hub
10. Museu Barbier–Mueller d'Art Precolombí

For sights & attractions on La Rambla See pp12–13

1 Barcelona Cathedral
Soaring over the Barri Gòtic is Barcelona's mighty Cathedral dating from 1298. See pp14–15.

2 Museu Picasso
Discover the youthful repertoire of one of the 20th-century's most revered artists. See pp24–5.

3 Palau de la Música Catalana

Cathedral spire

The city's most prestigious concert hall is a monument to both *la musica Catalana* and to *Modernisme*. See pp26–7.

4 Plaça de Sant Jaume
The site of the Plaça de Sant Jaume *(see p36)* was once the nucleus of Roman Barcino. With these roots, it seems fitting that the square has become home to Barcelona's two most important government buildings: the Palau de la Generalitat (seat of the Catalan government) and the Ajuntament (city hall). Look for the detailed carved relief of Sant Jordi, Catalonia's patron saint, on the 15th-century Generalitat façade. Within is the lovely 15th-century Capella de Sant Jordi *(see p39)*, designed by architect Marc Safont. A highlight of the Gothic Ajuntament is the lavish red-and-gold Saló de Cent, where the Council

of One Hundred ruled the city from 1372 to 1714. Also of note is the Pati dels Tarongers, a graceful patio with orange trees. ◎ *Palau de la Generalitat • Pl de Sant Jaume • Map M4 • Open 10:30am–1:30pm 2nd & 4th Sat & Sun of month for guided tours (ID/passport required) • Free* ◎ *Ajuntament • Pl de Sant Jaume • Map M4 • Open 10am–1:30pm Sun for guided tours (11am in English) • Free*

5 Conjunt Monumental de la Plaça del Rei
In the heart of the Barri Gòtic is the beautifully preserved, medieval Plaça del Rei *(see p36)*, presided over by the 13th- to 14th-century Palau Reial (royal palace). The impressive palace complex includes the Saló del Tinell, a massive hall crowned by Gothic arches, where Ferdinand and Isabel welcomed Columbus after his 1492 voyage to the Americas. The medieval Capella de Santa Àgata has a beautiful 15th-century altarpiece by Jaume Huguet. A visit to the Museu d'Història de la Ciutat gives access to the Palau Reial and to one of the largest underground excavations of Roman ruins on display in Europe. ◎ *Pl del Rei • Map M4 • Open 10am–8pm Tue–Sat, 10am–3pm Sun (Oct–May: closes 2–4pm, 7pm) • Adm • DA*

Left **Italianate façade, Palau de la Generalitat** Right **Mosaic pillar, Palau de la Música Catalana**

For more on Barri Gòtic squares **See pp36–7**

El Born

If you're hankering for a proper martini or perhaps some alternative jazz, then look no further than El Born, a musty-turned-hip neighbourhood, which was "reborn" several years ago. Students and artists moved in, attracted by cheap rents and airy warehouses, fostering an arty vibe that now blends in with the area's old-time aura.

Experimental design shops share the narrow streets with traditional, balconied buildings strung with laundry. The bustling Passeig de Born, lined with bars and cafés, leads onto the lively Plaça Comercial, where the cavernous Born Market (in operation 1870–1970) is now being converted into a cultural centre and exhibition space.

Plaça Reial (1850s)

6 Plaça Reial

Late 19th-century elegance meets sangria-swilling café society in the arcaded Plaça Reial, one of Barcelona's most emblematic and entertaining squares. The *plaça* is planted with towering palm trees and encircled by stately, 19th-century buildings. The *Modernista* lampposts were designed by a young Gaudí in 1879. At the square's centre is a wrought-iron fountain representing the Three Graces. The square is the best place to start a big night out, with a cluster of restaurants, bars and cafés that draw the hoi polloi – including all sorts of shady pickpockets. ✆ *Map L4*

7 Museu Frederic Marès

This fascinating museum houses the life collection of wealthy Catalan sculptor Frederic

Medieval arch, Museu Frederic Marès

Marès. No mere hobby collector, the astute (and obsessive) Marès amassed holdings that a modern museum curator would die for. Among them, an impressive array of religious icons and statues – dating from Roman times to the present – and the curious "Museu Sentimental", which displays anything from ancient watches to fans and dolls. Also worth a visit during summer is Cafè d'Estiu *(see p78)* on the museum's patio. ✆ *Pl de Sant Iu 5–6 • Map N3 • Adm • Closed for refurbishment until summer 2011, but highlights of the collection are projected onto giant screens in the courtyard. The Café d'Estiu remains open.*

8 Església de Santa Maria del Mar

The spacious, breathtaking interior of this 14th-century church, designed by architect Berenguer de Montagut, is the city's premier example of the austere Catalan Gothic style. The church is dedicated to Saint Mary of the Sea, the patron saint of sailors, and an ancient model ship hangs near one of the statues of the Virgin. Dubbed "the people's church", this is the city's most popular spot for exchanging wedding vows. ✆ *Pl de Santa Maria 1 • Map P5 • Open 9am–1:30pm, 4:30–8pm*

9 Disseny Hub

Housed in a pair of adjoining medieval palaces, the gallery features temporary exhibitions showcasing aspects of architecture, graphic and communication design, product design and fashion design. It also hosts detailed talks on design themes. The goal is to promote knowledge and understanding of the design world. The small but ultra-cool museum shop sells funky clothes, accessories and design collectables. ✆ C/Montcada 12–14 • Map P4 • Open 10am–7pm Tue–Sat, 10am–8pm Sun • Adm; free 3–8pm Sun • DA

10 Museu Barbier-Mueller d'Art Precolombí

Pre-Columbian art and artifacts, spanning 3,000 years, are exhibited in the 16th-century Palau Nadal. Sculpture, ceramics and detailed gold and silver pieces represent the rich artistic traditions of the Aztecs, Mayans and Incas. Temporary exhibits explore the diversity of these civilizations. ✆ C/Montcada 12–14 • Map P4 • Open 11am–7pm Tue–Fri, 11am–8pm Sat & Sun, • Adm; free 1st Sun of month and every Sun 3–8pm • DA

Interior, Església de Santa Maria del Mar

Roman Barcelona

Morning

🕐 Starting at the Jaume I metro, enter the ancient walled city of Barcino on C/Llibreteria, once the main road to and from Rome. Head right up C/Veguer to **Plaça del Rei** (see p36) and descend into a fascinating underground web of Roman walls and waterways via the **Museu d'Història de Barcelona** (see p71). Also visible here are the remains of a 2nd-century workshop and an ancient bodega, a source of much Roman merrymaking. Back above ground, pause for a café sol at the terrace of **Café–Bar L'Antiquari** (see p78) and bask in Barcelona's Gothic glory days. Stroll towards the Cathedral's spires along C/de la Pietat. Turn right onto C/Bisbe, once a Roman thoroughfare, then right again on Av de la Catedral to visit the **Pia Almoina** (see p15), where you can view a section of the Roman aqueduct and ride a glass elevator past Roman wall remains. Backtrack to Plaça Nova, once the Roman gateway to Barcino, cross the plaça and continue along C/Arcs.

Afternoon

🍴 Stop for lunch at the **Reial Cercle Artístic**, a late 19th-century artists' society. Ignore the "members only" sign; the restaurant is open to the public, and its tranquil balcony terrace provides a welcome breather from the crowds far below. After lunch, head up Av del Portal de l'Àngel and turn left onto C/Canuda to **Plaça de la Vila de Madrid** (see p37). The square is a fitting end to your Roman ramble, for here are the necropolis remains, where Romans were laid to rest.

For more museums **See pp40–41**

Left **Carrer del Bisbe** Centre **Església de Sant Just i Sant Pastor** Right **Plaça de Sant Felip Neri**

🔟 Best of the Rest

1 Carrer del Bisbe
Medieval Carrer del Bisbe is flanked by the Gothic Cases dels Canonges (House of Canons) and the Palau de la Generalitat *(see p71)*. Connecting the two is an eye-catching Neo-Gothic arched stone bridge (1928). ◈ *Map M3*

2 Carrer de Santa Llúcia
At weekends, amateur opera singers perform on this medieval street, home to the Casa de l'Ardiaca *(see p15)*, which has a ravishing little patio. ◈ *Map M3*

3 El Call
El Call was home to one of Spain's largest Jewish communities until their expulsion in the 15th century. The dark streets of this ghetto are so narrow it is said you can tie a handkerchief across their width. ◈ *Map M4*

4 Carrer Montcada
The "palace row" of La Ribera is lined with Gothic architectural gems, including the 15th-century Palau Aguilar, home to the Museu Picasso *(see pp24–5)*, and the 17th-century Palau Dalmases with its Gothic chapel. ◈ *Map P4*

5 Plaça de Ramon Berenguer el Gran
This square boasts one of the largest intact sections of Barcelona's Roman walls. ◈ *Map N3*

6 Carrer Regomir & Carrer del Correu Vell
You'll find splendid Roman remains on Carrer Regomir, most notably within the medieval Pati Llimona. Two Roman towers are revealed on nearby Carrer del Correu Vell, and there are Roman walls on the leafy Plaça Traginers. ◈ *Map M5*

7 Plaça de Sant Felip Neri
Sunlight filters through tall trees in this hidden oasis of calm. The *plaça* is home to the Museu del Calçat *(see p41)*. ◈ *Map M3*

8 Carrer Petritxol
This well-maintained medieval street is lined with traditional *granges* and *xocolateries* (cafés and chocolate shops). Also here is the famous Sala Parés art gallery, founded in 1877, which once exhibited Picasso, Casas and other Catalan contemporaries. ◈ *Map L3*

9 Església de Sant Just i Sant Pastor
This Gothic church (1342) has sculptures dating back to the 9th century, and 5th-century visigothic baptismal fonts. ◈ *Map M4*

10 Església de Santa Anna
Mere paces from La Rambla is the unexpected tranquillity of this Romanesque church, with a leafy, 15th-century, Gothic cloister. ◈ *Map M2*

For more Barcelona squares **See pp36–7**

Left **Escribà Confiteria i Fleca** Centre **La Manual Alpargatera** Right **Guantería Alonso**

Shops: Gifts, Garments & Goodies

1 Escribà Confiteria i Fleca
If the glistening pastries and towering chocolate creations aren't enough of a lure, then the *Modernista* store-front certainly is. Buy goodies to go, or enjoy them on the spot in the small café. ◈ *La Rambla 83 • Map L3*

2 Como Agua de Mayo
Try this tiny boutique for original fashion and footwear by Spanish designers. The style is feminine and glamorous and the prices are surprisingly affordable. ◈ *C/Argenteria • Map N4*

3 Cocotte
Divine women's fashions, accessories and toiletries are found in this loft-style store. Among the labels are top Spanish and French names, such as Hoss, Intropia and See by Chloé. ◈ *C/Rec 65 • Map P5*

4 Atalanta Manufactura
This shop's delicate, hand-painted silks are created in an on-site workshop. Unusual designs include a Klimt-inspired, gilded silk. ◈ *Pg del Born 10 • Map P5*

5 La Manual Alpargatera
What do the Pope, Jack Nicholson and legions of *Barcelonins* have in common? They buy their espadrilles (*alpargatas*) here. ◈ *C/Avinyó 7 • Map M4*

6 Casa Colomina
Sink your teeth into *torró*, the Spanish nougat-and-almond speciality. Casa Colomina, established in 1908, offers a tantalizing array. ◈ *C/Portaferrissa 8 • Map L3*

7 Cereria Subirà
Founded in 1761, this is Barcelona's oldest shop. Today you'll find it crammed with every kind of candle imaginable. ◈ *Baixada Llibreteria 7 • Map N4*

8 L'Arca de l'Àvia
Amazing antique clothing from flapper dresses to boned corsets, silk shawls, puff sleeved shirts and pin-tucked shirt fronts. There's also a selection of antique dolls and fans. ◈ *C/Banys Nous 20 • Map M3*

9 Guantería Alonso
This long-established shop is still the place to visit if you are looking for colourful hand-painted fans, handmade gloves, delicately embroidered shawls, ornamental combs and other traditional Spanish accessories. ◈ *C/Santa Anna 27 • Map M2*

10 Vila Vinateca
One of the city's best wine merchants stocking wines and spirits. An adjoining shop sells top quality Spanish delicacies, including hams, cheeses and olive oil. ◈ *C/Agullers 7*

For tips on shopping and standard opening hours **See p139**

Left **La Vinya del Senyor** Right **Schilling**

TOP 10 Cocktail & Conversation Spots

1 Schilling
Fronted by large windows overlooking the throngs on Carrer Ferran, this spacious bar draws a sociable mix of both visitors and locals. ⊗ C/Ferran 23 • Map M4

2 Bar L'Ascensor
An old-fashioned, dark-wood *ascensor* (elevator) serves as the entrance to this dimly-lit, convivial bar frequented by a cocktail-swilling crowd. ⊗ C/Bellafila 3 • Map M4

3 Café del Born Nou
This café is located opposite the Mercat del Born, and offers coffee and cakes, as well as a range of salads, sandwiches and light meals. It attracts a relaxed, arty crowd, who linger over their newspapers with a coffee.
⊗ Plaça Comercial 10

4 Ginger
An elegant bar that serves fine wines, champagne, cava, cocktails and a variety of original tapas to a glamorous crowd.
⊗ Palma de Sant Just 1 • Map N4
• Closed Mon, Sun

5 Glaciar
Occupying a prime corner of Plaça Reial, this atmospheric café-bar brings in all types. Grab a spot on the terrace with a front-row view of the *plaça* activities.
⊗ Pl Reial 3 • Map L4

6 María Mulata
Intimate and inviting, this bar serves good mojitos and caipirinhas. Cinema night is on a Monday, on the weekend DJ sessions take over and Sundays are for chilling out. ⊗ C/Ample 27 • Map M5

7 La Vinya del Senyor
A classy, yet cosy, bar attracting wine lovers from all over the city, who come to sample a rich array of Spanish and international varieties in the company of other wine aficionados.
⊗ Pl Santa Maria 5 • Map N5

8 Cactus Bar
The main draw of this little bar is the terrace with a couple of tables underneath an elegant stone arcade, which have a perfect view of Passeig del Born. ⊗ Passeig del Born 30 • Map P4

9 Gimlet
The original cocktail bar in El Born, the intimate, 1950s-style Gimlet pours nice (read: potent) cocktails to a local clientele.
⊗ C/Rec 24 • Map P4

10 Mudanzas
This long-time favourite hang-out has circular marble tables, black-and-white tiled floors and an informal, "everybody's welcome" vibe. ⊗ C/Vidrieria 15 • Map P5

Unless otherwise stated, bars, clubs & music venues are open daily.

Left **Sidecar Factory Club** Right **Jamboree**

TOP 10 Clubs & Music Venues

1 Jamboree
This Barri Gòtic institution has live jazz every night (11pm–1am). It then evolves into a dance club, with DJs spinning everything from hip-hop to R&B and salsa. ⊗ *Pl Reial 17 • Map L4 • Adm*

2 Sala Monasterio
This small and atmospheric basement bar has a little stage for live gigs. World music, jazz and blues are most popular, but the eclectic programme features most kinds of music. ⊗ *Passeig Isabel II No. 4*

3 El Pilé 43
This hip little bar is packed with funky 1960s and 1970s retro furniture, all of which is for sale. Sink into a sofa, sip a mojito and ponder which items could be squeezed into a suitcase. ⊗ *C/ Aglà 4 • Map L4*

4 Harlem Jazz Club
Dark and smoky, this kickback jazz haunt features a choice line-up of jazz and blues, flamenco fusion, reggae and African music. ⊗ *Comtessa de Sobradiel 8*
• Map M5 • Usually free
• Closed Mon, concerts start 10:30pm

5 Fantàstico Club
Pop, electro pop, and candy-coloured decor make this club a hit. ⊗ *Passatge Escudellers 3 • Map L5*

6 Karma
The hippie origins and 1970s glamour at this club are as popular as ever. ⊗ *Pl Reial 10*
• Map L4 • Adm • Closed Mon

7 Magic
Live music is played at this rock club at weekends by new, up-and-coming Spanish bands. After the show, the dancing goes on until 5:30am. ⊗ *Pg Picasso 40*
• Map P4 • Adm • Closed Sun–Wed

8 Sugar
This red-lit, busy cocktail bar is conveniently located near the Plaça Reial, and is a very popular pre-club hangout.
⊗ *C/Rauric 21*

9 Al Limón Negro
The eclectic "Black Lemon" restaurant-club features ethnic and world music concerts, performance art and occasional art exhibitions. ⊗ *C/Escudellers Blancs 3*
• Map L4 • Closed Mon

10 Sidecar Factory Club
Barcelona's music scene is like a motorbike to which Sidecar is inseparably bound. They say the American 6th fleet once hired the whole venue and made merry. Music, theatre, cabaret, video and good food can all be found.
⊗ *Pl Reial 7 • Map L4*
• Adm • Closed Sun

For Barcelona's best nightlife **See pp46–7**

Left **Terrace, Café-Bar L'Antiquari** Centre **Ice cream, Café d'Estiu** Right **Cafè-Bar del Pi**

🔟 Cafés & Light Eats

1 Cafè d'Estiu
Tucked away on the patio of the Museu Frederic Marès *(see p72)* is this alluring, sun-strewn terrace café, replete with stone pillars, climbing ivy and orange trees. ✆ Pl de Sant Lluc 5–6 • Map N3 • Closed Mon & Oct–Mar • DA

2 La Báscula
This quirky café, set in an old chocolate factory, has several vegetarian dishes and a range of tasty cakes on the menu. ✆ C/ Flassaders 30 • Map P4 • 93 319 98 66

3 Cafè-Bar L'Antiquari
In summer, bask in the old town's medieval atmosphere at the Plaça del Rei terrace. By night, sip Rioja in the intimate, rustic basement bodega. ✆ C/Veguer 13 • Map N4

4 Cafè-Bar del Pi
The Església de Santa Maria del Pi casts a shadow over this café's terrace. And if you're in that kick-back-and-do-nothing mode, street artists keep you entertained. ✆ Pl Sant Josep Oriol 1 • Map M4 • Closed Tue, 7–30 Jan

5 Tetería Salterio
Sit back and relax with tea and sweet Arab cakes. Do not miss the Sado, an Oriental style pizza with a variety of fillings. ✆ Sant Domenec del Call 4 • Map M4 • Closed Mon

6 Café Bliss
Take a break from exploring the Gothic Quarter at this friendly café. It serves divine cakes, light meals and snacks. Ask for a table outside. ✆ Plaça Sants Just i Pastor • Map N4 • 93 268 10 22

7 Drac Café
The best option for a coffee in the Parc de la Ciutadella is this charming outdoor café. Serves salads, dips and sandwiches. ✆ Parc de la Ciutadella • Map Q4

8 Caelum
Uptairs sells honey, preserves and other foods made in convents and monasteries all over Spain. Downstairs you can sample all the delicacies in a café on the site of 15th-century baths. ✆ C/Palla 8 • Map M3 • Closed Mon lunch

9 Venus Delicatessen
Colourful and inviting, this café-restaurant serves great coffee and tea as well as fresh fare, including innovative salads such as "Erotica", with asparagus, tuna and tomato. ✆ C/Avinyó 25 • Map M5 • Closed Sun, 7–30 Jan

10 La Granja Pallaresa
This family-run *xo-colateria* has long been serving up thick hot chocolate and *xurros* (fried dough strips) for dunking. ✆ C/Petritxol 4 • Map L3

For more cafés in the Barri Gòtic **See pp42–3**

Price Categories

For a three-course meal for one with half a bottle of wine (or equivalent meal), taxes and extra charges.

€	under €15
€€	€15–25
€€€	€25–35
€€€€	€35–45
€€€€€	over €45

Cal Pep

Restaurants & Tapas Bars

1 Agut d'Avignon
A French-Catalan restaurant housed in a 17th-century building. Home-style cuisine with a twist includes duck with figs and goose flavoured with pears. ◈ C/Trinitat 3 • Map M4 • 93 302 60 34 • Closed three weeks in Jan • €€€€€

2 Cal Pep
Taste delicious tapas, including the finest cured hams, at this established eatery. ◈ Pl de les Olles 8 • Map P5 • 93 310 79 61 • Closed Sat dinner, Sun, Mon lunch • €€€€

3 Cafè de l'Acadèmia
Superb Catalan cuisine and top-notch desserts are served at this restaurant in an 18th-century building. ◈ C/Lledó 1 • Map N4 • 93 315 00 26 • Closed Sat & Sun • €€

4 Comerç 24
The highlight of this innovative restaurant is the constantly changing menu. Each platillo (little plate) blends unique flavours to create an exquisite dish. ◈ C/Comerç 24 • Map P4 • 93 319 21 02 • Closed Sun and Mon • €€€€

5 Senyor Parellada
Excellent Catalan cuisine, including speciality bacalao (cod) and butifarra (sausage), is the deal at this restaurant. ◈ C/Argenteria 37 • Map N4 • 93 310 50 94 • €€€

6 Agut
For over 75 years, this friendly, family restaurant has been delighting patrons with excellent Catalan cuisine at decent prices. ◈ C/Gignàs 16 • Map M5 • 93 315 17 09 • Closed Sun eve & Mon, one week in Jan, Aug • DA • €€€€

7 Taller De Tapas
This is part of an excellent small chain with several branches. There is a set lunch menu, or try the seafood tapas, which is particularly good. ◈ Plaça de Sant Josep Oriol 9 • Map M3 • 93 301 80 20 • €€

8 Salero
The "Salt Cellar" has an all-white interior offset by flickering candles. An innovative menu features Mediterranean-Asian fusion cuisine. ◈ C/Rec 60 • Map P5 • 93 319 80 22 • Closed Sun • €€€

9 El Xampanyet
An old-fashioned bar popular for the fizzy cava and range of simple tapas. ◈ C/Montcada 22 • Map P4 • 93 319 70 03 • Closed Sun eve, & Mon • €€

10 Govinda
This soothing eatery offers vegetarian Indian main dishes and delectable desserts, but no alcohol. ◈ Pl Vila de Madrid 4 5 • Map M2 • 93 318 77 29 • Closed Sun eve & Mon eve • DA • €€

Unless otherwise stated, all restaurants accept credit cards.
For tips on dining and standard opening hours See p138

Left **Plaça de Joan Coromines** Right **Columns, Església de Sant Pau del Camp**

El Raval

THE SLEEK, SHINY, WHITE WALLS *of the Museu d'Art Contemporani (MACBA) juxtapose the decrepit, ramshackle tenement buildings; Asian grocery stores sell herbs and spices next to what were once the most decadent brothels in Europe; and smoky, decades-old bars share dark, narrow streets with high-ceilinged art galleries showcasing video installations. The old-town barri of El Raval is a traditional working-class neighbourhood in flux. Over the last decade it has been undergoing an enthusiastic urban renewal, led by the arrival of the MACBA. The barri now even has its very own Rambla, a pedestrian street called La Rambla del Raval. Not surprisingly, all of this has sparked a real-estate boom, with renovated old-fashioned flats now commanding top-tier prices and acting as a magnet to the city's young, savvy crowd.*

Stained-glass window, Museu Marítim

Sights

1 Museu d'Art Contemporani

2 Centre de Cultura Contemporània & Foment de les Arts Decoratives

3 Museu Marítim

4 Palau Güell

5 La Rambla del Raval

6 Carrer Nou de la Rambla

7 Carrers Tallers & Riera Baixa

8 Barri Xinès

9 Antic Hospital de la Santa Creu

10 Església de Sant Pau del Camp

For sights & attractions on La Rambla **See pp12–13**

1 Museu d'Art Contemporani

An eclectic array of work by big-name Spanish and international contemporary artists is gathered in the city's contemporary art museum. Excellent temporary exhibitions feature everything from mixed media to sculpture and photography. *See pp28–9.*

Central salon cupola, Palau Güell

2 Centre de Cultura Contemporània & Foment de les Arts Decoratives

Housed in the 18th-century Casa de la Caritat, the CCCB is a focal point for the city's thriving contemporary arts scene. It hosts innovative art exhibitions, lectures, film screenings and more, including multimedia and technology fairs during the popular Festival del Sònar *(see p65).* A medieval courtyard is dazzlingly offset by a massive, angled glass wall, which has been cunningly designed to reflect the city's skyline. Nearby, Foment de les Arts Decoratives *(see p84)* is an umbrella organization of art and design groups, founded in 1903 and housed in the restored, Gothic-style, 16th-century Convent dels Àngels. Here you'll find exhibits, lectures and debates (open Mon–Fri). *See pp28–9.*

3 Museu Marítim

Barcelona's mighty seafaring legacy comes to life at this impressive museum housed in the vast, 13th century Drassanes Reials (Royal Shipyards). Wander beneath looming Gothic arches and relive Barcelona's maritime history through exhibits of model ships, old maps and figureheads. A highlight is the full-scale replica of the royal galley, commanded by Don Juan of Austria during the Battle of Lepanto in 1571. Entrance also includes a visit to the Pailebot *Santa Eulàlia (see p98),* a restored wooden sailing ship dating from 1918. 🌑 *Av de les Drassanes • Map K6 • Open 10am–8pm daily • Adm*

4 Palau Güell

For an artist, a wealthy patron spells survival. The luck of young Gaudí turned when count Eusebi Güell recognized his talents. In 1886, Güell commissioned Gaudí to build a mansion that would set the count apart from his wealthy neighbours. The result is the Palau Güell, one of Gaudí's earliest works. An imposing façade gives way to an elaborate interior of lavish pillars and carved wooden ceilings, while the rooftop has a melange of mosaic chimneys. Due to restoration work, only the stables are open to visitors. The building is due to reopen in summer 2011. 🌑 *C/Nou de la Rambla 3–5 • Map L4 • Open 10am–2:30pm Tue–Sat • Free*

Puzzle table, Museu d'Art Contemporani

For more on Antoni Gaudí See p11

La Rambla del Raval

This palm tree-lined, pedestrian walkway is the latest attempt by city planners to spark a similar social environment to that of the city's famed La Rambla *(see pp12–13)*. So far it is off to a creaking start, with barely a fraction of the crowds that ply the original Rambla. Its advocates, however, are quick to point out that La Rambla del Raval is far better than the two dark, run-down streets that formerly existed here. New shops, bars and cafés mean it could well rival its cousin in years to come. ✪ *Map K4*

Carrer Nou de la Rambla

In the first half of the 19th century, El Raval's main street was a notorious strip of cabarets, brothels and other nocturnal dens. Today it still bustles with transactions, but of a different sort. Frayed-at-the-edge local eateries, ethnic grocery stores, and discount clothing and shoe shops dot the street. And nightspots, such as the atmospheric London Bar *(see p86)*, which have conserved their age-old identity and fixtures, lure partying visitors. ✪ *Map J5*

Carrers Tallers & Riera Baixa

Looking for bootleg CDs of Madonna's European tour? Or

Record shop, Carrer Tallers

Shoppers, Carrer Taller

vintage blue-and-white French navy tops once favoured by the likes of Picasso? Dotting Carrers Tallers and Riera Baixa, in the heart of El Raval, is a host of vintage music and clothing shops selling everything from vinyl to the latest CDs, original Hawaiian shirts and Dickies workwear. On Saturdays from 11am to 9pm, Carrer Riera Baixa hosts its own market, when the stores display their wares on the street. ✪ *Map L1 & K3*

Barri Xinès

The first thing locals will say when you ask about the Barri Xinès is that it no longer exists; the second is that the name has no real connection with the Chinese *(Xinès)*. Both statements are true. This barri, unfolding south from Carrer Sant Pau towards Drassanes, was once one of Europe's most infamous neighbourhoods, inhabited by the poor and working-class and rife with prostitutes, pimps, strippers and drug dealers. Today, due to enthusiastic clean-up efforts, mere vestiges remain of the barri's previous life (though some alleys still hint at illicit activity). As for the name, the area has nothing to do with the Chinese, but was named in the barrio's early-1900s heyday as a general reference to its large immigrant population. Today you can browse in cheap thrift shops and small grocery stores by day and bar-hop your way through the area by night. Ⓢ *Map K4*

9 Antic Hospital de la Santa Creu

A rich reminder of the neighbourhood's medieval past is this Gothic hospital complex (1401), which is today home to the National Library and various cultural organizations. Within, you can wander a pleasant garden surrounded by Gothic pillars. Ⓢ *Entrances on C/Carme & C/Hospital 56 • Map K3 • Courtyard open 9am–8pm daily • Free*

Cloister, Església de Sant Pau del Camp

10 Església de Sant Pau del Camp

Deep in the heart of El Raval is this Romanesque church, one of the oldest in Barcelona. Originally founded as a Benedictine monastery in the 9th century and subsequently rebuilt, this ancient church reveals a 12th-century cloister. Ⓢ *C/Sant Pau 101 • Map J4 • Open 10am–1:30pm, 4–7pm Tue–Sat. Mass 8pm Sat, noon Sun • Adm*

A Ramble in El Raval

Morning

Start your ramble mid-morning by perusing the innovative temporary art exhibits at the **CCCB** *(see p81)*. Here the two world's have meshed harmoniously. The eye-catching blend of old-meets-new in this cutting-edge art space provides a fitting introduction to El Raval's new identity. Head south along C/Montalegre to the Plaça dels Àngels. Sip a coffee beneath the Gothic arches of the restored Convent dels Àngels, which houses the café-restaurant and art and design exhibition rooms of **Foment de les Arts Decoratives** *(see p81)*. Round off your art amble with a trip down nearby C/Doctor Dou, which is speckled with commercial art galleries. If you're looking for contemporary art to jazz up your home, pop into **Ras** *(see p84)*.

Afternoon

From here, it's a short saunter to **Mercat de La Boqueria** *(see p12)*. Walk along C/Carme, turn left onto C/Jerusalem, and go into the back entrance of this cavernous market. Make a beeline for El Quim de La Boqueria (stall 584–585) where you can pull up a stool and dig into fresh fare from baby prawns drizzled in olive oil and garlic to steamed mussels. After, head to the medieval gardens of the **Antic Hospital de la Santa Creu**, off C/Hospital, and take in the Gothic ambience of pillared arcades and courtyards. Then, get to **Marsella** *(see p86)* and kick-start the evening with an absinthe before making for **London Bar** *(see p86)* with its *Modernista* decor.

Around Town – El Raval

Left **Galeria dels Àngels** Right **Window, Foment de les Arts Decoratives**

🔟 Galleries & Design Shops

Galeria dels Àngels
Emerging and established contemporary artists from home and abroad are shown at this cutting-edge photography, painting and sculpture gallery. ◈ C/Pintor Fortuny, 27 • Map L2 • Closed Sun & Mon

Transformer
This store on one of the most arty streets in El Raval stocks an innovative range of lamps, furnishings, ceramics and handmade jewellery. It is a good place to find unusual gifts. ◈ C/Doctor Dou 16 • Map L2 • 93 301 89 05

Espai Ras
Exhibits at this architecture and design gallery and bookstore include architectural models, video installations and graphic design. ◈ C/Doctor Dou 10 • Map L2 • Closed Sun & Mon

Bagués Joieria
Iconic Barcelona jeweller since 1839 with an international reputation. Each piece is hand-made using traditional methods. ◈ La Rambla 105 • Map L3 • Closed Sun

Nomon
This shop sells a range of stylish, often enormous, contemporary wall clocks, some made of unusual materials such as granite. ◈ C/dels Àngels 14 • Map K2 • 93 318 65 85

La Capella
This Gothic chapel is now a contemporary art gallery, run by the city and dedicated to emerging artists. ◈ C/Hospital 56 • Map K3 • Open noon–2pm & 4–8pm Tue–Sat, 11am–2pm Sun

Foment de les Arts Decoratives (FAD)
Check out the ongoing exhibitions hosted by FAD, a century-old arts, crafts and design organization. ◈ Pl Àngels 5–6 • Map K2 • Closed Sun

La Xina A.R.T.
The very latest on the contemporary art scene features at this innovative gallery, started by four local artists in the late 1990s. ◈ C/Doctor Dou 4 • Map L2 • Closed Sun & Mon, Tue–Fri mornings

Loring Art
Multimedia and digital design are spotlighted at this trendy bookshop space. ◈ C/Gravina 8 • Map L1 • Closed Sat & Sun

The Air Shop
A range of fun inflatable products by young designers are for sale and on display here: flower vases and accessories to furniture and all kinds of personalised items. ◈ C/Àngels 20 • Map K2 • Closed Sun & Mon am

Art aficionados gather at galleries for openings once a month (Tue–Thu). Enquire at individual galleries for more information.

Left **Mies & Felj** Right **Shop window, Revólver Records**

🔟 Vintage & Second-Hand Shops

1 Mies & Felj
A labour of love for two Catalan brothers and a Dutch woman, this shop is packed with vintage fur-lined leather jackets, Chinese dresses and racks of old jeans.
🏷 *C/Riera Baixa 4–5 • Map K3*

2 HoLaLa
Rummage for an outfit at this three-floor vintage store, with everything from original silk kimonos to army pants and colourful 1950s bathing suits.
🏷 *C/Tallers 73 • Map L1*

3 Discos Edison's
This record shop has been attracting eclectic music hounds since 1979 with a fantastic vinyl collection, including Catalan folk, Broadway tunes and Spanish pop. 🏷 *C/Riera Baixa 10 • Map K3*

4 Lailo
In this theatre-turned-vintage store, you'll find everything from glitzy 1950s cocktail dresses to 1920s costumes. 🏷 *C/Riera Baixa 20 • Map K3*

5 Revólver Records
The speciality here is classic rock – as shown by the wall art depicting The Rolling Stones and Jimi Hendrix. One floor houses CDs, the other a huge selection of vinyl. 🏷 *C/Tallers 11 • Map L2*

6 Wilde Vintage
This dimly-lit, boudoiresque boutique is lined with vintage sunglasses in every shape and colour, from aviator shades to a pair of cat's-eyes specs from the 1960s. 🏷 *C/Joaquin Costa 2 • Map K2*

7 Blow by Le Swing
If you're looking for Chanel shoes, a Dior coat or a YSL evening gown, this chic, boudoir-style boutique is definitely the store for you. There are some wonderful accessories too.
🏷 *C/Doctor Dou 11 • Map L2*

8 Smart & Clean
Hip young Barcelonians swear by this secondhand store with clothes mostly from the 60s and 70s. 🏷 *C/Riera Baixa 7 • Map K3*

9 Discos Tesla
This tiny, but well-stocked, record and CD store focuses on alternative music from decades past. It is the kind of place where you can hum a few lines of a song and the owner will track it down. 🏷 *C/Tallers 3 • Map L2*

10 GI Joe Surplus
One of Spain's few army and navy surplus stores, where you can find bags, backpacks and clothing from the Russian, Israeli and US militaries.
🏷 *Ronda Sant Antoni 49 • Map K1*

For tips on shopping and standard opening hours See p139

85

Left **Zelig** Right **Zentraus**

🔟 Bars & Clubs

1 Bar Almirall
The *Modernista* doors swing open to a young, friendly crowd at Barcelona's oldest watering hole. Founded in 1860, the bar has many original fittings, plus eclectic music and strong cocktails. ⊛ *C/Joaquin Costa 33 • Map K2*

2 Zelig
Intimate and welcoming, this gay-friendly cocktail bar is a great place to start the night. There are excellent cocktails – including a mean mojito – and light snacks. ⊛ *C/Carme 116 • Map K2*

3 Bar Resolis
Formerly an old-fashioned neighbourhood bar, this is now an appealing boho-chic tavern with a small terrace. Wine and cocktails accompany delicious tapas. ⊛ *C/Riera Baixa 22 • Map K3*

4 Marsella
This dimly lit *Modernista* bar serves up cocktails and absinthe to long-time regulars and first-timers. ⊛ *C/Sant Pau 65 • Map K4*

5 Zentraus
One of the most stylish bars in the area, Zentraus has a trendy red-black-and-white decor and cool lighting. A restaurant until 1am, the tables are cleared once the DJ gets going. ⊛ *Rambla de Raval 41 • Map K4*

6 Betty Ford's
A laidback cocktail bar on lively Carrer Joaquin Costa, Betty Ford's has a soothing chill-out vibe. ⊛ *Carrer Joaquin Costa 56 • Map K1*

7 Moog
Big-name DJs spin techno and electronica, but for a boogie to classic 1980s hits head for the second floor. ⊛ *C/Arc del Teatre 3 • Map L5 • Adm*

8 Boadas Cocktail Bar
This smooth little cocktail bar, founded in 1933, continues to mix the meanest martinis in town for an elbow-to-elbow crowd. ⊛ *C/Tallers 1 • Map L2 • Closed Sun*

9 London Bar
This cluttered bar has long been *de rigueur*, once with the likes of Picasso, Hemingway and Miró. Sip cocktails and enjoy the original *Modernista* furnishings. ⊛ *C/Nou de la Rambla 34 • Map K4 • Closed Mon*

10 La Penúltima
A small, quirky bar featuring a collection of Barbie and Ken dolls in unusual positions. It's a gay-friendly spot, and is perfect for the first drink of the night. Alternative music is predominantly played. ⊛ *C/Riera Alta 40 • Map J2*

For Barcelona's best nightlife **See pp46–7**

Price Categories

For a three-course meal for one with half a bottle of wine (or equivalent meal), taxes and extra charges.

€	under €15
€€	€15–25
€€€	€25–35
€€€€	€35–45
€€€€€	over €45

Ca L'Isidre

Good-Value Eats

1 Biblioteca
The walls at this elegant restaurant are lined with antique books. Food is prepared with fresh market ingredients, and you can watch the cooks at work in the open kitchen. Book in advance. ✏ C/Junta de Comerç 29 • Map K4 • Closed Sun

2 Ànima
A sleek, minimalist restaurant that serves sophisticated Mediterranean cuisine. Great value lunch menu. ✏ C/Àngels 6 • Map K2 • 93 342 49 12 • Closed Sun & lunch in Aug • €€€

3 Ca L'Isidre
Picasso, Tapiès and even Woody Allen have dined on Catalan fare at this long-time artists' hang-out. ✏ C/Flors 12 • Map J4 • 93 441 11 39 • Closed Sat (in summer), Sun, Easter, Aug, Christmas • €€€€€

4 Silenus
Mediterranean food is served in a loft-style space hung with local artists' work. Try the ostrich. ✏ C/Àngels 8 • Map K2 • 93 302 26 80 • Closed Sun • €€€

5 Las Fernández
The original menu features dishes from the El Bierzo area in León, such as steak with Bierzo peppers. ✏ C/Carretas 11 • Map J3 • 93 443 20 43 • Closed Mon, daily lunch, three weeks Aug • €€€

6 El Jardí
Located in one of the prettiest spots in the city, El Jardí serves delicious, light cuisine, such as soups, salads and crêpes. ✏ C/de Hospital • Map K3 • Closed Mon • €

7 Imprevist
In an old warehouse, this café-restaurant, owned (and decorated) by Catalan artists, offers a global menu. ✏ C/Ferlandina 34 • Map J2 • 93 342 58 59 • Closed Sun lunch • €€€

8 Mama Cafè
Organic Mediterranean dishes (many vegetarian) are served in this airy café-restaurant Contemporary art is projected onto the wall. ✏ C/Doctor Dou 10 • Map L2 • 93 301 29 40 • Closed Sun & lunch Aug • €€€

9 Libélula
The contemporary, rustic decor complements the fresh Mediterranean fare here. Organic produce is used where possible, and menus change according to the season. ✏ C/Reina Amalia 28 • Map J4

10 L'Havana
Despite the name, this eatery serves superb Catalan cuisine. Try the selection of classic dishes such as pigs' trotters, or the fresh fish of the day. ✏ C/Lleó 1 • Map K2 • 93 302 21 06 • Closed Sun eve, Mon • €€

For tips on dining and standard opening hours See p138

Left **Palau Nacional** Right **Estadi Olímpic**

Montjuïc

AMED THE "JEWISH MOUNTAIN", *after an important Jewish cemetery that existed here in the Middle Ages, this sizeable and mountainous park rises 213 m (700 ft) above the port. The park itself was first landscaped for the 1929 International Exhibition, when the elegant Palau Nacional and the strikingly modern Mies van der Rohe Pavilion were also built. During the following decade, the area fell into general disuse and soon became synonymous with decline. Together with the grim shadow cast over the hill by the castle, which for years acted as a slaughterhouse for Franco's firing squads, it is little short of miraculous that Montjuïc is now one of Barcelona's biggest tourist draws. However, as the main site for the 1992 Olympics, held on its southern slopes, Montjuïc was given a comprehensive face-lift and the area was transformed into a beautiful green oasis, with two fabulous art museums and a host of stunning sports facilities.*

Statue, Castell de Montjuïc

All these elements are interconnected by a network of exterior escalators and interlaced with quiet, shady gardens, which offer dazzling views over Barcelona and a welcome respite from the bustle of the city.

🔟 Sights

1. Palau Nacional & Museu Nacional d'Art de Catalunya
2. Fundació Joan Miró
3. Font Màgica
4. Castell de Montjuïc
5. Estadi Olímpic
6. Teatre Grec
7. Palau Sant Jordi
8. Pavelló Mies van der Rohe
9. Poble Espanyol
10. Caixa Forum

For more on Barcelona's history **See pp30–31**

Fountains, Palau Nacional

1 Palau Nacional & Museu Nacional d'Art de Catalunya

The Palau Nacional is home to the Museu Nacional d'Art de Catalunya which exhibits Catalonia's historic art collections. Boasting one of Europe's finest displays of Romanesque art, the museum includes a series of breathtaking, 12th-century frescoes, rescued from Catalan Pyrenean churches and painstakingly reassembled in a series of galleries here. See pp18–19.

2 Fundació Joan Miró

One of Catalonia's most representative painters, Joan Miró (1893–1983), donated many of the 11,000 works held by the museum. Housed in a stark, white building designed by his friend, architect Josep Lluís Sert, the collection – the world's most complete array of Miró's work – has been extended to include 25 new pieces by him. See pp22–3.

3 Font Màgica

Below the cascades and fountains that splash down from the regal Palau Nacional is the Magic Fountain, designed by Carles Buigas for the International Exhibition of 1929. As darkness descends, countless jets of water are choreographed in a mesmerizing sound and light show. When the water meets in a single jet it can soar to 15m (50ft). The extravagant finale is often accompanied by a recording of Freddie Mercury and Montserrat Caballé singing the anthem Barcelona as the fountain fades from pink to green and back to white before silently and gracefully disappearing. ◐ Av de la Reina Maria Cristina • Map B4 • May–Sep: every 30 minutes 9:30–11:30pm Thu–Sun; Oct–Apr: every 30 minutes 7–8:30pm Fri & Sat • Free • DA

Castell de Montjuïc

4 Castell de Montjuïc

Dominating Montjuïc's hill, this gloomy castle was once a prison and torture centre for political prisoners. At the end of the Spanish Civil War, 4,000 Catalan nationalists and republicans were shot in the nearby Fossar de la Pedrera, now a grassy field overlooked by thick stone walls. After such a tragic history, the castle is entering a happier phase: it is being developed into an international peace centre, but visitors can still climb the sturdy bastions for superb views of the port below. ◐ C/Castell • Map B6 • Open Tue–Sun • Free

The funicular connects Metro Paral·lel with the Fundació Joan Miró and the cable cars that continue up to the Castell de Montjuïc.

5 Estadi Olímpic

The stadium was first built for the 1936 Workers' Olympics, which were cancelled with the outbreak of the Spanish Civil War *(see p31)*. Today, the original Neo-Classical façade is still in place, though the stadium was rebuilt for the 1992 Olympic Games *(see p31)*. It is home to Espanyol football team *(see p61)*. The nearby Museu Olímpic i de l'Esport is an interactive museum dedicated to all aspects of sport. ⊗ *Av de l'Estadi • Map B5 • Museum: open 10am–6pm (to 8pm Apr–Sep) Tue–Sat, 10am–2.30pm Sun. Stadium not open to visitors. • Adm • DA*

6 Teatre Grec

This beautiful, open-air amphitheatre *(see p60)* was inspired by the Classical ideas of what was known as *Noucentisme*. This late 19th-century architectural movement was a reaction to the overly-decorative nature of *Modernisme*. With its leafy, green backdrop and beautiful gardens, there are few places more enchanting than this to watch *Swan Lake* or listen to some jazz. The theatre is used for shows during the summertime Festival del Grec *(see p66)*, when it also becomes home to a luxurious outdoor restaurant. ⊗ *Pg Santa Madrona • Map C4 • 10am–dusk • Free (when there are no shows)*

Barcelona Chairs, Pavelló Mies van der Rohe

7 Palau Sant Jordi

The star of all the Olympic installations is this steel-and-glass indoor stadium *(see p66)* designed by Japanese architect Arata Isozaki. Holding around 17,000 people, the stadium is the home of the city's basketball team *(see p61)*. The esplanade – a surreal forest of concrete and metal pillars – was designed by Aiko Isozaki, Arata's wife. Further down the hill are the indoor and outdoor Bernat Picornell Olympic pools *(see p60)*; which are open to the public. ⊗ *Av de l'Estadi • Map A4 • Open 10am–6pm (to 8pm May–Sep) Sat & Sun • Free • DA*

Palau Sant Jordi

8 Pavelló Mies van der Rohe

You might wonder exactly what this box-like pavilion of stone, marble, onyx and glass is doing bang in the middle of Montjuïc's monumental architecture. Years ahead of its time, this surprisingly rationalist gem represents Germany's contribution to the 1929 Exhibition. Built by Ludwig Mies van der Rohe (1886–1969), the elegant pavilion was soon demolished, only to be reconstructed in 1986. Inside, the elegant sculpture *Morning* by Georg Kolbe

You can board the Montjuïc Bus Turístic (see p133), which ferries visitors up the hill from Plaça d'Espanya and back (April to October).

Poble Espanyol

(1877–1947) is reflected in a small lake. ☉ Av Marquès de Comillas • Map B4 • Open 10am–8pm daily • Adm

Poble Espanyol

This Spanish *poble* (village) has been recreated from a hotch-potch of scaled-down famous buildings and streets from around Spain. Although a bit tacky, it has become a centre for arts and crafts, including an impressive glass-blowers' workshop. There are restaurants and cafés aplenty, and a couple of trendy nightclubs (see p95). ☉ Av Marquès de Comillas • Map A3 • Open 9am–8pm Mon, 9am–2am Tue–Thu, 9am–4am Fri, 9am–5pm Sat, 9am–midnight Sun • Adm

Caixa Forum

The Fundació La Caixa's impressive collection of contemporary art is housed in a former textile factory, designed by Modernista architect Puig i Cadafalch. The collection began in 1985 and assembles some 800 works by Spanish and foreign artists, which are shown in rotation along with temporary international exhibitions. ☉ Av Marquès de Comillas • Map B3 • Open 10am–8pm daily (until 10pm Sat) • Free • DA

A Day in Montjuïc

Morning

To get to the **Fundació Joan Miró** (see pp22–3) before the crowds and with energy to spare, hop on the funicular from Paral·lel metro station. From here it is a short walk to the museum, where you'll need an hour and a half to absorb the impressive collection of Miró paintings, sketches and sculptures. When you've had your fill of contemporary art, refuel with a *cafè amb llet* (see p43) on the restaurant terrace before backtracking along Av de Miramar and jumping on the cable car up to **Castell de Montjuïc** (see p89). Wander the castle gardens and look out over the city and the bustling docks. Return to Av de Miramar by cable car and follow the signs to the **Palau Nacional** (see p89), where you can lunch on typical Catalan cuisine with a modern twist in the elegant Oleum (see p95).

Afternoon

Afterwards, spend an hour perusing the **MNAC**'s (see pp18–19) extraordinary Romanesque art collection. When you exit, turn right and then follow the signs to the Olympic complex. The **Estadi Olímpic** is worth a look, but the silver-domed **Palau Sant Jordi** steals the limelight. Nearby, at Bernat Picornell, spend the late afternoon cooling down with a dip in the fantastic open-air pool. If it's summer, there may even be a film showing. From here it is just a short stroll to the **Poble Espanyol** where you can settle in at a terrace bar in Plaça de Mayor and sip a *cuba libre* as night descends.

Around Town – Montjuïc

PAR   BALTASP   MELCHIOR

Left **Jardins Mossèn Jacint Verdaguer** Right **Castell Jardins**

🔟 Parks & Gardens

1 Jardins Mossèn Costa i Llobera
These are among Europe's most important cactus gardens. They are particularly impressive as the sun sets, when surreal and shapes and shadows emerge. 🔊 *Map C5*

2 Jardí Botànic
These wild gardens offer splendid vistas and hundreds of examples of typical Mediterranean vegetation. 🔊 *Map A4 • Open Feb, Mar, Oct: 10am–6pm daily; Apr, May, Sep: 10am–7pm daily; Jun–Aug: 10am–8pm daily; Nov–Jan: 10am–5pm daily • Adm; free last Sun of month & every Sun from 3pm*

3 Jardins Mossèn Cinto Verdaguer
The best time to visit these wonderfully elegant gardens is in spring when the plants are in blossom and the colours and aromas are in full force. 🔊 *Map C5*

4 Jardins del Castell
Cannons among the rose bushes, and pathways along the walls of a flower-filled moat, are the highlights of these gardens, which ring the castle. 🔊 *Map B5*

5 Jardins del Teatre Grec
Reminiscent of the Hanging Gardens of Babylon, this gracious oasis surrounding the Greek amphitheatre is officially known as La Rosadela. 🔊 *Map C4*

6 Jardins de Miramar
Opposite the Miramar, these gardens are scattered with

stairways leading to enchanting leafy groves with vistas. 🔊 *Map C5*

7 Jardins Laribal
This multi-level park hides a small *Modernista* house, by Puig i Cadafalch, and the Font del Gat – a drinking fountain, which has inspired many local songs. 🔊 *Map B4*

8 Jardins de Joan Maragall
An avenue lined with sculptures by Frederic Marès and Ernest Maragall is the main delight here. The garden also has the last of the city's *ginjoler* trees. 🔊 *Map B4 • Open 10am–3pm Sat & Sun*

9 Muntanya de Montjuïc
A multitude of secret paths leads through wild gardens on Montjuïc's south side, the only part of the mountain that remains untamed. 🔊 *Map A5*

10 El Mirador del Llobregat
A viewing area with small gardens nearby, this is the only place in the city where you can see the plains of the Llobregat stretching below. 🔊 *Map A3 • DA*

Unless otherwise stated, parks & gardens are usually open 10am–dusk daily.

Price Categories

For a three-course	**€** under €15
meal for one with half	**€€** €15–25
a bottle of wine (or	**€€€** €25–35
equivalent meal), taxes	**€€€€** €35–45
and extra charges.	**€€€€€** over €45

Interior, Font de Prades

TOP 10 Restaurants, Cafés, Bars & Clubs

1 Oleum
Dine on refined Mediterranean cuisine under the dome of the Palau Nacional and enjoy amazing views across the city. ◈ *Palau Nacional • Map B4 • 93 289 06 79 • Closed Mon, eves • DA • €€€*

2 Bar Seco
A simple café serving cakes and snacks, with more substantial dishes at lunchtime. There's a summer terrace, organic wines and beers and free Wi-Fi. ◈ *Passeig Montjuïc 74 • Map C5 • 93 329 63 74 • Closed Mon–Wed eve • €€*

3 Fundació Joan Miró Restaurant
A great terrace, views of Miró's sculptures, plus modern Mediterranean food. ◈ *Parc de Montjuïc • Map B5 • 93 329 07 68 • Closed eve • DA • €€*

4 Rias de Galicia
A giant aquarium is full of lobster, crabs and more, all waiting to be plucked out and served up sizzling on a plate. ◈ *C/Lleida 9 • Map C4 • 93 424 81 52 • €€€€€*

5 La Tomaquera
A neighbourhood classic that serves Catalan home cooking at bargain prices. Arrive early or be prepared to queue. ◈ *C/Margarit 58 • Map C4 • Closed dinner Sun, Mon, Aug, Easter week • €€*

6 El Lliure
The Lliure theatre has a good-value café with an adjoining restaurant. In summer there are tables on the terrace. ◈ *Passeig Santa Madrona 40-46 • Map B4 • Closed Mon eve, Sat lunch, Sun • €€€*

7 La Terrrazza
Dance music rules at one of Barcelona's most popular nightclubs, housed in a Balearic-style mansion inside the Poble Espanyol. ◈ *Poble Espanyol • Map A3 • Closed Sun, mid-Oct–mid-Jun • Adm*

8 Font de Prades
By far the best food in the Poble Espanyol. ◈ *Poble Espanyol • Map A3 • 93 426 75 19 • Closed Mon, three weeks Jan • €€€*

9 Restaurant Forestier
Located in the AC Miramar, this elegant restaurant has wonderful views over the harbour and city. ◈ *Pl. Carlos Ibáñez, 3 • Map C5 • 93 281 16 00 • €€€€*

10 Quimet & Quimet
This tiny bodega has standing room only, but serves tasty tapas and wonderful wines. ◈ *C/Poeta Cabanyes • Map C4 • 93 442 31 42 • Closed Sat eve, Sun, Aug • €*

Unless otherwise stated, all restaurants accept credit cards. Admission to Poble Espanyol is free if you have a restaurant reservation.

Left **L'Aquàrium** Right **Swing Bridge, between La Rambla & Moll D'Espanya**

Port Vell, Barceloneta & Port Olímpic

THE HEADY ALLURE OF THE MEDITERRANEAN *permeates Barcelona, and a dip into its azure waters is only a few metro stops (or a brisk walk) away. Barcelona's beaches were once hidden behind an industrial wasteland, but things changed radically in preparation for the 1992 Olympics. The rallying cry was to create a new Barcelona oberta al mar (open to the sea); the result is phenomenal, as is the presence of large crowds seeking sun and sea. Tons of sand were transported to create miles of silky beaches from the fisherman's quarter of Barceloneta to Port Olímpic and beyond. Palm trees were planted, water cleanliness standards implemented and, this being design-obsessed Barcelona, numerous contemporary sculptures erected. The city's first two skyscrapers, the Torre Mapfre office building and the five-star Hotel Arts (see p143), punctuate the port's skyline, while the nearby Port Olímpic throbs with scores of bars, clubs and restaurants.*

Barceloneta beach

🔟 Sights & Attractions

1. Beaches
2. Museu d'Història de Catalunya
3. Rambla de Mar
4. L'Aquàrium
5. Barceloneta
6. Boat & Cable Car Trips
7. Pailebot Santa Eulàlia
8. Submarine Ictíneo II
9. El Centre de la Vila-Port Olímpic
10. World Trade Center

Take a boat tour of the port area **See p133**

Beaches

Fancy a splash in the Mediterranean? Trot down to the end of La Rambla, wander along the palm tree-lined Moll de la Fusta, down restaurant-packed Passeig Joan de Borbó, et voilà, the sea beckons. Over four km (2.5 miles) of blue flag beaches stretch north from Barceloneta to Port Olímpic and beyond. Facilities are top-notch, including showers, deck chairs, beach volleyball courts and lifeguards. Convenience, however, means crowds, so finding a spot among the masses of oiled bodies can be a challenge, particularly in the summer. ✈ Map E6

Museu d'Història de Catalunya

Housed in the Palau de Mar, a renovated portside warehouse, this museum offers a broad, interactive exploration of Catalonia's history since prehistoric times. Kids *(see p63)* especially will have a ball with the engaging exhibits, such as a Civil War-era bunker and a recreated Catalan bar from the 1960s with an ancient *futbolín* (table football) game. ✈ Pl Pau Vila 3, Palau de Mar • Map N6 • Open 10am–7pm Tue–Sat (to 8pm Wed), 10am–2:30pm Sun • Adm €4, free first Sun of month • DA

Rambla de Mar

Saunter along the Rambla de Mar, a floating wooden pier that leads to Maremagnum, a flashy mall that has many shops and restaurants. Nearby the giant IMAX® cinema shows 3-D films on megascreens generally on

Museu d'Història de Catalunya

nature-, adventure- and sports-related topics. ✈ Moll d'Espanya • Map E5 ✈ Maremagnum: shops open 10am–10pm daily; restaurants until 1am daily ✈ IMAX: shows from 12:20–10:25pm daily • Adm • DA

L'Aquàrium

Come face to face with the marine world of the Mediterranean at Barcelona's impressive aquarium, the largest in Europe. The highlight is the 80-m (262-ft) long underwater tunnel, which has a moving walkway that transports visitors through the deep blue unknown, while sharks glide menacingly close. A huge hit with the kids is the Explora! floor, with interactive exhibits that allow you to explore the ecosystems of the Mediterranean. ✈ Moll d'Espanya • Map E6 • Open Jul & Aug: 9:30am–11pm daily; Sep–Jun: 9:30am–9pm Mon–Fri (to 9:30pm Sat & Sun) • Adm

Yachts, Port Olímpic

The top floor café at the Museu d'Història de Catalunya has sweeping views of the city, the port area & Montjuïc.

5 Barceloneta

A portside warren of narrow streets, small squares and ancient bars, this traditional neighbourhood of *pescadors* (fishermen) and *mariners* (sailors) seems worlds apart from the megamalls and disco lights of nearby Port Olímpic. A refreshing foray through this tight-knit community yields a glimpse into

Yachts & skyscrapers, Port Olimpic

the way Barcelona was 150 years ago. Older couples still pull chairs out onto the street to gossip and watch the world go by, and small seafood restaurants serve a *menú del dia* of whatever's fresh off the boat. Running the length of Barceloneta's western edge is Passeig Joan de Borbó, which is lined with restaurants serving *mariscs* (shellfish) and paellas. ◎ *Map F5*

6 Boat & Cable Car Trips

See Barcelona's port activity from a different perspective, either from the air or the sea. The *Transbordador Aeri* cable

Street scene, Barceloneta

cars offer sweeping bird's-eye views of Barcelona and its coast, while the old-fashioned Les Golondrines boats and the Orsom Catamaran and speedboat sweep you around the port area. ◎ *Telefèric, from Torre Jaume I & Torre San Sebastià • Map D6 & E6 • Adm ◎ Les Golondrines, Portal de la Pau • Map E5 • roughly 30 mins from 11:30am • 93 442 31 06 • Adm ◎ Orsom, Portal de la Pau • www.barcelona-orsom.com • Map E5 • Call 93 441 05 37 for times • Adm • DA*

7 Pailebot Santa Eulàlia

Bobbing in the water at the Moll de la Fusta (Timber Quay) is this renovated, three-mast schooner, originally christened *Carmen Flores*. It first set sail from Spain in 1918. On journeys to Cuba, the ship used to transport textiles and salt, and return with tobacco, coffee, cereals and wood. In 1997, the Museu Marítim *(see p81)* bought and restored the ship as part of an ongoing project to create a collection of seaworthy historical Catalan vessels.

◎ *Moll de la Fusta • Map L6 • Open noon–5:30pm Mon–Fri • Adm*

8 Submarine Ictíneo II

In 1859, Catalan Narcís Monturiol invented one of the world's first submarines, a replica of which stands on the Moll d'Espanya. Hard to believe, but in an earlier version of this wooden, fish-shaped submarine, powered by two internal steam engines, Monturiol made a number of successful underwater journeys.

For more on boat and cable cars trips **See p133**

He invented the submarine as a means of gathering coral; later, he tried to sell it to the army. However, he finally sold his invention in parts and died penniless. ◈ *Moll d'Espanya • Map E5*

9 El Centre de la Vila-Port Olímpic

This shopping complex offers a slew of shops, cafés and fast food restaurants. Best of all, it houses the cinemas of the Icària Yelmo Cineplex *(see p67)*, one of the largest cinemas in town to show VO (non-dubbed) films.
◈ *Salvador Espriu 61 • Map H5*
• Mall shops open 10am–10pm Mon–Sat

Pailebot Santa Eulàlia

10 World Trade Center

This massive, circular structure is an iconic building in Port Vell. It is home to shops, offices, congress and convention halls, a five-star hotel and, fashionable restaurant and nightclub, The Sugar Club. In the central courtyard is a "rhythmic" fountain that spurts out streams of water at differing velocities. Nearby, you can board cable cars and soak up splendid views from the top of Torre Jaume I. ◈ *Moll de Barcelona • Map D6 • DA*

Exploring the Port

Morning

🕙 Begin your port *passeig* (stroll) with a visit to the **Museu Marítim** *(see p81)*, where you can see Barcelona's status as one of the most active ports in the Mediterranean. From here, head towards the Monument a Colom *(see p12)*, and stroll the Moll de la Fusta to admire the **Pailebot Santa Eulàlia**, which has been immaculately restored by the museum. Saunter down the **Rambla de Mar** *(see p97)*, an undulating wooden drawbridge that leads to the glitzy Maremagnum mega-mall. At the start of the pier, embark on the **Orsom Catamaran**, where you can grab a drink and snack and soak up the rays and the port skyline, while sprawled out on a net just inches above the water. Back on land, about 90 minutes later, stroll down the Moll d'Espanya and turn towards the traditional fisherman's quarter of **Barceloneta**, an atmospheric pocket of narrow streets and timeworn bars. Get a real taste of old-style Barcelona at the boisterous tapas bar, **El Vaso de Oro** (C/Balboa 6). Wedge yourself in at the bar and savour some tasty seafood morsels.

Afternoon

Revived, head to Pg Joan de Borbó and make for the beach. Douse yourself in the Med, then siesta in the afternoon sun. Pick yourself up with sangria at the beachside **Salamanca Chiringuito** (at the end of Pg Joan de Borbó), where you can bury your feet in the sand and watch the waves lap on the shore as the sun dips into the horizon.

➜ You can't miss Frank Gehry's massive, glistening *Peix* sculpture on Passeig Marítim **See p41**

Left **Club Catwalk** Right **Razzmatazz**

TOP 10 Bars & Beach Clubs

1 Club Catwalk
One of the hottest clubs in town, this has two floors: one for the bar and chilling out, and the other for dancing to hip hop, R 'n' B, electronica and house. ⊗ *Ramón Trías Fargas 2–4 • Map G6 • Closed Mon–Wed • DA • Adm*

2 CDLC
Right by the beach, with a terrace on which to relax, this is a restaurant that becomes a club after dinner. Guest DJs feature every week. ⊗ *Passeig Marítim de la Barceloneta 32 • Map G6*

3 Bar Jai Ca
The TV blares and kids race around in this relaxed neighbourhood favourite. Delicious tapas are on offer. ⊗ *C/Ginebra 13 • Map F5 • 93 268 32 65*

4 Kennedy Irish Sailing Club
When you tire of dance music, try this Irish bar with a popular terrace; regular live gigs in summer. ⊗ *Moll Mistral 26–27 • Map G5 • Closed Mon*

5 Arola
A luxurious, summer-only poolside bar at the plush Hotel Arts, the Arola has huge white beds covered with silk cushions, DJ sessions, and a range of perfectly mixed cocktails. ⊗ *C/ Marina 19–21 • Map G5 • 93 483 80 90*

6 Le Kasbah
With Arabic decoration, soft lights and house music, this bar in the Palau del Mar building provides a city oasis. ⊗ *Plaça de Pau Vila 1 • Map F6 • Closed Mon*

7 Mar Bella beach bars
Head to one of the *xiringuitos* (beach bars) on Barcelona's hippest beach and enjoy the DJ sessions. ⊗ *Platja Nova Mar Bella*

8 Eclipse
The spectacular bar on the 26th floor of the landmark Hotel Vela offers some of the most magnificent views of the city. ⊗ *Hotel Vela Plaça de la Rosa dels Vents 1 • Map F6 • 93 295 28 00*

9 Shôko
A Japanese restaurant during the day, this club by the beach provides all kinds of music in a great setting. ⊗ *Passeig Marítim de la Barceloneta 36 • Map E6 • Closed Mon–Tue and in winter*

10 Razzmatazz
Concerts – from rock to jazz – feature several nights a week at this trendy club, which boasts five different spaces offering a range of musical styles, such as the Razz Club, Loli.ta and the Loft. ⊗ *C/Almogàvers 122 (The Loft: C/ Pamplona 88) • Map H4 • Razz Club and Loft closed Sun–Thu*

For Barcelona's best nightlife See pp46–7

Agua

Price Categories

For a three-course meal for one with half a bottle of wine (or equivalent meal), taxes and extra charges.	€ under €15
	€€ €15–25
	€€€ €25–35
	€€€€ €35–45
	€€€€€ over €45

🔟 Restaurants & Tapas Bars

1 Set Portes
Founded in 1836, this large institution serves some of the finest Catalan cuisine in the city, including paellas. ◈ Pg Isabel II 14 • Map N5 • 93 319 30 33 • DA • €€€€€

2 Agua
The spacious terrace at this restaurant boasts views of the sea. Superb seafood and Mediterranean fare feature on the menu. ◈ Pg Marítim 30 • Map G6 • 93 225 12 72 • DA • €€€€

3 Can Manel la Puda
The oldest restaurant on this strip serves Catalan cuisine, specializing in catch-of-the-day dishes. ◈ Pg Joan de Borbó 60–61 • Map F6 • 93 221 50 13 • Closed Mon • €€€

4 Somorrostro
This chic restaurant serves a daily changing menu prepared with fresh ingredients. Warm ambience and decor. ◈ Sant Carles 11 • Map F6 • 93 225 00 10 • Closed lunch (except Sun), Tue, two weeks Jan • €€€

5 Kaiku
Decorated with fishing prints and nets, Kaiku is known for its tasty seafood, particularly the arros del xef (chef's rice). Book early for a table on the terrace. ◈ Plaça del Mar 1 • Map E6 • 93 221 90 82 • Closed eve, Mon • €€€

6 Salamanca
This may feel like a tourist trap at first, with its packed dining rooms and photo-covered walls, but the food is top notch. There are plenty of meat dishes on offer. ◈ C/Almirall Cervera 34 • Map F6 • 93 221 50 33 • €€€€

7 Can Ganassa
An old-style, family-run tapas bar that has been serving fresh seafood tapas to locals for decades. ◈ Pl de la Barceloneta 4–6 • Map F6 • 93 225 75 86 • €

8 Merendero de la Mari
Located in the historic Palau del Mar building, this restaurant serves seafood and some of the best paellas in the area. ◈ Plaça Pau Vila, 1 • Map F6 • 93 221 31 41 • €€€€

9 Suquet de l'Almirall
This family-run gem serves excellent arroz de barca (rice in broth, with seafood) and suquet (seafood and potato stew). ◈ Pg Joan de Borbó 63 • Map F6 • 93 221 62 33 • Closed Sun eve, Mon, three weeks Aug • DA • €€€€€

10 Lluçanès
Located in Barceloneta's revamped municipal market, award-winning Lluçanès offers exquisite Catalan cuisine in contemporary surroundings. ◈ Plaça de la Font • Map F6 • 93 224 25 25 • €€€€

Unless otherwise stated, all restaurants accept credit cards.
For tips on dining and standard opening hours See p138

Left **Fountain, Rambla de Catalunya** Right *Modernista* **hotel entrance**

Eixample

I F THE OLD TOWN IS THE HEART *of Barcelona and the green mountains of Tibidabo and Montjuïc the lungs, the Eixample is the city's nervous system – its economic and commercial core. The area began to take shape in 1860 when the city was permitted to expand beyond the medieval walls (see p30). Its design, based on plans by Catalan engineer Ildefons Cerdà, comprises hundreds of symmetrical grid-like squares. Construction continued into the 20th century at a time when Barcelona's elite was patronizing the city's most daring architects. Modernisme was flourishing and the area became home to the cream of Barcelona's Modernista architecture, with myriad elegant façades and balconies. Today, a wealth of enchanting cafés, funky design shops, gourmet restaurants and hip bars and clubs draws the professional crowd, which has adopted the neighbourhood as its own.*

🔟 Sights

1. Sagrada Família
2. La Pedrera
3. Mansana de la Discòrdia
4. Hospital de la Santa Creu i de Sant Pau
5. Fundació Tàpies
6. Palau Baro de Quadras
7. Fundació Francisco Godia
8. Rambla de Catalunya
9. Universitat de Barcelona
10. Museu Egipci

Spires, Sagrada Família

For more on Modernista architecture **See pp32–3**

1 Sagrada Família
Gaudí's wizardry culminated in this enchanting, wild, unconventional temple, which dominates the city skyline *(see pp8–10)*.

2 La Pedrera
A daring, surreal fantasyland, and Gaudí's most remarkable civic work *(see pp20–21)*.

3 Mansana de la Discòrdia
At the heart of the city's *Quadrat d'Or* (Golden Square) lies this stunning block of houses. Literally "the block of discord", the Mansana de la Discòrdia is so-called because of the dramatic contrast of its three flagship buildings. Built between 1900 and 1907 by the three *Modernista* greats, rival architects Gaudí, Domènech i Montaner and Puig i Cadafalch, the buildings were commissioned by competing bourgeois families. Domènech is represented by the ornate Casa Lleó Morera *(see p33)*; Puig makes his mark with the Gothic-inspired Casa Amatller *(see p33)*; and Gaudí flaunts his architectural prowess with Casa Batlló *(see p33)*. All boast superb interiors, but Casa Lleó Morera is closed to the public. Casa Amatller runs tours of the top floor studio and the exhibition area. The houses at Nos. 37 and

Windows, Casa Battló, Mansana de la Discòrdia

39 add to the overall splendour of the block. The Perfume Museum is at No. 39 *(see p41)*. ✆ *Pg de Gràcia 35–45 • Map E2*

4 Hospital de la Santa Creu i de Sant Pau
Still a fully functioning hospital, it was built in two stages from 1905 by Domènech i Montaner and his son. A tribute to *Modernisme* – and Domènech's answer to Gaudí's Sagrada Família – the sumptuous design comprises eight pavilions and various other buildings linked by underground tunnels. The pavilions, each different, recall the history of Catalonia with murals, mosaics and sculptures. Interlacing the buildings are gardens creating beautiful outdoor oases. The courtyards and gardens are open to visitors. Part of the Ruta del Modernisme *(see p133)*. ✆ *C/ Sant Antoni Maria Claret 167 • Map H1*

Left **Hospital de la Santa Creu i de Sant Pau** Right **Casa Lléo Morera, Mansana de la Discòrdia**

For more on Antoni Gaudí **See p11**

Main entrance, Fundació Francisco Godia

Fundació Tàpies
Paintings and sculptures by Antoni Tàpies (b. 1923), Catalonia's foremost living artist, are housed in this early *Modernista* building *(see p32)*. For a glimpse of what awaits inside, look up: crowning the museum is the artist's eye-catching wire sculpture *Cloud & Chair* (1990). The collection of over 300 pieces covers Tàpies' whole range of work, including impressive abstract pieces such as *Grey Ochre on Brown* (1962). Temporary exhibitions are also held here, with past shows by Mario Herz, Hans Hacke and Craigie Horsfield. ◎ *C/Aragó 255 • Map E2 • 93 487 03 15 • Open 10am–8pm Tue–Sun • Adm • DA • Free under 16*

Palau Baró de Quadras
Built by the architect Puig i Cadafalch, this *Modernista* mansion has a Gothic influence with its medieval-style turrets adorned with gargoyles. The mansion now houses the Casa Asia, and is open to the public for regular exhibitions on Asian themes. The building is located between two important streets and has two completely different façades. ◎ *Avda Diagonal 373 • Map E2 • 93 368 08 36 • Open 10am–8pm Tue–Sat, 10am–2pm Sun*

Ildefons Cerdà

Ildefons Cerdà's design for the new city, comprising a uniform grid of square blocks, received backing in 1859. Reflecting Cerdà's utopian socialist ideals, each block was to have a garden-like courtyard, surrounded by uniform flats. Real estate vultures soon intervened and the court-yards were converted into warehouses and factories. Today these green spaces are gradually being reinstated.

Fundació Francisco Godia
Although Francisco Godia (1921–90) was best known for his prowess behind the wheel – notably as an F1 racing driver – his passions extended to the art world. His once private collection now forms this museum and en-compasses a range of art from medieval times to the 20th century: from Jaume Huguet's altarpiece *St Mary Magdalene* (c. 1445) to a range of Spanish ceramics and works by 17th-century fresco-painter Luca Giardano. ◎ *C/Diputació 250 • Map E3 • 93 272 31 80 • Open 10am–8pm daily • Adm*

Cloud & Chair sculpture, Fundació Tàpies

8 Rambla de Catalunya

This elegant extension of the better-known Rambla is a more up-market version. Lined with trees that form a leafy green tunnel in summer, it boasts scores of pretty façades and shops, including the *Modernista* Farmàcia Bolos (No. 77). The avenue teems with terrace bars and cafés, which are ideal for people-watching. *See also p50.* ◈ *Map E2*

Interior courtyard, Universitat de Barcelona

9 Universitat de Barcelona

Until 1958, this was the only university in Barcelona – today it is one of six. The graceful building (1861–89) occupies two blocks of the Eixample and has a distinct air of academia. The interior gardens with their fountains and patios make for a cool, shady hideaway on hot afternoons. ◈ *Pl de la Universitat • Map E3*

10 Museu Egipci

Spain's most important Egyptology museum houses more than 350 exhibits from over 3,000 years of Ancient Egypt. Exhibits include terracotta figures, human and animal mummies, and a bust of the lion goddess Sekhmet (700–300 BC). ◈ *C/València 284 • Map E2 • Open 10am–8pm Mon–Sat, 10am–2pm Sun • 93 488 01 88 • www.museuegipci.com • Adm*

The Modernista Route

Morning

🕐 Pop into the decrepit chess bar El Pato Loco (cnr Diputació & Aribau) to get a sepia picture of Barcelona that hasn't changed for a century. Wake up with a *café solo* and watch the old men playing speed-chess, then stroll around the gardens of the **Universitat**. Head east along Gran Via past the elegant Palace Barcelona Hotel *(see p143)* and right down C/Bruc for your first real taste of Catalan Art Nouveau, with Gaudí's **Casa Calvet** *(see p107)* on C/Casp. Turn right onto C/Casp and walk three blocks west to the majestic Pg de Gràcia; then go right again three blocks to the impressive buildings known as the **Mansana de la Discòrdia** *(see p103)* and the **Perfume Museum** *(see p41)*. Sniff around **Regia** perfume shop *(see p106)* before continuing north to marvel at Gaudí's **La Pedrera** *(see pp20–21)*. Feeling peckish? Stop at **Tragaluz** on Ptge de la Concepció *(see p109)*. The set menu is an enjoyable way to experience this glitterati hang-out.

Afternoon

After lunch, head north on Pg de Gràcia, turn right along Diagonal, taking in the fairy-tale **Casa de les Punxes** at No. 416 *(see p33)*. Walk along Diagonal, making a detour left at Pg Sant Joan to see **Palau Macaya** at No. 108. Then stroll along C/Mallorca to the **Sagrada Família** *(see pp8–11)*. Here you can take in the Nativity Façade and rest weary legs in the Plaça de Gaudí before climbing the bell towers for a breathtaking view of the city.

Left **Light, Dos i Una** Centre **Shoppers, Passeig de Gràcia** Right **Furniture, Vinçon**

TOP 10 Design Shops

1 Vinçon
The cream of the crop in Spanish design with out-of-this-world designs for the most everyday objects. Furniture is displayed in a 1900 upper-class apartment. Breathtaking.
✎ Pg de Gràcia 96 • Map E2

2 L'Appartement
A spacious, white-painted store packed with gorgeous furnishings and knick-knacks at reasonable prices: from quirky, cool lights and sculptures to bags, jewellery and t-shirts. ✎ C/Enric Granados 44 • Map E2 • Closed Sun & Mon

3 Regia
The biggest perfume shop in the city has over one thousand scents, including all the leading brands and other surprises. Also home to the Perfume Museum (see p41). ✎ Pg de Gràcia 39 • Map E2

4 Dos i Una
A designer gift shop with a steel-tiled floor and a psychedelic colour scheme. Concentrates on selling "made in Barcelona" items, which make for unusual souvenirs.
✎ C/Rosselló 275 • Map E2

5 Muxart
Excellent and arty shoe shop for men, women and kids in a country famed for its leather.
✎ C/Rosselló 230 • Map E2

6 Biosca & Botey
Exceptionally elegant shop selling all kinds of lamps, from Art-Nouveau mushrooms to ultra-modern steel shades. ✎ Rambla de Catalunya 125 • Map E2 • DA

7 Pilma
Breathtaking designer shop selling quality modern furniture and interior accessories by big names, as well as cutting-edge creations by Catalan designers.
✎ Av Diagonal 403 • Map E1

8 DBarcelona
An eclectic range of gadgets and gifts in a shop that doubles as an exhibition space for up-and-coming designers and more established artists.
✎ Av Diagonal 367 • Map F2

9 Kowasa
A specialist photography bookshop with over 7,000 titles, including foreign magazines. The ambience is friendly and intimate and browsing is encouraged.
✎ C/Mallorca 235 • Map E2 • DA

10 Sadur
The owner designs and sells leather accessories, many with a Barcelona theme: wallets, bags and a few paths, well made and well priced. ✎ C/Bruc 150 • Map F2

For tips on shopping and standard opening hours See p139

Left **Dance Floor, City Hall** Right **OmmSessions Club**

Top 10 After-Dark Venues

1 La Fira
Decked out in vintage fairground memorabilia, this striking bar rates high on novelty factor. Order a *cuba libre* while swaying in a swing. Lively atmosphere, unique setting. Ⓢ *C/Provença 171 • Map D2 • Closed Mon • Adm*

2 Minusa Club
This is a refreshingly relaxed music bar in an otherwise rather snooty neighbourhood. Good for afternoon coffee, it fills up in the evenings when DJs get the crowd going with funk and ol ectropop. Ⓢ *C/València 166 • Map D2*

3 Dry Martini
A classic and elegant venue where extraordinarily professional barmen are ready to prepare your favourite cocktail. Quiet jazz sounds play in the background. Ⓢ *C/Aribau 162 • Map D2*

4 OmmSessions Club
Located in possibly the most fashionable address in town, the OmmSessions Club attracts a young, international crowd. Ⓢ *C/Rosselló 265 • Map E2*

5 Velvet
Large, popular and populist disco bar with lavish decor, luxury fittings and music ranging from Elvis to Abba. Ⓢ *C/Balmes 161 • Map E2 • Adm*

6 Luz de Gas
A classic late-night watering hole, this half concert hall, half bar has live music nightly – from blues to jazz and soul. Ⓢ *C/Muntaner 246 • Map D1 • DA*

7 Ideal
Luxurious cocktail lounge opened by legendary barman José María Gotarda in the 1950s and now run by his son. More than 80 varieties of whisky. Ⓢ *C/Aribau 89 • Map D2 • Closed Sun*

8 City Hall
This popular club has two dance floors. Club nights cover a range of music styles, from electro pop to drum 'n' bass. Ⓢ *Rambla de Catalunya 2-4 • Map E3*

9 Museum
This is currently the hottest gay bar in town. The black-and-gold faux Baroque decor is offset with huge video screens showing disco divas. Ⓢ *C/Sepúlveda 178 • Map D3 (Sepúlveda)•Open 10pm–3am daily*

10 Les Gens que j'Aime
The ideal place to have a drink while enjoying soft music, after walking around Passeig de Gràcia and Rambla Catalunya. Ⓢ *València 286 • Map E2 • Open 6pm–2:30am daily (3am weekends)*

For Barcelona's best nightlife **See pp46–7**

Left **Laie Llibreria Cafè** Right **Casa Alfonso**

TOP 10 Cafés

1 Laie Llibreria Cafè
A cultural meeting place with a lively atmosphere, airy terrace and foreign newspapers. There's an excellent set lunch and live jazz (on Thursdays). ® C/Pau Claris 85 • Map E3 • Closed Sun & Mon eve

2 Cafè del Centre
Said to be the oldest café in the Eixample, with dark wooden interiors that have not changed for a century. An unpretentious spot for a quiet coffee. ® C/Girona 69 • Map F3 • Closed after 9pm

3 Casa Alfonso
This classy café has been in business since 1929. Arguably the best *pernil* (serrano ham) in the city. ® C/Roger de Llúria 6 • Map F3 • Closed Sun

4 Cacao Sampaka
An infinite array of chocolate, including innovative combinations such as chocolate with Parmesan cheese or olive oil. ® C/Consell de Cent 292 • Map E3 • Closed Sun, mornings in Aug

5 Mauri
One of the best pastry shops in town. Enjoy a hot drink with an elaborate dessert in *Modernista* surroundings. ® Rambla Catalunya 102 • Map E2 • Closed Sun eve

6 Galeria Cosmos
Located on a semi-pedestrianized street, this art gallery café offers sandwiches, cakes and tapas. Free Wi-Fi. ® C/Enric Granados 3

• Map E2 • Open 10am–10pm Mon–Thu, noon–2am Fri & Sat, noon–10pm Sun

7 Palace Barcelona
This elegant *Modernista* hotel, formerly the Ritz, is the perfect place for breakfast in the conservatory or afternoon tea in the Grand Hall. It's thoroughly luxurious, but pricey. ® Gran Via de les Corts Catalanes 668 • Map F3 • DA

8 Bauma
A mixed crowd drifts in to read the paper or smoke a Havana cigar with a post-lunch *carajillo* (coffee and cognac). ® C/Roger de Llúria 124 • Map F2 • Closed Sat • DA

9 Mantequería Ravell
A deli-style shop offering incredible breakfasts, including eggs with foie gras, at a huge communal table. Wine and traditional hams and cheeses are also available. ® C/Aragó 313 • Map F2 • Closed Mon & Sat after 6pm, Tue & Wed after 9pm, Sun

10 Tragarrapid
A chic café below the Tragaluz restaurant. Up-market tapas and coffee served with style. ® Ptge de la Concepció 5 • Map E2

For tips on dining and standard opening hours See p138

Price Categories

For a three-course meal for one with half a bottle of wine (or equivalent meal), taxes and extra charges.

€	under €15
€€	€15–25
€€€	€25–35
€€€€	€35–45
€€€€€	over €45

Casa Calvet

TOP 10 Restaurants & Tapas Bars

1 Tragaluz
Popular with the fashionable crowd, this design-conscious, restaurant with a huge skylight (tragaluz) serves imaginative Mediterranean cuisine. ⊗ Ptge de la Concepció 5 • Map E2 • 93 487 01 96 • €€€€€

2 La Semproniana
Set in an old printworks, this place serves food that's a cross between Catalan and nouvelle cuisine – with a sense of playfulness. Try the black pudding lasagne. ⊗ C/Rosselló 148 • Map E2 • 93 453 18 20 • Closed Sun • €€€€ • DA

3 Cinc Sentits
Indulge the five senses (cinc sentits in Catalan) at this stylish restaurant, where diners are wowed with modern interpretations of classic Catalan cuisine. ⊗ C/Aribau 53 • Map D2 • 93 323 94 90 • Closed Sun & Mon • €€€€€

4 Velódromo
This historic bar was reopened by Catalan celebrity chef Charles Abellan. The menu features sophisticated versions of Catalan classics. The original 1930s furnishings have been preserved. ⊗ C/Muntaner 213 • Map D1 • €€

5 Noti
Apart from the superb French-Mediterranean cuisine and stylish decor, Noti also has an adjoining cocktail bar. ⊗ C/Roger de Lluria 35–37 • Map F3 • 93 342 66 73 • Closed Sat lunch, Sun • €€€€ • DA

6 Casa Calvet
Catalan food with a modern twist is served in Gaudí-designed dining rooms. ⊗ C/Casp 48 • Map F3 • 93 412 40 12 • Closed Sun • €€€€€ • DA

7 Moo
Run by the Roca brothers, Moo serves creative Catalan recipes prepared with the finest local ingredients. Book in advance. ⊗ C/Rosselló 265 • Map E2 • 93 445 40 00 • €€€€ • DA

8 Inopia
Tucked away in a residential neighbourhood, Inopia serves traditional tapas. Long queues. ⊗ C/Tamarit 104 • Map C3 • 93 424 52 31 • Closed Tue–Fri lunch, Sun, Mon • €€€ • DA

9 Cervecería Catalana
Just a few steps from Rambla de Catalunya, with some of the best tapas in town and a variety of beers. ⊗ C/Mallorca 236 • Map E2 • 93 216 03 68 • €€€ • DA

10 Paco Meralgo
This bright, modern tapas bar has a gourmet menu based on recipes from around the country. ⊗ C/Muntaner 171 • Map D1 • 93 430 90 27 • €€

Unless otherwise stated, all restaurants accept credit cards.
For tips on dining and standard opening hours **See p138**

Left **Cloister, Monestir de Pedralbes** Right **Exterior, Palau de Pedralbes**

Gràcia, Tibidabo & Zona Alta

THE ZONA ALTA *(Uptown)* is an area covering several neighbourhoods that, as the name suggests, are in the hilly part of the city. From the moneyed streets of Pedralbes and Tibidabo to bohemian Gràcia, this entire northern area of the city offers stunning views and regal attractions. But what really sets this area apart from the rest of the city is its 15 parks; the best are Gaudí's stunning and imaginative Parc Güell, and the colossal natural park of Collserola, which spreads out like green baize over Tibidabo mountain. Gràcia stands out as the city's most cosmopolitan neighbourhood. Its strong political tradition and gypsy community have long drawn artists and writers to the labyrinthine streets, and it is now home to scores of innovative boutiques, bars and squares, which teem with life most nights of the week.

Parc d'Atraccions del Tibidabo

🔟 Sights & Attractions

1. Parc d'Atraccions del Tibidabo
2. Monestir de Pedralbes
3. Torre de Collserola
4. Museu del FC Barcelona & Camp Nou Stadium
5. Palau Reial de Pedralbes
6. Parc Güell
7. Temple Expiatori del Sagrat Cor
8. Parc de Collserola
9. Tramvia Blau
10. Jardins del Laberint d'Horta

The best way to visit this area is on the Bus Turístic **See p133**

1 Parc d'Atraccions del Tibidabo

Take the funicular up to the top of Tibidabo's 517-m (1,695-ft) mountain to visit this traditional amusement park, which first opened in 1908. Although there are a couple of stomach-churning, white-knuckle rides, the real attractions are the quaint, old-fashioned ones, including a beautifully conserved carousel and a Ferris wheel. Here also is the Museu dels Autòmates *(see p41)*, with automatons, mechanical models and a scale model of the park. ◈ Pl de Tibidabo • Map B1 • Opening times vary, call 93 211 79 42 for details • www.tibidabo.es • Adm • DA

2 Monestir de Pedralbes

Named after the Latin *petras albas*, which means white stones, this outstandingly beautiful Gothic monastery was founded by Queen Elisenda de Montcada de Piños in the early 14th century. Her alabaster tomb lies in the wall between the church and the particularly impressive three-storey Gothic cloister. An interesting glimpse of medieval life is provided by the furnished kitchens, cells, infirmary and refectory, all of which are well preserved. ◈ C/Baixada Monestir 9 • Map A1 • Open 10am–2pm Tue–Sat

(until 5pm Apr–Sep), 10am–8pm Sun • Adm; free 1st Sun of the month and every Sun 3–8pm • DA

3 Torre de Collserola

This slender telecommunications tower was designed by British architect Norman Foster.

Torre de Collserola

The needle-like upper structure rests on a concrete pillar and is anchored by 12 huge steel cables. Rising to a height of 560 m (1836 ft) above sea level, the top is reached by a glass-fronted elevator. On a clear day, you can see Montserrat and the Pyrenees. ◈ Parc de Collserola • Map B1 • Check website for opening hours. • www.torrede collserola.com • Adm • DA

4 Museu del FC Barcelona & Camp Nou Stadium

Barcelona's most visited museum is a must for fans of the beautiful game. With football memorabilia of every conceivable kind, you can learn all about the club's history. Work donated by some of Catalonia's leading artists is also on display. Admission includes access to Barça's 120,000-seater stadium, an impressive monument to the city's love-affair with the game. ◈ Entrance 9 Stadium, Av Aristides Maillol • Map A2 • Open 10am–6:30pm Mon–Sat (to 8pm Apr–Oct), 10am–2:30pm Sun • Adm

Camp Nou Stadium

Gràcia

Until the end of the 19th century, Gràcia was a fiercely proud independent city. Despite locals' protests, it became part of Barcelona proper in 1898, but has always maintained a sense of separatism and has been a hotbed of political activity. It is now home to a booming cottage industry nurtured by a growing band of artisans. Don't miss the barri's annual fiesta *(see p65)* in the second week of August.

Palau Reial de Pedralbes

The former main residence of Count Eusebi Güell was donated to the Spanish royal family in 1919. Open to the public since 1937, this majestic palace houses the Museu de Ceràmica, the Museu de Textil and the Museu de les Arts Decoratives. The former has a fine collection of Catalan and Moorish ceramics; the Museu de les Arts Decoratives has period furniture, plus a number of artifacts dating from the Middle Ages onwards, and the Museu de Textil focuses on fashion and costume. The magnificent gardens include a fountain designed by Gaudí. ◈ Av Diagonal 686 • Map A2 • Museums open 10am–6pm Tue–Sat, 10am–8pm Sun • Adm (free 1st Sun of the month & every Sun 3–8pm) • DA

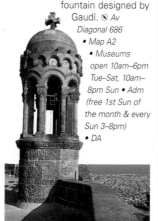

View, Temple Expiatori del Sagrat Cor

Parc Güell

Declared a UNESCO World Heritage Site in 1984, this heady brew of architectural wizardry includes *trencadís* tiling, a serpentine bench, fairy-tale pavilions, Gothic archways, and the columned Sala Hipóstila (originally intended as a market hall). In true Gaudí style, playfulness and symbolism pervade every aspect of the park. The Casa-Museu Gaudí, where Gaudí lived for 20 years, is dedicated to the architect's life. ◈ C/d'Olot • Map B2 • Open 10am–dusk daily • Free ◈ Casa-Museu Gaudí • Map B2 • Open Oct–Mar: 10am–5:45pm; Apr–Sep: 10am–7:45pm • Adm €5.50

Museu de Ceràmica, Palau Reial

Temple Expiatori del Sagrat Cor

Visible from almost anywhere in Barcelona, the Temple of the Sacred Heart was built by Enric Sagnier between 1902 and 1911. It has a dramatic sculpture of Jesus and an elaborately decorated door that verges on the psychedelic. Take the elevator up the main tower, or climb the steps to the outside terrace for breathtaking views. ◈ Pl del Tibidabo • Map B1 • Open 10am–8pm daily (Elevator open 10:30am–2pm & 3–7pm daily) • Adm

Parc de Collserola

Beyond the peaks of Tibidabo mountain, this 6,500-ha (16,000-acre) natural park of wild forest

Parc del Laberint d'Horta

and winding paths is an oasis of calm. It is great for hiking and biking (see p59), with sign-posted paths and nature trails. ❧ Info point: C/Església 92 • Map B1

Tramvia Blau
9 The city's blue trams, with their old-fashioned, wooden interiors are attractions in themselves. The route, from the FGC station to Plaça Doctor Andreu, passes many *Modernista* mansions to the top of Avinguda Tibidabo. ❧ Av Tibidabo • Map B1 • Trams run 10am–8pm (Oct–May 6pm) daily (mid-Sep–late June Sat, Sun & bank hols only) • Adm

Parc del Laberint d'Horta
10 In 1802, the Marquès d'Alfarràs hosted a huge party in these wonderful Neo-Classical gardens to celebrate the visit of Carles IV. Designed by Italian architect Domenico Bagotti, they incorporate a lake, a waterfall, canals and a wonderful cypress-tree maze. ❧ C/German Desvalls • Map C1 • Open 10am–dusk daily • Free (Wed & Sun), Adm (all other days)

Museu de les Arts Decoratives, Palau Reial

Exploring the Heights

Morning
🕐 Taking the northern route of the Bus Turístic (see p133) is the easiest way to negotiate the vast northern area of the city; it also gives discounts on entrance to major sights en route. Start off at Plaça de Catalunya (tickets can be bought on board) and sit on the top deck for a good view of the *Modernista* magic along Pg de Gràcia. Make the whimsical **Parc Güell** your first stop and spend the morning ambling around Gaudí's otherworldly park. Get back on the bus and continue north to the southern end of Av Tibidabo. Walk about 500 m (1600 ft) up Av Tibidabo and stop off for a leisurely lunch in the garden of the palatial **El Asador d'Aranda** (see p117).

Afternoon
After you've had your fill of fine Castilian cuisine, continue strolling up Av Tibidabo to Plaça Doctor Andreu where you can hop on the steep funicular train to go higher still to Plaça de Tibidabo. Pop into the **Parc d'Atraccions** (see p111) for a ride on the dodgems or the Ferris wheel. Then head to the landmark **Torre de Collserola** (see p111), where a glass elevator whisks you up to an observation deck for spectacular views. Return to Plaça Doctor Andreu on the funicular and treat yourself to a *granissat* (see p43) in one of the terrace bars. Then go down Av Tibidabo on the charming **Tramvia Blau** and catch the Bus Turístic back to the city centre.

For more on Barcelona's parks See p56–7

Left **Món de Mones** Right **El Piano**

🔟 Gràcia Boutiques

1 Naftalina
Of all the cottage industry boutiques in Gràcia, Naftalina has the most stylish interior – befitting the equally stylish, handmade designer clothes. Chic, elegant, understated women's wear with an emphasis on textured fabrics. ⊗ *C/La Perla 33*

2 Ninas
Nina, an American designer, sells simple, modern women's clothes made from fine fabrics. The shop is housed in a gorgeous *Modernista* building which was once a butcher's, and has a workshop at the back. ⊗ *C/Verdi 39*

3 Llena eres de Gràcia
For gorgeous women's fashions, accessories and evening wear at surprisingly reasonable prices, try this colourful boutique. The clothes are very wearable but most have a quirky twist. ⊗ *C/Ros de Olano 52*

4 José Rivero
José provides his own original in-house creations for men and women; he also sells crafted accessories, including handbags, by young local designers. ⊗ *C/Astúries 43*

5 Multiart
This fabric workshop sells colourful, hand-printed textiles, bedlinen, and clothes for men and women. It also runs educational dress-making workshops. ⊗ *C/Sant Joaquim 23*

6 Món de Mones
For colourful jewellery and accessories, try the "World of Monkeys" (*món de mones* in Catalan) near the Plaça del Sol. The designer, Teresa Roig, uses a variety of materials from glass to felt to create her original designs. ⊗ *C/Xiquets de Valls 9*

7 Camiseria Pons
One of the oldest shops in this area, this men's specialist shop sells shirts by top Spanish and international designers, including Ralph Lauren. ⊗ *Gran de Gràcia 49*

8 Mushi Mushi
From hard-to-find, small labels to the best international collections, this pretty little boutique stocks a fine selection of women's fashion. It also offers a small range of shoes, bags and accessories. ⊗ *Plaça Rius i Taulet 5*

9 El Piano
El Piano sells elegant and stylish women's clothes with a retro flair made by Catalan designer Tina García. It also stocks clothes by other independent designers. ⊗ *C/Verdi 20 bis*

10 Zucca
One of two branches in Barcelona, Zucca offers a superb range of colourful fashion accessories. The stock includes plastic flowers for your hair and stick-on navel rings. ⊗ *C/Torrent de l'Olla 175*

Around Town – Gràcia, Tibidabo & Zona Alta

Most of Gràcia's small boutiques accept commissions.

Left **Sign, Cafè Salambó** Right **Tea urns, Teteria Jazmín**

Gràcia Cafés

1 Cafè del Sol
This café-bar is a cut above the others in the lively, bohemian Plaça del Sol. The atmosphere buzzes, the conversation inspires and the excellent coffee keeps on coming. ◎ *Pl del Sol 16 • DA*

2 Cafè Salambó
Scrumptious sandwiches and a tasty range of salads are the draw at this beautiful, wooden, trendy bar-cum-café. There are pool tables upstairs. ◎ *C/Torrijos 51 • DA*

3 Teteria Jazmín
An aromatic café that serves hundreds of different teas; the most unusual is the mint tea served with pine-kernels. Typical Morrocan dishes (*tagines* and *couscous*) are also available. ◎ *C/Maspons 11 • Closed Mon, Tue, two weeks Sep*

4 La Cafetera
Of all the cafés on Plaça de la Virreina, this one, with its outdoor terrace and tiny patio full of potted plants, is easily the most pleasant for a quiet and leisurely morning coffee and a sandwich. ◎ *Pl de la Virreina 2*

5 Aroma
It's always a pleasure to smell the coffee being freshly ground at this cream-walled and wood-beamed café. Hundreds of coffees to choose from, with takeaway packets available. ◎ *Travessera de Gràcia 151 • DA*

6 Vreneli
The cosy Plaça de Rius i Taulet boasts several café terraces to choose from. Vreneli is the most interesting one, with a mixture of Mexican, Swiss and Spanish fare. No alcohol is served. ◎ *Pl Rius i Taulet 8 • Closed Mon • DA*

7 Blues Cafè
The walls at this dusky, atmospheric café-bar are plastered with black-and-white photos of John Lee Hooker and Leadbelly, among others. The music, electric or acoustic, is always the blues. ◎ *C/Perla 35*

8 Cafè del Teatre
This is an ideal place to find a young, friendly crowd and good conversation. The only connection with the theatre here seems to be the velvet curtains on the sign over the door of this scruffy, but busy, café. ◎ *C/Torrijos 41*

9 La Nena
This café is popular with parents, thanks to the room with tables and games for children. Their range of homemade cakes, juices and hot drinks makes this a neighbourhood favourite. ◎ *C/Ramón y Cajal 36 • Map F1*

10 Sureny
A sophisticated addition to this square, Sureny is simple but stylish, with a tantalizing selection of tapas and plenty of wines available by the glass. ◎ *Pl Revolució 17 • Closed Mon • DA*

Left **Mirasol** Right **Gràcia Nightlife, Plaça del Sol**

Hip Drinking Spots

1 Mirasol

Possibly Gràcia's most classic bar, the atmospheric Mirasol has been a bohemian hang-out for decades. In summer, there's outdoor seating on the *plaça*. ॐ *Pl del Sol 3 • Closed Sun • DA*

2 Universal Café

Open until 5:30am, Universal Café is a late-night, two-level bar with a spacious, airy interior. The image-concious crowd comes to flirt and dance to house (upstairs) and acid jazz (below). ॐ *C/Marià Cubí 182 • Closed Sun • Occasional adm*

3 Mirablau

A slightly older, well-heeled set, who adhere to the smart dress code, come to this club-bar for a combination of cocktails and amazing views of the city. ॐ *Pl Dr Andreu*

4 Elephant

Lavish, stylish and totally unique, Elephant is one of the best clubs in the city for a fun night out. In summer, you can lounge in the garden on huge, white beds. ॐ *Passeig dels Til.lers 1*

5 Bar Elèctric

A longstanding favourite on the Gràcia scene, Bar Elèctric is a bar as well as a small venue for live gigs, featuring rock, pop and world music acts. It is a cheerful, scruffy neighbourhood bar, which is packed at weekends. ॐ *Travessera de Gràcia 23 • Map D1*

6 Sala BeCool

A favourite in the chic Sant Gervasi neighbourhood, Sala BeCool offers a wide-ranging programme of DJ sessions, club nights and live gigs. ॐ *Plaça Joan Llongueras 5 • Map C1*

7 Otto Zutz

Barcelona's media crowd flocks to this New-York-style club to chatter in the corners upstairs and shoot pool downstairs. The huge dance floors throb with house music. ॐ *C/Lincoln 15 • Closed Sun & Mon • Adm*

8 La Cervesera Artesana

This friendly micro-brewery offers a good range of imported beers in addition to their own excellent brews. The Iberian Pale Ale, a mellow amber beer, is well worth a try. ॐ *C/Sant Agustí 14 • Map F1*

9 Heliogàbal

This cult, live music venue is best on Thursday or Sunday nights when you can hear anything from an indie band to a poetry slam. Prices are very reasonable too. ॐ *C/Ramón y Cajal 80 • Map F1*

10 Bikini

Opening from midnight onwards, this huge venue has three spaces, which offer dance and Latin music and a cocktail lounge. Regular live music includes some of the best acts in Europe. ॐ *C/Deu i Mata 105 • Closed Mon • Adm • DA*

Around Town – Gràcia, Tibidabo & Zona Alta

Normal closing times for bars is 2:30am, 3am weekends. Clubs open until 4:30/6am. For more on Barcelona's nightlife **See pp46–7**

Price Categories

For a three-course meal for one with half a bottle of wine (or equivalent meal), taxes and extra charges.

€	under €15
€€	€15–25
€€€	€25–35
€€€€	€35–45
€€€€€	over €45

Interior, Flash Flash

🔟 Restaurants & Tapas Bars

1 El Asador d'Aranda
Housed in the magnificent *Modernista* Casa Roviralta, this restaurant is a magnet for business-folk. Order the delicious lamb roasted in an oak-burning oven and dine in the beautiful garden. ✎ *Av Tibidabo 31 • 93 417 01 15 • Closed Sun dinner • €€€€*

2 Bar-Restaurante Can Tomàs
This tapas bar, in the Sarrià neighbourhood, is an institution. It has the well-deserved reputation of making some of the best tapas in town. Particularly recommended are the *patates braves*. ✎ *C/ Major de Sarrià 49 • 93 203 10 77 • Closed Wed • No credit cards • €€*

3 Hofmann
Run by the talented chef Mey Hofmann, this restaurant serves seriously delicious Catalan cuisine. Save room for the exceptional desserts. ✎ *C/La Granada del Penedès 14–16 • 93 218 71 65 • DA • €€€€€*

4 Neichel
Top-class in every way, Neichel lures a moneyed clientele with *nouvelle cuisine* and a luscious interior. Reserve in advance. ✎ *C/Boltrán i Rózpide 1 • 93 203 84 08 • Closed Sun & Mon • €€€€€*

5 Taverna El Glop
This tavern-like eatery serves traditional Catalan food. Its *calçots* (chargrilled, gigantic spring onions with spicy romesco sauce) are legendary (served only in spring). ✎ *C/St Lluis 24 • 93 213 70 58 • DA • €€*

6 Àbac
At the foot of Tibidabo mountain, Àbac offers French-Mediterranean cuisine prepared by award-winning chef, Xavier Pellicer. ✎ *Avinguda Tibidabo 1 • 93 319 66 00 • Closed lunch Sun, Mon, Fri lunch • DA • €€€€€*

7 Flash Flash
Truites (omelettes) rule here, from the classic (Spanish) to the inventive (garlic and asparagus). The owners claim to have used five million eggs in just over 30 years. ✎ *C/Granada de Penedès 25 • 93 237 09 90 • DA • €€€*

8 La Balsa
In the quiet Bonanova district, La Balsa is a beautiful spot, with two garden terraces. Fine Basque, Catalan and Mediterranean dishes are on the menu. ✎ *C/Infanta Isabel 4 • 93 211 50 48 • Closed Sun dinner, Mon lunch & lunch in Aug • €€€€€*

9 Tram Tram
Housed in a handsome old town house, this restaurant serves, innovative, contemporary Catalan cuisine. ✎ *C/Major de Sarria 121 • 93 204 85 18 • Closed Sat lunch, Sun, Mon, fortnight in Aug • €€€€*

10 Botafumeiro
The fish tanks at this sea-food restaurant are teeming with crabs and lobster destined for plates. Try the tender *pulpo Gallego* (Galician octopus). Reservations are essential. ✎ *C/Gran de Gràcia 81 • 93 218 42 30 • DA • €€€€€*

Unless otherwise stated, all restaurants accept credit cards.
For more on dining and standard opening hours See p138

Left **Monestir de Santes Creus** Right **Cadaqués**

Beyond Barcelona

STEEPED IN TRADITION, *with its own language and an enormous sense of pride in its separate identity, Catalonia is immensely rich in both cultural heritage and physical geography. It is no exaggeration to say that Catalonia really does have everything. To the north are the 3,000-m (9840-ft) peaks of the Pyrenees. The coastline is dotted with hundreds of beautiful sandy beaches and intimate rocky coves with crystal-clear waters. These staggering natural treasures are complemented by a wealth of fabulous churches and monasteries, many set in stunning, isolated mountain scenery. For the gourmet, the regional cuisine is particularly rewarding, while the locally-produced cava easily holds its own against its French champagne counterparts.*

Teatre-Museu Dalí

Sights & Attractions

1. Montserrat
2. Teatre-Museu Dalí, Figueres
3. Vall de Núria
4. Alt Penedès
5. Begur & Around
6. Tarragona
7. Girona
8. Empúries
9. Port Aventura
10. Costa Daurada & Sitges

For tips on getting around Catalonia **See p132**

Beyond Barcelona

Montserrat

The dramatic mount of Montserrat, with its remote Benedictine monastery (dating from 1025), is a religious symbol and a place of pilgrimage for the Catalan people. The Basilica houses a statue of Catalonia's patron virgin, La Moreneta, also know as the "Black Virgin". Some legends date the statue to AD 50, but research

Basilica, Monestir de Montserrat

suggests it was carved in the 12th century. The monastery itself was largely destroyed in 1811 during the War of Independence, and rebuilt some 30 years later. Montserrat forms part of a ridge of mountains that rise suddenly from the plains. Take the funicular to the mountain's unspoilt peaks, where paths run alongside spectacular gorges to numerous hermitages. ⊗ *Tourist Info: Pl de la Creu • 93 877 77 01*

Teatre-Museu Dalí, Figueres

Salvador Dalí was born in the town of Figueres in 1904. Paying tribute to the artist is the fantastic Teatre-Museu Dalí, which is full of his eccentric works. Housed in a former theatre, the country's second-most-visited museum (after the Prado in Madrid) provides a unique insight into the artist's extraordinary creations, from *La Cesta de Pan* (1926) to *El Torero Alucinogeno* (1970). Thirty minutes' drive away, near the beach town of Cadaqués, the Dalí connection continues. Here you can visit the Casa-Museu Salvador Dalí, the artist's summer house for nearly 60 years until his death in 1989.

⊗ *Pl Gala-Salvador Dalí, Figueres • 972 67 75 00 • Open Mar–Jun, Oct: 9:30am–6pm Tue–Sun (daily in Jun); Jul–Sep: 9am–8pm daily, Nov–Feb. 10:30am–6pm Tue–Sun • Adm* ⊗ *Casa-Museu Salvador Dalí, Port Lligat • 972 25 10 15 • Closed early Jan to mid-Mar • Guided visits only, Tue–Sun (15 Jun–15 Sep daily) by reservation • Adm •www.salvador-dali.org*

Vall de Núria

This enchanting Pyrenean hideaway, surrounded by crests reaching as high as 3,000-m (9,840-ft), is a ski resort in winter and a peaceful oasis attracting hikers and nature-lovers in summer. The mountain resort centres on a religious sanctuary and has a youth hostel and apartments for rent. The valley is only accessible via a silent cog railway, which trundles above the clouds through breathtaking scenery. ⊗ *Tourist Info: Railway Station, Vall de Núria • 97 273 20 20 • Rack railway train from Ribes de Freser, 10 km N Ripoll*

Rainy Taxi, Teatre-Museu Dalí

Anywhere in Catalonia can be reached by car from Barcelona in less than three hours.

4 Alt Penedès

Catalonia's most famous wine region is the *cava*-producing area of the Penedès. The *cava* brands of Cordoníu and Freixenet have become household names worldwide. Many of the area's wineries and bodegas are open to the public. One of the most spectacular is the Cordoníu bodega, housed in a *Modernista* building designed by Puig i Cadafalch, with a phenomenal 26 km (16 miles) of cellars on five floors. ⊗ *Tourist Info: C/Cort 14, Vilafranca del Penedès • 93 818 12 54 • The tourist office has details on all winery visits in the region, including the Cordoníu winery*

5 Begur & Around

The elegant hilltop town of Begur, with its ruined 14th-century castle, looks down over pristine wetlands and some of the prettiest coves on the Costa Brava. The town's population quadruples in summer as visitors make this their base for exploring nearby beaches and small, isolated coves. Many of the area's beaches stage jazz concerts throughout the summer. This is perhaps the best stretch of coastline in Catalonia. ⊗ *Tourist Info: Av Onze de Setembre 5 • 972 62 45 20*

6 Tarragona

Entering the city of Tarragona, past the oil refineries and its huge industrial port, it's hard to envisage the astounding archaeological treasures that await. Once the capital of Roman Catalonia, the city's main attractions today are from this era. Highlights include an impressive amphitheatre and the well-kept Roman walls that lead past the Museu Nacional Arque-

Riu Onyar, Girona

ològic and the Torre de Pilatos, a tower where Christians were supposedly imprisoned before being thrown to the lions. Also in Tarragona is the Catedral de Santa Tecla *(see p124)*. ⊗ *Tourist Info: C/Fortuny 4 • 977 23 34 15 • www.tarragonaturisme.cat*

7 Girona

Said to have the highest living standards in Catalonia, Girona is a pleasant town surrounded by lush green hills. Hidden away in the old town, the atmospheric Jewish quarter (known as El Call) is one of the best-preserved medieval enclaves in Europe. Girona's cathedral is a must *(see p124)*. ⊗ *Tourist Info: Rambla de la Llibertat 1 • 972 22 65 75*

Codorníu *cava*

8 Empúries

After Tarragona, Empúries is Catalonia's second most important Roman site. Occupying an impressive position by the sea, it includes more than 40 hectares (99 acres) scattered with Greek and Roman ruins, the highlights of which are the remains of a market street, various temples and part of a Roman amphitheatre. Coupled with lovely nearby beaches, it's an ideal spot for those looking to mix a bit of history with a dip in the sea. ✪ *Empúries • 972 77 02 08 • Open Jun–Sep: 10am–8pm daily; Oct–May: 10am–6pm daily • Adm*

9 Port Aventura

Universal Studios' theme park is divided up into five areas: China, Far West, Mediterranean, Polynesia and Mexico, each offering rides and attractions. Thrill-junkies will appreciate one of Europe's biggest roller coasters, Dragon Kahn (China). There are also shows, and the entire experience is like being on a film set. ✪ *Av Pere Molas, Vila-seca, Tarragona • 902 20 22 20 • Open mid-Mar–Oct daily, call for seasonal hours • Adm • DA*

10 Costa Daurada & Sitges

With its wide sandy beaches and shallow waters, the Costa Daurada differs from the northern Catalonian coastline. The sleepy town of Torredembarra is a pleasant and rarely busy family resort, but the jewel in the crown is undoubtedly Sitges. It's the summer home to Barcelona's chic crowd, as well as being a popular gay resort (see p49). All this gives it a cosmopolitan, frenetic feel, but the town never reaches the tacky excesses of some of the Costa Brava's resorts. ✪ *Tourist Info: C/Sínia Morera • 938 10 93 40 • www.sitgestur.cat*

Waterfront, Sitges

A Scenic Drive

Morning

🕐 From Barcelona take the AP7 motorway until exit 4, then take the C260 to Cadaqués. The journey should take about two and a half hours in all. Just before dropping down to the town, stop at the viewpoint and take in the azure coastline and the whitewashed houses of this former fishing village. Once in **Cadaqués**, now one of Catalonia's trendiest beach towns, wander the quaint boutique-filled streets. After a splash in the sea and a coffee on one of the chic terrace cafés, take the road leaving Port Lligat and head for the **Cap de Creus** *(see p125)* lighthouse. Drive through the desolately beautiful landscape of this rocky headland before doubling back and heading off to Port de la Selva. The road twists and winds interminably, but the picture-perfect scenery will leave you speechless.

Afternoon

Stop in the tiny, mountain-enclosed Port de la Selva for an excellent seafood lunch at the Cala Herminda. Then drive to the neighbouring village of Selva del Mar with its tiny river and have a post-prandial coffee on the terrace of the Bar Stop before continuing up to the **Monestir Sant Pere de Rodes** *(see p124)*. You'll be tempted to stop several times on the way up to take in the views. Don't, because the best is to be had from the monastery, which offers an incredible sweeping vista of the whole area. There are plenty of well-signposted walks around the mountain top here and it is worth staying put to see the sun set slowly over the bay.

Following pages **Inner Courtyard, Monestir de Montserrat**

Left **Chapterhouse detail, Monestir de Santes Creus** Right **Monestir de Poblet**

Churches & Monasteries

Monestir de Montserrat
Catalonia's holiest place is the region's most visited monastery. It boasts some Romanesque art and a statue of the "Black Virgin" *(see p119)*. ⊗ *Montserrat* • *93 877 77 77* • *Adm* • *DA to Basilica*

Monestir de Poblet
This busy, working monastery contains the Gothic Capella de Sant Jordi, a Romanesque church, and the Porta Daurada, a doorway that was gilded for Felipe II's visit in 1564. ⊗ *off N240, 10 km W of Montblanc* • *97 787 00 89* • *Adm*

Monestir de Ripoll
The west portal of this monastery (879) has reputedly the finest Romanesque carvings in Spain. Of the original buildings, only the doorway and cloister remain. ⊗ *Ripoll* • *972 70 23 51* • *Adm*

Monestir de Santes Creus
The cloister at this Gothic treasure (1150) is notable for the beautifully sculpted capitals by English artist Reinard Funoll. ⊗ *Santes Creus, 25 km NW of Montblanc* • *695 18 68 73* • *Closed Mon* • *Adm* • *Tue free*

Monestir de Sant Pere de Rodes
The dilapidated charm of this UNESCO World Heritage Site may have dwindled since its face-lift, but nothing detracts from the views it offers over Cap de Creus and Port de la Selva. ⊗ *22 km E of Figueres* • *972 38 75 59* • *Closed Mon* • *Adm*

Sant Climent i Santa Maria de Taüll
These two churches are perfect examples of the Romanesque churches that pepper the Pyrenees. Dating from 1123, most of the original frescoes are now in the MNAC in Barcelona *(see pp18–19)*. ⊗ *138 km N of Lleida* • *973 69 40 00*

Catedral de La Seu d'Urgell
Dating from around 1040, this cathedral is one of the most elegant in Catalonia. ⊗ *La Seu d'Urgell* • *973 35 32 42* • *Adm* • *DA*

Catedral de Santa Maria
This cathedral is remarkable for possessing the widest Gothic nave anywhere in Europe and the second widest of any type after the Basilica in the Vatican. ⊗ *Old Town, Girona* • *972 21 58 14* • *Adm* • *Sun free*

Catedral de Santa Tecla
At 104-m (340-ft) long, Tarragona's cathedral is the largest in the region. Its architecture is a mixture of Gothic and Romanesque, and it is crowned by a huge octagonal bell tower. ⊗ *Old Town, Tarragona* • *977 23 86 85* • *Closed Sun except for 11am mass* • *Adm*

Sant Joan de les Abadesses
This pretty French Romanesque-style monastery in the Pyrenees harbours a prestigious collection of Romanesque sculpture. ⊗ *Sant Joan de les Abadesses* • *972 72 05 99* • *www.santjoandelesabadesses.com* • *Adm*

Beyond Barcelona

124

Usual opening hours for monasteries and churches are 10am–1pm & 3–7pm Mon–Sat, 10am–1pm Sun. Call to confirm seasonal times.

Parc Natural de la Zona Volcànica de la Garrotxa

National Parks & Nature Reserves

1 Parc Nacional d'Aigüestortes i Estany de Sant Maurici
The magnificent peaks of Catalonia's only national park are accessible from the resort of Espot. You'll find ponds and lakes 2,000 m (6,560 ft) up. 🚩 *148 km N of Lleida*

2 Delta de l'Ebre
This giant delta is a patchwork of paddy fields. The wide expanse of the River Ebre is a nature reserve for migratory birds and has scores of bird-watching stations. 🚩 *28 km SE of Tortosa*

3 Parc Natural de la Zona Volcànica de la Garrotxa
It is 10,000 years since La Garrotxa last erupted and the volcanoes are long since extinct. The largest crater is the Santa Margalida, at 500 m (1,640 ft) wide. It is magical here in spring when thousands of butterflies emerge. 🚩 *40 km NW of Girona*

4 Cap de Creus
As the Pyrenees tumble into the Mediterranean, they create a rocky headland, which juts out 10 km (6.25 miles). It forms Catalonia's most easterly point and offers spectacular views of the craggy coastline. 🚩 *36 km E of Figueres*

5 Parc Natural del Cadí-Moixeró
Covered in a carpet of conifers and oaks, this mountain range has surprisingly lush vegetation. Several peaks are over 2,000 m (6,560 ft) high. 🚩 *20 km E of La Seu d'Urgell*

6 Parc Natural del Montseny
Forming Catalonia's most accessible natural park, these woodland hills are well-equipped for walkers and mountain bikers, with a huge network of trails. Climb the well-signposted and popular Turó de l'Home, which is the highest peak. 🚩 *48 km NW of Barcelona*

7 Massis de Pedraforca
A nature reserve surrounds this huge outcrop of mountains, a favourite of rock climbers with peaks rising to 2,500 m (8,200 ft). 🚩 *64 km N of Manresa*

8 Serra de l'Albera
On the eastern part of the border between Spain and France, the tree-covered slopes of Albera are speckled with interesting ruins. 🚩 *13 km N of Figueres*

9 Parc Natural dels Aiguamolls de l'Empordà
This nature reserve hides bird-watching towers. Those in the Laguna de Vilaüt and La Bassa de Gall Marí allow bird-lovers to observe herons, moorhens and other bird species nesting in spring. 🚩 *15 km E of Figueres*

10 Parc Natural de Sant Llorenç del Munt
Surrounded by industry and within easy reach of Barcelona, this is a surprisingly untamed park inhabited by large numbers of wild boar. Walk up Cerro de la Mola to see the Romanesque monastery. 🚩 *12 km E of Manresa*

Rafting, La Noguera Pallaresa

TOP 10 Outdoor Activities

1 Rafting & Kayaking
One of Europe's best rivers for white-water sports is La Noguera Pallaresa in the Pyrenees. Late spring is the best time to go, as the mountain snow thaws. *Yeti Emotions, Llavorsí, 14 km N of Sort • 973 62 22 01 • www.yetiemotions.com*

2 Scuba Diving
Reserva Natural de les Illes Medes has thousands of species and coral reefs. Glassbottomed boats cater to non-divers. *Aquàtica, L'Estartit • 972 75 06 56 • www.aquatica-sub.com*

3 Watersports & Sailing
Good sailing can be found in Sitges, along with yachts for rent, classes for the novice, canoeing and windsurfing. *Club de Mar Sitges, Pg Marítim, Sitges • 93 894 09 05 • www.clubdemardesitges.com*

4 Skiing
La Molina is the most accessible Pyrenean ski-resort from Barcelona, but Baqueira-Beret is where the jet-set goes. Both offer all levels of skiing (including off-piste) from December. *La Molina, 25 km S of Puigcerdà • 972 89 20 21 • www.lamolina.com • Baqueira-Beret, 14 km E of Vielha • 902 41 54 15 (snow reports: 973 63 90 25) • www.baqueira.es*

5 Golf
The Costa Brava is one of Europe's top golf destinations; the best courses are around Platja d'Aro. *Santa Cristina d'Aro • 972 83 70 55 • Platja d'Aro • 972 81 67 27*

6 Horse Riding
Montseny National Park *(see p125)* is ideal for horse riding, with a number of centres. *Can Marc, 6 km W of Sant Celoni • Closed Mon • 938 48 27 13*

7 Ballooning
A balloon journey over the volcanic area of La Garrotxa is an unbeatable way to get a bird's-eye view of Catalonia. *Vol de Coloms • 972 68 02 55, or 689 471 872 • www.voldecoloms.cat*

8 Boat trips
Take a picturesque cruise from Calella and Blanes to Tossa de Mar, stopping at the old town and the castle of Tossa de Mar. *Dofi Jet Boats, Blanes • 972 35 20 21 www.dofijetboats.com • boats every hour daily from Blanes (twice daily from Calella) • Closed Nov–Feb*

9 Windsurfing, Rowing & Golf
Used for rowing competitions in the 1992 Olympics, the huge Canal Olímpic is now a leisure complex offering a host of activities. *Canal Olímpic • Av Canal Olímpic, Castelldefels • 93 636 28 96 • www.canalolimpic.com*

10 Foraging for Mushrooms
From late September to late October, thousands of Catalans flock to the hills in search of the highly prized *rovelló*. There are also poisonous varieties, so amateurs should get a guide through the Diputació de Barcelona.

Diputació de Barcelona has information on activities in Catalonia, from gastro tours to guided walks. www.turismedecatalunya.com

Price Categories

For a three-course meal for one with half a bottle of wine (or equivalent meal), taxes and extra charges.

€	under €15
€€	€15–25
€€€	€25–35
€€€€	€35–45
€€€€€	over €45

Anchovy tapas, El Pescadors

🔟 Places to Eat

1 El Taller
A renovated historic townhouse in Tossa de Mar's walled old town now houses this charming restaurant. Fine Mediterranean seafood and meat dishes in an informal setting. ◎ C/Pou de la Vila 9, Tossa de Mar • 972 34 03 26 • Closed Sun night, Mon & Tue in winter

2 El Racó de Can Fabes
Celebrated chef Santi Santamaria prepares sublime traditional French-Catalan food at this three-Michelin-star countryhouse restaurant. ◎ Sant Joan 6, Sant Celoni, Montseny • 93 867 28 51 • Closed Sun eve & Mon • €€€€€

3 La Torre del Remei
A *Modernista* palace provides an elegant setting for wonderfully presented Catalan food. The game dishes are sublime. ◎ Camí Reial, Bolvir, Cerdanya, 3 km SW of Puigcerdà • 972 14 01 82 • DA • €€€€€

4 El Mirador de les Caves
This restaurant is set in a castle overlooking Catalonia's wine country. Traditional cuisine is complemented by bottles of local wine and *cava*. ◎ Els Casots, 4 km S of Sant Sadurní d'Anoia • 93 899 31 78 • Closed Sun eve & Mon eve • €€€€€

5 Fonda Europa
Established over 150 years ago, Fonda Europa was the first in a line of successful Catalan restaurants. Ample portions include pig's trotters. ◎ Anselm Clavé 1, Granollers • 93 870 0312 • DA • €€€

6 Restaurant Sangiovese
Exceptional Catalan cuisine prepared with the freshest local produce in a sleek, designer setting. The best reason to visit Mataró. ◎ C/Sant Josep 31, Mataró • 937 41 02 67 • €€€€

7 Carme Ruscalleda Sant Pau
Carme Ruscalleda is considered one of the finest chefs in Spain. Head to the pretty, seaside village of Sant Pol de Mar, where her restaurant offers sublime Catalan cuisine. ◎ C/Nou 10, Sant Pol de Mar • 93 760 06 62 • Closed Sun, Mon, Thu lunch, three weeks in May, three weeks in Nov • €€€€€

8 Els Pescadors
"The Fishermen", a traditional *Empordà*-style restaurant, offers local specialities, including an array of blue fish dishes. ◎ Port d'en Perris 3, l'Escala • 972 77 07 28 • Closed Sun eve (winter), Thu & Nov • €€€€€

9 El Celler de Can Roca
The Roca brothers provide exciting, contemporary Catalan cuisine that is complemented by an exceptional wine list. ◎ C/Can Sunyer 48, Girona • 972 22 21 57 • €€€€

10 Cal Ton
A comfortable restaurant in the heart of Catalonia's biggest wine region, this serves fresh, contemporary cuisine. The *menu degustació* is recommended. Excellent wine list. ◎ C/Casal 8, Vilafranca del Penedès • 938 90 37 41 • €€€€

Unless otherwise stated, all restaurants accept credit cards. For more on dining and standard opening hours **See p138**

STREETSMART

BARCELONA'S TOP 10

Left **Airport sign** Right **Iberia logo**

Tips on Getting To Barcelona

1 By Air
British Airways, Iberia and easyJet offer direct flights from the UK to Barcelona. From the US, flights usually involve one stopover (in Madrid). Qantas flies from Australia and New Zealand to Barcelona via a series of stopovers. ⊗ *British Airways: 90 211 13 33 • www.britishairways.com*
⊗ *Iberia: 90 240 05 00*
• *www.iberia.es*
⊗ *easyJet: 807 260 026 (premium rate) • www.easyjet.com* ⊗ *Delta: 901 116 946 • www.delta.com*
⊗ *United Airlines: 900 813 996 • www.united.com*

2 Barcelona Airport
Prat de Llobregat airport's three adjoining terminals are 12 km (7 miles) south of the city centre. ⊗ *90 240 47 04*
• *www.aena.es*

3 From the Airport
One of the most convenient ways from the airport to the city centre is by Aerobús, which depart every 6 minutes from 6am to 1am, and make various stops, terminating in Plaça de Catalunya. There are two Aerobús lines, A1 and A2, one for each terminal. RENFE trains leave the airport every 30 minutes, stopping at Estació de Sants and Passeig de Gràcia; both link up with the metro. A taxi from the airport into the city centre costs €20–25. ⊗ *Aerobús: 93 415 60 20* ⊗ *RENFE: 902 320 320*

4 By Train
Trains run throughout Spain and Europe from Estació de Sants and Estació de França. Sants has several services, including lockers, ATMs and bureaux de change, but França has none. RENFE is Spain's national train company. ⊗ *Estació de França, Av Marqués de l'Argentera • Map Q5* ⊗ *Estació de Sants, Pl dels Països Catalans • Off map* ⊗ *RENFE: 90 232 03 20 (24 hours) • www.renfe.es*

5 By Bus
Both Eurolines and Linebús serve Barcelona from numerous European cities, including Rome, Paris and London. Buses usually operate from Barcelona's main bus station, Estació del Nord, and also from Estació de Sants. ⊗ *Estació del Nord, C/Ali Bei 80 • Map R2* • *90 226 06 06 • www.barcelonanord.com* ⊗ *Eurolines: 93 490 00* ⊗ *Linebús: 90 233 55 33*

6 By Car
Barcelona is linked to the rest of Spain and Europe by *autopistes* (toll highways) and toll-free roads. The tolled AP7 runs between Barcelona and the border of France.

7 Domestic travel
The city is connected to the rest of Spain by train, bus and plane. Iberia flies to and from many domestic destinations and offer a shuttle service between Madrid and Barcelona with up to 30 flights a day. Spanair, Vueling and Air Europa serve Barcelona from the rest of Spain. RENFE and several bus companies link Barcelona to most of Spain's major cities.
⊗ *Spanair: 90 213 14 15*
• *www.spanair.com*
⊗ *Air Europa: 90 240 15 01*
• *www.aireuropa.com*
⊗ *Vueling: 902 33 39 33*
• *www.vueling.com*

8 Cheap Travel
Book long before your departure date to cut costs. If you're flexible and open to stopovers, you're likely to find better deals. The internet is great for cheap fares (try www.travelocity.com or www.cheaptickets.com). Many airlines offer discounts if you buy online.

9 Planning
Citizens from the US, Canada, the UK, Ireland, Australia and New Zealand need a valid passport. For non-EU citizens, a visa is required if you intend to stay in Spain for longer than three months. If you're taking any kind of medication, bring your prescription.

10 When to Visit
If you're in search of sun, visit Barcelona during the summer, but remember that many businesses close through August. To avoid the summer crowds, visit around May or October.

Left **Metro sign** Centre **Barcelona taxi** Right **Tram**

Tips on Getting Around Barcelona

1 Metro
Barcelona's six-line metro system is convenient, fast, easy to use and extensive. The metro stays open all night on Saturdays. 🕾 *93 318 70 74 • www.tmb.net • Open 5am–midnight Mon–Thu, 5am–2am Fri, 5am–midnight Sun*

2 FGC
The FGC (Ferrocarrils de la Generalitat de Catalunya) is the city's commuter rail system, serving northern and eastern Barcelona. The FGC shares several key stations with the metro, including Plaça de Catalunya and Plaça d'Espanya, and has the same prices and similar hours. 🕾 *93 205 15 15 • www.fgc.cat • Open 5am–midnight Mon–Thu, 5am–2am Fri–Sat, 6am–midnight Sun*

3 Bus
Barcelona's bus system covers the entire city. Bus stops are clearly marked and buses have their destinations on the front. For information on routes and schedules call 010 or pick up a bus guide from tourist offices. 🕾 *93 318 70 74 • www.tmb.net • 6am–10pm daily*

4 Nightbus
There are about 17 Nitbús (nightbus) routes across the city, many of which pass through Plaça de Catalunya. 🕾 *93 318 70 74 • www.tmb.net*

5 Tickets & Passes
A single fare on the metro, FGC, bus or nightbus costs €1.40. The T-10 personal ticket costs €7.85 and permits 10 journeys on metro, FGC and bus, providing the total journey is completed within 1 hour 15 minutes. One-, two-, three-, four- and five-day passes are also available, which provide unlimited travel on public transport. Tickets are available from attendants and machines at all metro stations.

6 Taxi
Hail a yellow-and-black taxi on any major street in town; a green light on the roof indicates that one is free. For two or more passengers, taxis are almost as cheap as the metro for short hops. A minimum fare applies. 🕾 *Taxi Radio: 93 303 30 33* 🕾 *Barna Taxi: 93 357 77 55*

7 On Foot
Barcelona is extremely compact and most areas are best negotiated on foot, especially the old town and Gràcia, where a leisurely stroll is the only way to soak up the architectural and cultural riches. Barcelona's waterfront, from the Port Vell to the Port Olímpic, is also made for walking. *See pp58–9.*

8 By Bicycle
Pedalling around the port, Barri Gòtic or Parc de la Ciutadella is a refreshing alternative to walking. There are over 70 km (43 miles) of bike lanes throughout the city, outlined on maps available from the tourist office and bike rental shops. Bikes are available to rent daily from Budget Bikes or Un Cotxe Menys. 🕾 *Budget Bikes: 93 304 18 85* 🕾 *Un Cotxe Menys: 96 268 21 05*

9 Transport for the Disabled
The airport bus is accessible to wheelchair users as are Lines 2 and 11 of the metro, all city buses, a few FGC stations and all nightbuses. Taxi Amic has cars and vans dedicated to wheelchair users – give advance notice. For information on transport for the disabled, call Informació Municipal de Persones amb Discapacitat (IMD). For details about specific routes, call 010 or check the TMB website. 🕾 *Taxi Amic: 93 420 80 88 • IMD: 93 413 27 75* 🕾 *TMB: 93 318 70 74 • www.tmb.cat*

10 Getting Around in a Wheelchair
Barcelona's Institut Municipal de Persones amb Discapacitat *(see p134)* has developed a detailed computer database that charts all the streets accessible to wheelchair users. Call 010, give your departure point and destination, and they'll advise you of a route and places accessible en route.

Citybus and metro guides are available at the underground transport information office at Universitat metro station.

Left **RENFE train ticket** Centre **Road sign** Right **RENFE sign**

Ways to Explore Catalonia

1 By Train
RENFE operates lines out of Barcelona in all directions, making it easy to escape the city. Most regional trains leave from Estació de Sants *(see p130)* and Estació Passeig de Gràcia. Call the RENFE information line for destinations and schedules. ◈ *Estació Passeig de Gràcia • Pg de Gràcia • Map E2* ◈ *RENFE • 902 32 03 20*

2 By Bus
Regional bus companies operate all over Catalonia. Most depart from Estació del Nord – call the station for information or check timetables online. ◈ *Estació del Nord: C/Ali Bei 80 • Map R2 • 90 226 06 06 • www.barcelonanord.com*

3 By Car
A car is essential if you wish to explore off the beaten track, particularly in the Pyrenees and the Catalonian heartland. There are many car rental companies, including the big names (Avis, Budget, Hertz). All have offices at the airport. Prices range from €300–450 for a medium-sized car for a week. You must be over 25, and have a valid driver's licence, a credit card and a passport. Booking your rental car from abroad or on-line is often cheaper. ◈ *Avis: 90 224 88 24 • www.avis.com* ◈ *Budget: 90 211 25 85 • www.budget.com* ◈ *Hertz: 90 240 24 05 • www.hertz.com*

4 By Bike
Mountain bikers will find a wealth of rugged terrain in the Pyrenees. The Turisme de Catalunya has maps and brochures as well as a website showing regional bike routes. Terra Diversions offer a range of tours (including self-guided) in Catalonia, and arrange bike rental. ◈ *C/Santa Tecla 1 • 93 416 08 05 • www.terradiversions.com*

5 Sea Cruises
"Sightsea" off the Costa Brava aboard glass-bottomed boats and other sea cruisers. L'Aventura del Nautilus conducts coastal sea cruises from L'Estartit to the Medes Islands off the Costa Brava. Excursiones Marítimes plies the Mediterranean from Calella and Blanes to Tossa de Mar, stopping at lovely coves along the way. ◈ *L'Aventura del Nautilus: L'Estartit, 100km N of Barcelona • 972 75 14 89* ◈ *Dofi Jet Boats: Calella, 40 km N of Barcelona; Blanes, 60 km N of Barcelona • 972 35 20 21*

6 Bus Tours
Discover Catalonia on organized bus tours, which include trips to the Monestir de Montserrat, Girona, the Teatre-Museu Dalí in Figueres and the Costa Brava. Also offered is a half-day tour of Montserrat, a half-day tour of the wine and cava regions, and trips to Vic and Manresa. Tours are organized by Barcelona tourist office, and can be booked online. Prices start at €65 for a full-day tour. ◈ *Barcelona Tourism: 93 285 38 32 • www.barcelonaturisme.com*

7 Main Roads
Main roads – usually single lane or dual carriageways – are designated with an N (for *Nacional*), or C (for *Catalunya*). Road information is available at www.gencat.net/transit (also in English).

8 Avoiding Traffic
The best time to get out of town is in the late morning. Avoid long holiday weekends *(pont)* and Friday evenings, when traffic is always heavy. Since most Spanish take their holidays in August, motorways are particularly busy around this period.

9 Tips for Families
RENFE offers a 40 per cent discount for children aged four to 11. Enquire when booking tickets.

10 Turisme de Catalunya
This well-stocked tourist office offers plenty of material on Catalonia, from maps to information on outdoor sports and festival listings. Changing exhibits on the region are also on display. ◈ *Palau Robert, Pg de Gràcia 105 • Map E2 • 012 • www.gencat.es/probert • Open 10am–7pm Mon–Sat, 10am–2:30pm Sun*

Left **Las Golondrines tour boat** Right **Bus Turístic, Plaça de Catalunya**

10 Tours & Trips

1 Bus Tours

The open-topped Bus Turístic has several routes. The red route explores northern Barcelona; the blue route takes in the southern area; and the (summer only) green route travels along the beach front. There is also a night tour available. You can hop on and off as many times as you like. Discounts to sights and shops are included. ✆ Depart from Pl de Catalunya • Every 5–25 mins 9am–7pm (8pm Apr–Oct) daily • Purchase on the bus, at tourist offices or online at www.barcelonaturisme.com

2 Walking Tours

The tourist office (see p134) organizes a selection of reasonably-priced guided walks from the main office in Plaça de Catalunya – these include tours of the Barri Gòtic, Modernisme tours, seaside tours, gourmet tours and a Picasso-themed tour. The Travel Bar (see p134) also conducts lively walking tours.

3 La Ruta Modernista

The Modernisme Route guidebook contains several itineraries, a map and discount vouchers for all admission fees. For the guide, tours and information, visit the Centre del Modernisme at the Tourist Information Office in Plaça Catalunya ✆ 010 • www.rutadel modernisme.com

4 Boat Tours

See the city from the sea on one of Las Golondrines' sightseeing boats. Trips lasting 35 minutes depart every half-hour; longer tours are available on a catamaran with an underwater view. Orsom operate catamaran and speedboat tours around the port. ✆ Las Golondrines: Portal de la Pau • 93 442 31 06 • www.las-golondrinas.com ✆ Orsom: Portal de la Pau • 93 441 05 37 • www.barcelona-orsom.com

5 Cable Cars

Cable cars (telefèric) depart from Montjuïc (Miramar station), Torre de Jaume I and Torre de Sant Sebastià, yielding stunning views of the city. ✆ 93 441 48 20

6 Night Kayaking

Kayak under the stars off Barcelona's shores on a summer's night – with a beer and pica pica (snack) en route. Base Nàutica arranges various outdoor water activities and provides all the necessary equipment and insurance. After kayaking, go back to base for a barbecue, cocktails and ambient, DJ-spun music. ✆ Base Nàutica Municipal, Platja Mar Bella • 93 221 04 32 • Jun–Sep: 9pm Thu–Sat

7 Helicopter Tours

Cat Helicopters offers three tours of Barcelona, which depart from their landing pad at the port. The five-minute Costa Tour costs €45, and takes in the city coastline. For some of the city's biggest sights, including the Sagrada Família, take the Skytour (10mins, €80); it can also be extended to Montserrat (35mins, €240). ✆ Heliport, Passeig de l'Escullera, Moll Adossat • 93 224 07 10

8 Bike Tours

Whiz about the old town and the Parc de la Ciutadella on group bike tours organized by bike rental shops. Un Cotxe Menys ("One Car Less"), Barcelona by Bike also runs bike tours in English. ✆ Un Cotxe Menys (Bike-tours Barcelona), C/Esparteria 3 • 93 268 21 05 • www.bicicletabarcelona.com ✆ Barcelona by Bike: 93 268 81 07 • Open all year • www.barcelonabybike.com

9 Horse-drawn Carriages

It may be a tourist trap, but riding up La Rambla on a horse and carriage can raise a smile, especially for kids. ✆ Depart from Pl de Portal de la Pau • 93 421 15 49

10 Bus Montjuïc Turístic

Explore Montjuïc on this sightseeing open-top bus, which departs from Plaça d'Espanya and climbs past all the main sights. Get on and off as you wish. ✆ 93 414 982 • Open Apr–Oct

Left **Tourist information sign** Centre **Newsstand on La Rambla** Right **Magazines**

TOP 10 Sources of Information

1 Tourist Information

Multilingual staff give out free maps and information at Barcelona's main tourist office on Plaça de Catalunya. They also have a hotel booking service, a bureau de change, internet access and a souvenir shop. Other offices are located in Estació de Sants and on Plaça de Sant Jaume. For information on the rest of Catalonia, visit the Turisme de Catalunya (see p132). For information over the phone on everything from museum opening hours to bus routes, call 010 or the Turisme de Barcelona's information line. 🇸 Turisme de Barcelona, Pl de Catalunya 1 • Map M1 • www.barcelonaturisme. com • 93 285 38 34 • Open 9am–9pm daily

2 Information Officers

In summer red-jacketed tourist information officers roam the city's busiest areas giving out maps and advice. There are also information points in Las Ramblas, Estació del Nord and Plaça Espanya.

3 Magazines

The weekly Guía del Ocio covers the city's nightlife (music, theatre, dance and film), has extensive restaurant listings and is available from all newsstands. Barcelona Metropolitan (free) is the city's leading English-language monthly magazine, featuring culture, the arts and restaurant and nightlife listings. b-guided gives the latest on trendy places to shop, eat and drink – in English and Spanish.

4 Consulates

Various nations have consulates in Barcelona. 🇸 UK: Av Diagonal 477 • 93 366 62 21 🇸 US: Pg Reina Elisenda 23 • 93 280 22 27 🇸 Australia: Pl Gala Placidia 1–3, 1st floor • 93 490 90 13 🇸 New Zealand: Travessera de Gràcia 64 • 93 209 03 99 🇸 Canada: Plaça Catalunya 9 • 93 412 72 36 🇸 Ireland: Gran Via Carles III 94 • 93 491 50 21

5 Institut de Cultura de Barcelona

Get the lowdown on cultural and arts events among others, from the Institut de Cultura in the Palau de la Virreina (see p13). 🇸 La Rambla 99 • 93 316 10 00 • Open 10am–8pm daily

6 Websites

Numerous websites cover Barcelona, including the official tourist office site (www.barcelona turisme.com). The in-depth www.bcn.cat is another excellent source. The website of Turisme de Catalunya (www. catalunyaturisme.com) has extensive coverage of Catalonia.

7 Travel Bar

This friendly bar, with internet access and amiable staff, is a good source of information. The bar hosts guided walking (see p133) and bike tours "intercambio" nights to practise your Spanish, and a popular bar crawl to the best bars of the old town. 🇸 C/Boqueria 27 • 93 342 52 52

8 University Bulletins

If you're after cheap, short-term accommodation or if you're looking to practise your Spanish, peruse the university notice boards posted around the building's cloisters. 🇸 Gran Via de les Corts Catalanes • 93 403 54 17

9 Libraries & British Institute

The city's main library is the Biblioteca de Catalunya; bring your passport to apply for a one-day pass. The Institut Britànic houses a library of English books and newspapers. 🇸 Biblioteca de Catalunya: C/Hospital 56 Institut Britànic: C/Amigó 83 • Closed Aug

10 Disabled Travellers

Disabled access in Barcelona is limited, though getting better – especially in old buildings. The Institut Municipal de Persones amb Discapacitat provides a list of places with wheelchair access and can offer advice on getting around. 🇸 Av Diagonal 233 • 93 413 27 75

Left **Postage stamp** Centre **Telephone** Right **Mailbox**

🔟 Communication Tips

Public Phones
There are public phones (*cabines*) throughout the city. Use coins or a phonecard.

Phonecards
Purchase a phonecard from a newsstand, phone centre or tobacco shop (*estanc*). The Telefónica phonecard comes in denominations of €6 and €12. Phone centres (*locutoris*) usually sell phone cards with a scratch-off pin number for cheap calls.

Long-Distance Calls
To make an international call, dial 00 followed by the country code (UK: 44; US/Canada: 1; Australia: 61; New Zealand: 64), the area code and the phone number. To call Spain from abroad, dial the international access code then 34 for Spain plus the full phone number. For operator assistance in making international calls from Spain, dial 11825. This is also the number to call if you want to make an international collect call as well as for international information and directory enquiries.

Local & Regional Calls
The cost of a local call from a phone booth to a land line is generally about 20 cents. Barcelona phone numbers all begin with the code 93; the rest of Catalonia is divided up into the provinces of Lleida (973), Girona (972) and Tarragona (977). For operator assistance, dial 11818.

Phone Centres
Phone centres (*locutoris*) provide a more comfortable – and usually cheaper – alternative to public pay phones. Phones are hooked up to a digital display showing the cost, which is paid at the end. You will find several in El Raval as well as around Sants station and in the Poble Sec neighbourhood.

Post
Post offices (*correus*) are usually open 8:30am–8:30pm Mon–Fri and 9:30am–1pm Sat, though hours may vary slightly. Barcelona's main post office is open longer hours. It also offers a range of services, including fax and express mail services (*urgente*). The city's mailboxes are bright yellow 🅢 *Main Post Office: Pl Antoni López • Open 8:30am–10pm Mon–Sat, noon–10pm Sun*

Poste Restante
You can receive mail at any post office, but it's safest to have it sent to the main one. Bring your passport (or a copy of it) to collect mail.
🅢 *Address letters to: Lista de Correos, 08070, Barcelona, Spain*

Internet Access
Internet centres are dotted all over Barcelona, many around Plaça de Catalunya and La Rambla. Most are open until 11pm, sometimes midnight. Phone centres (*locutoris*) usually also provide Internet access. The city council offers more than 300 Wi-Fi points around the city, including at parks and beaches, which allow free Internet for at least 1 hour (see *www.bcn.cat/barcelonawifi for more information*). Several cafés, hostels, hotels and bars offer Wi-Fi, although some charge for the service.
🅢 *Workcenter: C/Roger de Llúria 2; Diagonal 439* 🅢 *Bornet Internet Café C/ Barra de Ferro 3*
• *93 268 15 07* • *www.bornet-bcn.com*

Courier Services
Courier services will pick up a package and deliver it anywhere in the world, usually within 1–5 days.
🅢 *Federal Express: 902 10 08 71* 🅢 *UPS: 902 88 88 20* 🅢 *DHL Worldwide Express: 902 12 24 24*

Fax
You can send and receive faxes at most post offices. Many Internet centres also offer fax services, at lower prices.

Left **Guardia Urbana** Centre **Pharmacy shop front** Right **Pharmacy sign**

⑩ Security & Health Tips

1 Emergencies
The national emergency number is 112, through which you can contact the *policia* (police), *bombers* (firemen) and *ambulància* (ambulance).

2 Police
Dial 091 to call the national police (Policia Nacional), and 092 for the local police (Guàrdia Urbana). If you need to report a crime, go to the nearest *comissaria*. ⊗ *Comissaria, Old Centre: C/Nou de la Rambla 76–78 • 93 306 23 00 • Eixample: Gran Via 256 • 93 424 26 88 • Also located in Plaça de Catalunya train station (underground) • Open 24 hours*

3 Personal Security
Although petty crime is rife, more serious incidences of violence are rare. Thieves occasionally carry knives – if threatened, hand over your belongings immediately.

4 Valuables
Leave all your valuables, including your passport, behind in a hotel safety deposit box. Take as little cash as possible and carry what you do have in a money belt hidden under clothes. Carry wallets in front pockets and ensure bags are strapped across your front. On the beach and in cafés and restaurants, always keep your belongings on your lap or tied to your person. Also be cautious of any odd or unnecessary human contact, verbal or physical, whether it's a tap on the shoulder or someone spilling their drink at your table. Thieves often work in twos, so while one is catching your attention, the other is swiping your wallet.

5 Hospitals
Hospital de la Creu Roja de Barcelona, Hospital de la Santa Creu i de Sant Pau *(see p103)* and Hospital Clinic all have 24-hour emergency rooms (called *urgències*). For an ambulance, dial 061. ⊗ *Hospital de la Creu Roja de Barcelona: C/Dos de Maig 301 • 93 433 15 51* ⊗ *Hospital de la Santa Creu i de Sant Pau • C/Sant Antoni Maria Claret 167 • 93 291 90 00* ⊗ *Hospital Clinic: C/Villaroel 170 • 93 227 54 00*

6 Doctors & Clinics
The tourist office can provide information on English-speaking doctors. There are many walk-in clinics in the city (usually private), including the Creu Blanca near Plaça de Catalunya, where there is no need to make an appointment. There is also a 24-hour clinic at Passeig Reina Elisenda de Montcada, 17. ⊗ *Creu Blanca: C/Pelai 40 • 93 412 12 12 • Open 8:30am–2pm, 4–8pm Mon–Sat*

7 Health Insurance
EU citizens can receive free medical care with a European health insurance card, which must be obtained before travelling. Non-EU citizens are strongly advised to take out medical cover.

8 Dental Treatment
Dental care is not covered by the EU health service. There are numerous dental clinics in Barcelona where you can walk in and get a consultation, including the Clínica Dental Barcelona, where dentists are generally on duty 9am–midnight daily. ⊗ *Clínica Dental Barcelona: Pg de Gràcia 97 • 93 487 83 29*

9 Pharmacies
Pharmacies *(farmàcies)* are marked by a large green or red cross, usually in neon. All chemists have trained pharmacists who can offer advice (places on and around La Rambla usually have a pharmacist who speaks English). Regular hours are generally 10am–10pm. One pharmacy per neighbourhood is open all night from 9pm until 9am on a rotating basis (information is listed on the front door of each). Some pharmacies are open 24 hours, including the Farmacia Clapés on La Rambla.

10 Drinking Water
Spain's tap water is perfectly safe to drink. Most visitors, however, generally prefer to drink bottled water.

CAIXA CATALUNYA

Left **Caixa de Catalunya logo** Right **Twenty-euro note**

Banking & Money Tips

1 The Euro
Since 1 January 2002, the official currency of Spain, and much of Europe, has been the Euro. For general information on the Euro check the European Union website.
🔊 http://ec.europa.eu

2 Banks
Banks are generally open 8am–2pm on week days. Some are open 4–8pm on Thursdays and 8am–2pm on Saturdays, except from July to September. Banks tend to offer better exchange and commission rates than bureaux de change, although rates do vary from bank to bank. There's a Caixa de Catalunya exchange in Plaça de Catalunya, next to the tourist office, which stays open until 9pm. Numerous small bank branches exchange money in Estació de Sants train station and the airport; these are open from 7 or 8am to 10pm daily.

3 Changing Money
Avoid changing money at bureaux de change in tourist areas as commission rates tend to be high or exchange rates poor. On the whole, banks offer better deals, but bureaux de change have the advantage of longer opening hours. Some, particularly those on La Rambla, are open until midnight.

4 ATMs
ATMs (cash machines) provide the easiest way to access money and are a good way to beat commission charges. Surcharges depend on your bank. Relying on ATMs also means that you can take out money in smaller denominations and avoid carrying large amounts of cash. Before travelling, check with your bank that your PIN number works with foreign ATMs. Nearly all take VISA or MasterCard (Access) cards.

5 Travellers' Cheques
Buy travellers' cheques in Euros. All banks cash travellers' cheques, as do larger stores. Always carry the cheque numbers separately from the cheques. American Express and Thomas Cook are two well-known providers of travellers' cheques. Thomas Cook has also introduced "cash passport cards", which can be used at ATMs.

6 Credit Cards
Visa and MasterCard are readily accepted in all but budget hotels, restaurants and shops. American Express and Diner's Club cards are rarely accepted, except in the largest hotels and shops. Credit card cash advances are available from any bank (or ATM if you have a PIN number). Note that the transaction fee for cash advances on credit cards can be high.

7 Emergency Numbers
If your credit card is lost or stolen, call the police and your credit card company. Most credit cards have a number to call collect from abroad, which is provided at the time of issue. 🔊 Visa: 900 99 11 24 🔊 MasterCard: 900 97 12 31 🔊 American Express: 902 37 56 37

8 Online Banking
The quickest and cheapest way to keep track of your bank account and credit card bills is by checking them online. It's best to set up your online account before travelling.

9 Emergency Cash
It is advisable to carry some emergency cash hidden inside your luggage, separate from your wallet.

10 Tipping
Tipping is not the norm in Spain, though expectations are higher of tourists. Locals tip as follows: in restaurants, it is usually about five per cent of the bill. For a light meal, they round up the bill to the nearest 50 cents. Taxi drivers are usually tipped five per cent and hotel porters about 50 cents per bag.

Left **Coffee and croissant** Right **Terrace café, Barri Gòtic**

TOP 10 Eating & Drinking Tips

1 Opening Hours
The Spanish eat much later than much of Europe; lunch starts around 2 or 3pm, with dinner any time after 9pm. Restaurants are usually open 1:30–4pm and 8:30–midnight. Many are closed one day of the week and during the month of August. Cafés and bars are open from around 7:30am, closing around 2am. It is difficult to get a drink or bite to eat after 4am.

2 The Menu
Multilingual menus are increasingly the norm. Many restaurants offer their best deal for lunch from Monday to Friday, so do as the Spaniards do and fill up from the *menú del dia* between 1:30 and 4pm. The fixed-price menu of the day usually includes three courses, wine and water.

3 Catalan Cuisine
Catalan cuisine is characterized by the meeting of *mar i muntanya* (surf and turf), and signature dishes include *llagosta i pollastre* (lobster and chicken). Side dish mainstays are *samfaina* (aubergine/eggplant, grilled peppers, tomatoes and onion in olive oil and garlic) and *escalivada* (sweet peppers, onion and garlic). Other Catalan favourites are *botifarra amb mongetes* (Catalan sausage with white beans) and *pa amb tomàquet* (bread

smeared with tomato and drizzled with olive oil). If innards are your thing, ask for *call* (tripe). For dessert, enjoy *crema catalana*, a custard topped with caramelized sugar.

4 Seafood & Paella
For prime seafood, head for the sea. Along Passeig Joan de Borbó in Barceloneta is a string of restaurants, many specializing in seafood and paellas. Seafood restaurants also abound in the Port Olímpic, where you can feast on fresh-off-the-boat fish and seafood on open-air terraces. Fresh seafood is served year-round, but the traditional day for paella is Thursday.

5 Vegetarian
Barcelona has a handful of vegetarian eateries. Carrer Pintor Fortuny, in El Raval, has a couple of options, including Biocenter (at number 25), with its all-you-can-eat salad bar. Vegetarians can also feast almost anywhere on an array of tapas, including *patates braves* (spicy potatoes) and *truita de patates* (potato omelette). If you eat fish, then you'll be spoiled for choice.

6 Seasonal Specialities
From the end of the year until mid-Spring, try the Catalan speciality of *calçots*, sweet grilled scallions usually in a *romesco* sauce (spicy tomato sauce). Another autumn

favourite are *bolets* (mushrooms), usually lightly grilled and served with a sprinkling of olive oil.

7 Etiquette
Some restrictions on smoking in bars or restaurants apply, and a complete ban is due to be introduced in 2011.

8 Tipping
Tipping is not expected in most establishments, so it's up to your own preference and how you rate the service. If leaving a tip, five per cent is usually acceptable. In upscale restaurants, however, a tip of 10 per cent is the norm. Catalans occasionally tip at the bar, perhaps leaving the small change from their drinks bill.

9 Children
The Spanish are relaxed about bringing children to restaurants and bars. Though kids' menus are rare, restaurants are often willing to serve half portions on request.

10 Disabled Access
All new restaurants must be wheelchair accessible by law, which includes access from the street to the dining room and at least one accessible bathroom. Contact the Institut Municipal de Persones amb Discapacitat *(see p134)* for a list of accessible restaurants. Always call ahead to check.

For Barcelona's best restaurants & tapas bars **See pp44–5**

Left **Shopper, Pg de Gràcia** Centre **Shoe shop, C/Portaferrissa** Right **Clothes boutique, Gràcia**

Shopping Tips

Opening Hours
Most stores are open 10am to 2pm and 4:30pm to 8pm Monday to Saturday. Department stores and other large shops don't close at lunch time.

Sales
Barcelona's big sales (rebaixes) come twice a year, from 1 July to the end of August and from 7 January until the end of February.

Reclaiming VAT
Non-EU citizens can claim an IVA (VAT) refund on most purchases over €90 when they leave Spain. Shops displaying the tax-free logo will provide a tax-refundable receipt, which you present before checking-in on departure. IVA (VAT) of 18 per cent (8 per cent on food) is included. IVA for hotels is 8 per cent, which is not always included in the price.

Leather
Leather items are a good buy in Spain and are of high quality. There are good shoe stores on Carrer Portal de l'Àngel, Carrer Pelai, Rambla de Catalunya and Passeig de Gràcia. Loewe is internationally famous for its quality leather goods. ◈ Loewe: Pg de Gràcia 35

Antiques
Antiques aficionados will be richly rewarded with a stroll along Carrer Banys Nous and Carrer de la Palla in the Barri Gòtic. For more antique finds, head to the Bulevard dels Antiquaris (see p50) on Passeig de Gràcia, home to over 60 antiques and arts shops. The antique markets, including the Mercat dels Antiquaris (see p53) and the Port Vell antique market, at weekends (10am–8pm), are also worth a browse.

Clothing
High-end clothing stores dot Passeig de Gràcia and Avinguda Diagonal. For trendier gear, head to Carrer Portaferrissa and Carrer Pelai. For the best original designs, check out the cool boutiques of La Ribera. Spain's success story is the wildly popular men's and women's contemporary clothing chain Zara, which is all over town (and all over Europe). Another universal favourite is Mango, targeted towards younger women, which also has branches all over the city. If you're looking to buy local, there are a number of top-end Catalan designers, including Antonio Miró. ◈ Zara: Pg de Gràcia 16 ◈ Mango: Pg de Gràcia 65 ◈ Antonio Miró: C/Consell de Cent 349

Sizes
Clothing sizes tend to be small in Spain. Size conversions for women's clothing are: US/UK 6/8 is 36; 8/10 is 38; 10/12 is 40; 12/14 is 42; 14/16 is 44. For men's clothing, the conversions are: US & UK 36 is 46; 38 is 48; 40 is 50; 42 is 52.

Music
FNAC has a vast music selection, as does the department store El Corte Inglés. Equally popular among locals are the small eclectic music shops along Carrer Tallers (see p82). Also worth a look are the CD and vinyl music shops on nearby Carrer Riera Baixa (see p82). ◈ FNAC: El Triangle, Pl de Catalunya 4 ◈ El Corte Inglés: Portal de l'Àngel 19–21

Late-night Shops
There are numerous late-night grocery stores selling the basics. Open Cor sells everything from fresh flowers to wrapping paper, beer and wine. ◈ Open Cor: Ronda de Sant Pere 33 and Gran de Gràcia, 29 • Open until 2am daily

Department Stores
Barcelona's leading department store is El Corte Inglés, which has branches across the city. You can find seemingly everything under one roof, including a supermarket and a gourmet food shop. ◈ El Corte Inglés: several locations, including Pl de Catalunya 14, Av Diagonal 471–473 & Av Diagonal 617–619

For Barcelona's best shopping areas See pp50–51

Left **Shop sale sign** Centre **Five-euro note** Right **Menú del Dia**

TOP 10 Barcelona on a Budget

1 Sightseeing Passes

The Barcelona Card offers up to 50 per cent off the city's main attractions, plus free travel on buses and the metro. It's available for two to five days at all tourist offices and El Corte Inglés department stores. The Articket, which costs €22 and is valid for six months, provides free entry to seven art museums, including MNAC (see pp18–19), MACBA (see pp28–9) and the Fundació Joan Miró (see pp22–3). The tourist office on Plaça de Catalunya (see p134) sells it, as do the museums.

2 Museums

Many museums offer free entry on the first Sunday of the month, including the Museu Picasso (see pp24–5) and MNAC (see pp18–19). Others are also free 3–8pm every Sunday. The tourist office has a list of all the free museum days. Most museums also offer a 30–50 per cent discount – or free admission – for people over 65.

3 Public Transport

The T-10 ticket permits 10 rides on metro, FGC and buses. It is the best option as it can be shared, and allows for transfers (within 75 minutes). Alternatively, you can purchase a two-, three-, four- or five-day pass, which provides unlimited travel on the same services. See p131.

4 Concerts & Opera

Enjoy rock-bottom prices for concerts and the opera (Sep–Jul) by buying seats with partial views – or no view at all. The Gran Teatre del Liceu (see p66) sells cheap tickets for opera and classical recitals. The Palau de la Música Catalana (see pp26–7) has reduced price early-evening weekend shows twice a month. For general information on cultural events – and special deals – call or visit the Institut de Cultura in the Palau de la Virreina (see p13). ✆ Gran Teatre del Liceu ticket office: 93 485 99 00 Institut de Cultura: 93 301 77 75

5 Eating

The most economical way to get a bite to eat is to pick up picnic goodies at one of the city's food markets (see pp52–3). The menú del dia (fixed lunch menu) offered from Monday to Friday at many restaurants is often very reasonable. Dining on the terrace can be more pricey than eating inside, where sitting at the bar is usually the cheapest option.

6 Fast Food

Bypass McDonald's and Burger King and sample Spain's cheaper fast food equivalents. Pans & Company and Bocatta are found all over town; both offer cheap meals, particularly if you eat between 10am and noon, and 4 and 7pm.

7 Drinking

Start out the night in your hotel with a bottle of Spanish wine from the supermarket. Then head to the Barri Gòtic or El Raval where there are plenty of cheap dive bars. Order a canya (tap beer) or a Spanish bottled beer, Estrella or San Miguel, which are usually cheaper than imported beers.

8 Hotels

Visit Barcelona during the low season, from October to April, and you'll find cheaper hotel deals (and air fares). The same can be true in August when many Spanish businesses close. Enquire about any special deals when booking a room.

9 Hotel Bars

You don't have to stay at the ritzy hotels to enjoy their luxurious environs. Most of the bars and cafés at the five-star hotels are open to the public. Try the Hotel Arts (see p143), or the Hotel W, with its great views (see p143), where you can sip a cocktail to the sound of classical piano.

10 Cinemas

Go to the cinema (see p67) on el dia del espectador (often Monday or Wednesday) or for a matinée (usually before 2:30pm), when tickets are cheaper.

Left **Overpriced eatery, La Rambla** Right **Traffic jam**

TOP 10 Things to Avoid

1 Dangerous Areas
Beware of underpopulated alleys and streets in the old town after dark, particularly in the Barri Gòtic and El Raval. These attract thieves who tend to operate in groups. Prime pickpocketing times are between 9pm and midnight, when most locals are eating dinner and only visitors are out on the streets. The early hours (3–6am), after the bars and clubs close, are also popular with thieves.

2 Overpriced Leather Shops
Avoid the pricey leather shops clustered on and around La Rambla. The leather is often poor quality and prices are high. Stop off at the tourist office for a list of approved leather shops, or head for established stores (see pp50–51).

3 La Rambla Scams
Don't get sidetracked by the raucous "find the hidden ball" games on La Rambla. Usually played on makeshift tables, presided over by a skilled, nimble-fingered trickster, it appears at first glance to be a lively game of chance. In reality, it's a confidence trick. The lively folk who cheer you on are all accomplices who are in on the act. Though you may win the first few rounds, you'll soon start to lose, and you'll walk away with a much lighter wallet. Also to be avoided are the gypsies who try to sell you flowers and often pick your pocket at the same time!

4 Overpriced Eats
Rip-off, touristy terrace restaurants line La Rambla. Most of these paella and tapas eateries cater solely to tourists, charging sky-high prices for mediocre meals. The side streets off La Rambla offer better food at more reasonable prices.

5 Crowds
Miss the crowds and interminably long queues at the city's most popular sights by visiting first thing in the morning when the sights open or towards the end of the day, an hour or two before closing time. To avoid the hordes on the beaches in summer go on weekday afternoons.

6 Money Exchange
Steer clear of the bureaux de change on La Rambla, Plaça de Catalunya and near major tourist sights. They usually charge much higher commission than banks. If they advertise no commission, exchange rates are generally poor.

7 Looking Like a Tourist
Avoid attracting attention to yourself as a tourist. Keep cameras hidden, try not to display large banknotes and don't wear valuable jewellery. When consulting a guidebook or map, keep a vigilant eye on your belongings.

8 Traffic
Avoid city traffic congestion by driving around late morning (10am–1pm) or late afternoon (5–7pm). Most office workers have a lunch break between 2pm and 4pm, which means that the roads are packed during this period. Similarly, avoid leaving town on Friday evenings, particularly during the summer. The best time to head out of the city is mid- to late-morning after 10am.

9 August
During the month of August, many Barcelona establishments shut down altogether, the locals disappear on holiday and the city fills with visitors. With so many restaurants, bars, shops and even some sights closed, not to mention the distinct lack of local life, August in Barcelona has its drawbacks. Always call first to check on opening times during this period.

10 Monday Sightseeing
Many of the top museums are closed on Mondays, including the Museu Picasso (see pp24–5) and the MNAC (see pp18–19). So always double-check opening times on this day.

141

Left **Room, Hotel Mesón Castilla** Right **Suite, Hotel Claris**

🔟 Accommodation Tips

1 Book Ahead
If visiting Barcelona in the high season (Mar–Jul & Sep), book ahead as the city's hotels, *pensions* and *hostals* (smaller, more basic guesthouses rated at one to three stars) usually fill to capacity. When reserving a room, ask about special deals as many hotels have these, especially in the low season (Oct–Mar & Aug).

2 Where to Find Budget Beds
There are scores of cheap *pensions* and *hostals* on La Rambla and its sidestreets in the Barri Gòtic and El Raval. Plaça Reial also has a cluster of budget accommodation options.

3 Pensions & Hostals
Room size (and comfort level) in *pensions* and *hostals* varies widely, but in the accredited budget places (the tourist office has a list of these), you'll find clean rooms and good security. Rooms come either *amb bany* (with a bath) or *sense bany* (without a bath); most have a washbasin.

4 Getting the Room you Want
Hotels and *hostals* give the best rooms to those who ask for them – so always inquire. Most *hostals*, particularly in the old town, have some rooms with lovely wrought-iron balconies, which can make all the difference to a small room. Ask for *una habitació exterior amb vistes* (a room with a view) or *amb balcó* (with balcony). If you're a light sleeper, opt for a *una habitació interior* (interior room).

5 Single Travellers
Single rooms in *hostals* and *pensions* are few and far between, but hotels are legally obliged to let double rooms to single occupants at a fixed price. All rates must be posted at reception or in the rooms.

6 Families
Many hotels offer discounts for children under 12 when they share their parents' room on a temporary bed.

7 Security
If you're going to be staying at youth hostels and campsites, carry a chain and padlock to tie your luggage to something sturdy. Always leave your valuables in a safe or locked box, which most places have.

8 Hotel Booking Service & Websites
The tourist office *(see p132)* in Plaça de Catalunya has a hotel booking service, which is useful if you arrive in high season without a reservation. It offers bookings in hotels of all categories, but most often in three-star hotels and above. A deposit is payable on reservation. The tourist office also produces a list of the best *pensions* and *hostals* for budget travellers. On the web, try www.barcelonahotels.es and www.barcelonaturisme.com.

9 Cases de Pagès
Discover rural Catalonia by staying at *Cases de Pagès* (country or farm houses), which offer B&B-style lodgings. They vary widely, from small, rural homes with a handful of rooms to luxurious, palace-sized farmhouses. Stop by the Turisme de Catalunya office *(see p132)* for a free list of the *Gîtes de Catalunya* and (to buy) the *Cases de Pagès* book, which has detailed listings and pictures of all such houses. This information is also accessible through its website (www.gencat.es/probert).

10 Refugis
Throughout the Pyrenees and other mountainous areas, you'll find *refugis* (basic mountain hostels for hikers and bikers). They offer simple, cheap accommodation, usually bunk beds in a dorm room. In the summer months, *refugis* fill up quickly, so it is advisable to book in advance. Ask at tourist offices for a list of local ones; or stop by Turisme de Catalunya *(see p132)*.

 Visitors seeking long-term accommodation, beware of agencies that charge for accommodation lists; they are invariably a scam.

Hotel Omm

Price Categories

For a standard, double room per night (with breakfast if included), taxes and extra charges.

€	Under €60
€€	€60–120
€€€	€120–180
€€€€	€180–240
€€€€€	Over €240

Luxury Hotels

1 Hotel Arts
Barcelona's grande dame five-star hotel is mere steps from the sea, with ample, sumptuous rooms and top-notch eating places. The first-floor, outdoor pool has stunning views. ⊗ C/Marina 19–21 • Map G5 • 93 221 10 00 • www.hotelartsbarcelona. com • DA • €€€€€

2 Abac Hotel and Restaurant
Arguably the city's finest restaurant, Abac is now part of a boutique hotel with 15 gorgeous rooms stylishly decorated with contemporary minimalism. There is a spa and a small, but immaculate, garden. ⊗ Avda Tibidabo 1 • 93 319 66 00 • www.abacbarcelona.com • €€€€€

3 Hotel Palace Barcelona
This deluxe hotel, is an emblem of tradition and style, with great service. The famous Restaurant Caelis offers an innovative gourmet menu. ⊗ Gran Via de les Corts Catalanes, 668 • Map F3 • 93 510 11 30 • www. hotelpalacebarcelona.com • DA • €€€€€

4 Hotel Majestic
Stately decor and faultless service are the hallmarks of this aptly named hotel. Exit through the heavy brass-and-glass doors and you're mere steps from the Eixample's Modernista gems. The rooftop swimming pool has views of the Sagrada Família and the Barcelona cityscape. ⊗ Pg de Gràcia 68 • Map E2 • 93 488 17 17 • www.hotelmajestic.es • DA • €€€€€

5 Hotel Omm
Designed by award-winning Catalan architect Juli Capella, this is one of the hottest hotels in the city. There is an excellent restaurant and bar (see p107), a great spa and stunning views from the rooftop deck and pool. ⊗ C/Rosselló 265 • Map E2 • 93 445 40 00 • www. hotelomm.es • €€€€€

6 Hotel W
Popularly known as the Hotel Vela (the sail hotel) for its billowing form, this sumptuous five-star option enjoys unparalleled sea views. With floor-to-ceiling windows it is easy to imagine you are at sea. All the fancy extras are here, from spa and rooftop pool to designer bars and restaurants. ⊗ Plaça de la Rosa dels vents 1 • Map E5 • 93 295 28 00 • www.starwoodhotels.com • €€€€€

7 Granados 83
Rooms at this designer hotel are decorated with African zebrawood, chocolate brown leather and original pieces of Buddhist and Hindu art. Suites have private terraces overlooking a plunge pool. There is a restaurant, and a pretty rooftop pool with a very fashionable bar. ⊗ C/Enric Granados 83 • Map E2 • 93 492 96 70 • www. derbyhotels.es • €€€€€

8 Casa Camper
A converted 19th-century mansion, this hotel oozes with innovative yet comfortable design touches. Big rooms, roof-terrace, extraordinary vertical garden and a free 24-hour bar. ⊗ Elisabets 11 • Map L2 • 93 342 62 80 • www.casacamper.com • DA • €€€€€

9 Hotel Rey Juan Carlos I
This massive complex includes a vast private garden and a conference hall for up to 2,500 people. The spacious rooms are sumptuously decorated in a contemporary style. The top floors offer unobstructed views of the city and mountains. ⊗ Av Diagonal 661–671 • Off map • 93 364 40 40 • www.hrjuan carlos.com • DA • €€€€€

10 Grand Hotel Central
This large, elegant hotel has a great location close to the Gothic Quarter and Born. But the real draw is the stunning rooftop pool with spectacular views of the city. ⊗ Via Laietana 30 • Map E4 • 93 295 79 00 • www.grandhotelcentral. com • €€€€€

Unless otherwise stated, all hotels accept credit cards, have en-suite bathrooms and air conditioning.

143

Left **Salon, Hotel Mesón Castilla** Right **Swimming Pool, Hotel Ducs de Bergara**

TOP 10 Historical Hotels

1 Hotel Mesón Castilla

A historical gem in the heart of El Raval, this family-run hotel is housed in an early-1900s mansion. A home-turned-hotel, it shines under the loving care of its management. From the opulent first-floor salon to the lovely rooms – each with antique furniture – this hotel offers a chance to step back in time. Enjoy breakfast on the outdoor patio. ✪ *C/Valldonzella 5 • Map L1 • 93 318 21 82 • www. mesoncastilla.com • €€€*

2 Hotel Ducs de Bergara

Housed in a lovely 1898 *Modernista* building, this luxurious hotel has well-appointed rooms. There's a large interior courtyard with a swimming pool. ✪ *C/Bergara 11 • Map L1 • 93 301 51 51 • www. hoteles-catalonia.es • DA • €€€€*

3 Gran Hotel La Florida

Set in a Modernista villa in the hills above Barcelona, this luxurious hotel has been beautifully renovated by the finest designers and architects. ✪ *Ctra Vallvidrera al Tibidabo 83-93 • 93 259 30 00 • www. hotellaflorida.com • €€€€€*

4 Hotel Neri

This 17th-century former palace at the heart of the Barri Gòtic offers an exclusive combination of history, the avant-garde and glamour. There is Internet access in all rooms, a library, solarium and a roof terrace with views to the Cathedral. ✪ *C/Sant Sever 5 • Map M3 • 93 304 06 55 • www. hotelneri.com • €€€€€*

5 Hotel Oriente

Opened in 1842, this Barri Gòtic institution has hosted its share of luminaries, including many opera greats from the nearby Liceu *(see p12)*. It was built on the site of an old Franciscan monastery and the ballroom was created out of the cloister. The hotel may be showing its age, but for many, its charm lies in the faded grandeur. ✪ *La Rambla 45 • Map L4 • 93 302 25 58 • www.hotelhusaoriente. com • €€€*

6 1898

A 19th-century tobacco factory houses this chic hotel, which has retained some original fittings and combined them with 21st-century amenities. These include pools, a fitness centre, and a good restaurant. ✪ *La Rambla 109 • Map L2 • 93 552 95 52 • www.barcelonahotel 1898.com • DA • €€€*

7 Hotel Duquesa de Cardona

Located in a 16th-century building, this stylish hotel combines the original structure with avant-garde decor and all the modern facilities. The rooftop terrace, which offers great views over the Port Vell, also has a plunge pool. ✪ *Passeig Colón 12 • Map M6 • 93 268 90 90 • www.hduquesade cardona.com • €€€€€*

8 Hotel Montecarlo

This friendly, family-owned hotel, with a 1930s façade, is particularly eye-catching lit up at night. Rooms are pleasant and bright, and many have balconies overlooking La Rambla. ✪ *La Rambla 124 • Map L2 • 93 412 04 04 • www.montecarlobcn. com • €€€*

9 Casa Fuster

Originally designed by Domènech i Muntaner, this hotel is one of the city's most prestigious and luxurious. The sumptuous *Modernista* details have been retained, but are combined with 21st-century amenities. ✪ *Passeig de Gràcia 132 • Map E1 • 93 255 30 00 • www.hotelcasafuster. com • €€€€€*

0 Hotel Claris

This 19th-century Eixample palace was once home to the counts of Vedruna. Inside is a small museum of pre-Colombian art, some of which also decorates the suites. Guests get free admission to the Museu Egipci *(see p105)*, run by the hotel owner. ✪ *C/Pau Claris 150 • Map E2 • 93 487 62 62 • www.derbyhotels.es • DA • €€€€€*

 It is always worth checking hotel websites for off-season promotional offers.

Price Categories

For a standard, double	€ under €60
room per night (with	€€ €60–120
breakfast if included),	€€€ €120–180
taxes and extra	€€€€ €180–240
charges.	€€€€€ over €240

Exterior, Hotel Colón

Central Stays

1 Hotel Colón
A handsome, family-owned Barri Gòtic hotel, the Colón has traditional decor with mirrors and oil paintings throughout. The magnificient views of the Cathedral and Plaça de la Seu from this homely, quaint place, are stunning. ◎ *Av de la Catedral 7* • *Map N3* • *93 301 14 04* • *www. hotelcolon.es* • *€€€*

2 Hotel 54 Barceloneta
The seaside neighbourhood of Barceloneta has traditionally had very few hotels. This trendy newcomer fills a welcome gap on two counts – it's perfectly located overlooking the yacht-filled port, and the modest but bright rooms are very reasonable. ◎ *Passeig Joan de Borbó 54* • *Map F6* • *93 225 00 54* • *www.hotel54barce loneta.com* • *€€€*

3 AC Miramar
Celebrity architect, Oscar Tusquets, is responsible for designing this spectacular hotel, which enjoys a unique location on Montjuïc hill. The stunning views, over the sea, and out to the sea, are absolutely breathtaking. There are beautiful gardens to relax in, a luxurious spa and an excellent restaurant. ◎ *Plaça Carlos Ibáñez 3* • *Map C5* • *93 281 16 00* • *www.hotelmiramar barcelona.es* • *€€€€€*

4 Hotel Banys Orientals
Behind the traditional frontage lies a modern, cosy hotel with free Internet access in every room. Plusher suites are available in a separate building. The Cathedral, Picasso museum and Barceloneta beach are close by. ◎ *C/ Argenteria 37* • *Map N4* • *93 268 84 60* • *www. hotelbanysorientals.com* • *€€*

5 Mandarin Oriental Barcelona
This ultra-luxurious hotel boasts rooms overlooking either the iconic Passeig de Gràcia or the gorgeous interior gardens. It has a spa, a roof terrace with splash pool and gourmet restaurant. ◎ *Passeig de Gràcia 38–40* • *Map E3* • *93 151 88 88* • *www.mandarinoriental. com/barcelona* • *€€€€€*

6 Park Hotel
A 1950s design classic with a gorgeous wraparound staircase, the Park Hotel was refurbished in the 1990s by the original architect's son. Rooms are small but comfortably furnished, and some have balconies. It is near the fashionable Born boutiques and clubs. ◎ *Avinguda Marquès de l'Argentera* • *Map F5* • *93 319 60 00* • *www.park hotelbarcelona.com* • *€€€*

7 Jazz
The modern Jazz hotel may not be the most stylish option, but it is centrally located and has many amenities including a small rooftop pool. It is great value for money, and the friendly staff are always on-hand to offer help and advice. ◎ *C/Pelai 3* • *Map L1* • *93 552 96 96* • *www. nnhotels.com* • *€€€*

8 Hotel Constanza
This elegant mid-sized hotel is located near all the main sights of Eixample. Some of the stylish rooms come with terraces and there is a good guest-only restaurant. ◎ *C/Bruc 33* • *Map F3* • *93 270 19 10* • *www.hotelconstanza. com* • *€€–€€€*

9 Soho
Top Spanish architect Alfredo Arribas, designed this swanky hotel. Located in Eixample, it's perfect for shopping, sightseeing and enjoying the nightlife. ◎ *Gran Via Corts Catalanes 543* • *Map D3* • *93 552 96 10* • *www. hotelsohobarcelona.com* • *€€€€*

10 Pullman Barcelona
Located on the beachfront, the Pullman has the perfect location for a summer city-break. It has all the facilities you would expect in a five-star hotel. Designed for business travellers, weekend bargains are often available. ◎ *Avenida Litoral 10* • *Map G6* • *93 221 65 65* • *www.pullman-barcelona-skipper.com* • *€€€€*

Left **Hostal Jardi** Right **Entrance hall, Hostal Oliva**

Budget Accommodation

Sol y k

A charming budget option in the heart of the Gothic quarter. A handful of individually decorated rooms with mosaic head-boards and original artworks set the Sol y k apart from other guest houses in this price bracket. Free Wi-Fi is available. ◈ C/Cervantes 2 • Map M5 • 93 318 81 48 • www.solyk.com • €

Hostal Oliva

From the lovely, *Modernista* elevator to the individually wrapped soaps imprinted with the Oliva logo, this cheerful, family-run *hostal* is one of Barcelona's best. The ornate *Modernista* building has bright rooms that are sparklingly clean; some have en-suite bathrooms. ◈ Pg de Gràcia 32 • Map E3 • 93 488 01 62 • www.lasguias.com/ hostaloliva • No credit cards • €€

Hostal Goya

A well-run *hostal* that has been accommodating visitors since 1952. The rooms are bright and modern with bold prints and some designer touches. Most rooms have en-suite bathrooms and some have air conditioning. ◈ C/Pau Claris 74 • Map N1 • 93 302 25 65 • www.hostalgoya.com • €€

Hostal Fernando

Spotless and bright, this central *hostal* has well-maintained doubles (with or without bath), plus dorm rooms that sleep 4 to 8 people. There are also left-luggage lockers. ◈ C/Ferran 31 • Map L4 • 93 301 79 93 • www.hfernando.com • €

Market

Close to the *Modernista* market of Sant Antoni, this is a very stylish hotel for the price. The rooms have an oriental feel, with glossy lacquered wood and a red-white-and-black colour theme. Market has a popular restaurant, where breakfast is served. Book well in advance. ◈ Passatge Sant Antoni Abat 10 • Map D3 • 93 325 12 05 • www. markethotel.com.es • €€

Hostal Jardí

Get your beauty sleep in the snug heart of the Barri Gòtic at this hotel. Simple yet spotless rooms, all with en-suite bathrooms, are done up in light wood and cool colours. The bright breakfast room has balconies overlooking the plaça. ◈ Pl Sant Josep Oriol 1 • Map M3 • 93 301 59 00 • €€

Hotel Praktic Rambla

A *Modernista* mansion has been handsomely restored to contain this chic, yet modestly priced, hotel. Original details, such as beautiful tiled floors and woodwork, have been preserved alongside modern amenities. Excellent central location. ◈ Rambla de Catalunya 27 • Map E3 • 93 343 66 90 • www.hotelpraktikrambla. com • €€

Bonic

A great budget option, this charming hotel has stylish rooms and many thoughtful extras, such as free tea, coffee, muffins, Internet access and dressing gowns. Bathrooms, however, are shared. ◈ C/Josep Anselm Clavé 9 • Map L6 • 62 605 34 34 • www.bonic-barcelona.com • €€

Chic and Basic

This converted 19th-century townhouse is a big hit with fashionistas. Rooms are minimalist white, with contemporary glass and steel bathrooms, and colourful LED lights that add a kitsch touch. The White Bar is also very popular. ◈ C/Princesa 50 • Map P4 • 93 295 46 52 • www. chicandbasic.com • €€

Gat Xino

This is the second *hostal* in the Gat Accommodation group, and is typical of their signature style: simple, modern design at great prices. It's worth splashing out on the suite, which has its own private terrace. ◈ C/Hospital 149 • Map K3 • 93 324 88 33 • www. gatrooms.es • €€

Unless otherwise stated, none of these establishments has air conditioning or en-suite bathrooms.

Price Categories

For a standard, double room per night (with breakfast if included), taxes and extra charges.

€	under €60
€€	€60–120
€€€	€120–180
€€€€	€180–240
€€€€€	over €240

First floor, Gothic Point Youth Hostel

Hostels and Student Residences

1 Gothic Point Youth Hostel

This bright, well-run, central hostel has dorm rooms sleeping 6 to 14. Breakfast is included in the price, and there's free 24-hour Internet access. There is air conditioning in all rooms. ⬡ C/Vigatans 5 • Map N4 • 93 268 78 08 • www.gothicpoint.com • €

2 Ideal Youth Hostel

Situated close to La Rambla, this is a modern hostel with dorms for four, six and eight people, each with balcony, en-suite toilet and shower. It also has single and double rooms. Breakfast is included as is free Internet access. There is a self-service laundrette. ⬡ C/Unió 12 • Map L4 • 93 342 61 77 • www.idealhostel.com • €

3 Feetup Hostel Garden House

This friendly hostel is located on the outskirts of the city, near the beautiful Gaudí-designed Park Güell. It's only a 15-minute metro ride into the centre of town. There is a lovely garden and roof terrace, and a relaxed, easygoing vibe. ⬡ C/d'Hedilla 58 • 93 427 24 79 • www.feetup hostels.com • €

4 Downtown Paraiso Hostel

Established by four former travellers, this friendly hostel is a hit with young backpackers. It is central, has no curfew, you don't need to rent sheets and blankets, and it offers a range of rooms, with or without bathrooms. ⬡ C/Junta de Comerç 13 • Map K4 • 93 302 61 34 • www.down townparaisohostel.com • €

5 Alberg Kabul

Kabul is a favourite with young backpackers, so it's often full (and noisy). Dorm rooms, all with air conditioning and some with balconies on the Plaça Reial (see p36), sleep 4 to 20 people. There's a laundry, free Internet access, lockers and a small cafeteria that serves cheap food during the day. ⬡ Pl Reial 17 • Map L4 • 93 318 51 90 • www.kabul.es • €

6 Barcelona Dream

This hostel may not be central, but it is only a 20-minute metro ride from the city centre. It is well-priced, close to the beaches, and the rooms accommodate between two and 12 persons. Kitchen and laundry facilities are included. ⬡ Ave. Alfonso XIII, Badalona • 93 399 14 20 • www. barcelonadream.net • €€

7 Centric Point Hostel

Housed in a renovated Modernista building, this hostel offers large dorms, as well as single and double rooms with private facilities. There is a common room with a bar, free Internet access and satellite TV. ⬡ Passeig de Gràcia 33 • Map E3 • 93 231 20 45 • www. equity-point.com • €

8 Melon District

Part-student residence and part-hostel, Melon District has rooms available to rent for short- or long-term stays. The rooms are not large, but have great facilities. There is a rooftop plunge pool. ⬡ Avda Paral.lel 101 • Map D4 • 93 217 88 12 • www. melondistrict.com • €

9 Mambo Tango

Toto and Marino, ex-travellers themselves, are behind this warm and welcoming hostel. It has dorms for four, six and eight people, breakfast and sheet-hire are included in the price, and extras include a home cinema. Party animals are actively discouraged, so you can count on a good night's sleep. ⬡ C/Poeta Cabanyes 23 • Map C4 • 93 442 51 64 • www. hostelmambotango.com • €

10 Itaca Hostel

In the heart of the Gothic Quarter, this is a clean and friendly hostel with space for 30 guests in double rooms, dorms (for up to six) and apart-ments. Bedding and lockers are included in the price and there is Wi-Fi available in the main building. ⬡ C/Ripoll 21 • Map N3 • 93 301 97 51 • www.itacahostel.com • €

Left **Camping Tamariu** Right **Swimming Pool, Aparthotel Bertran**

TOP 10 Campsites and Aparthotels

1 Camping Roca-Grossa

Situated between the mountains and the sea, this modern campsite has good installations and access to the nearby beach. It has a large swimming pool, restaurant and bar and is 1 km from the lively resort of Calella. Bungalows are also available. Ⓢ *Ctra, N-II km 665, Calella • 93 769 12 97 • www.rocagrossa.com • Closed Oct–Mar • €*

2 Camping Sitges

A small and well-kept campsite with swimming pool, supermarket and playground. It is located 2 kms (1 mile) southward from Sitges, and is close to its famous beaches. Ⓢ *Ctra, Comarcal 246, km 38, Sitges • 93 894 10 80 • www.camping sitges.com • Closed mid-Oct–Feb • €*

3 Camping Masnou

Located 12 kms (7.5 miles) to the north of Barcelona, this family-owned camp site faces the sea and has a small beach nearby. Facilities include a supermarket, restaurant and bar. Ⓢ *Camilo Fabra 33 (N-II, km 663), El Masnou • 935 55 15 03 • Credit cards from €100 • DA • €*

4 Camping Tamariu

This well-kept camp site is on the Costa Brava, near the lovely beach town of Tamariu. It is 200 m (656 ft) from the beach and within sauntering distance of the town for bars, restaurants and grocery shops. Ⓢ *Costa Rica 2, near Tamariu, 5 km E of Palafrugell • 97 262 04 22 • www.campingtamariu. com • Closed Oct–Apr • €*

5 Camping Barcelona

Twenty-eight kms (17.5 miles) north of Barcelona is this campsite next to a small beach. It is also close to several larger beaches. The camp site is about 1 km (0.6 mile) from the train station. Bungalows are also available. Ⓢ *Carretera A2, km 650, 8 km E of Mataró • 93 790 47 20 • www. campingbarcelona.com • Closed Nov–Mar • DA • €*

6 Camping Globo Rojo

Close to the beaches of Canet de Mar and with a swimming pool, tennis court, football pitch as well as all kinds of sporting activities. Great for kids. Ⓢ *Ctra, N-II km 660, 9, Canet de Mar • 93 794 11 43 • www. globo-rojo.com • Closed Oct–mid-Mar • DA • €*

7 Citadines

If you're smitten with Barcelona, try an aparthotel for a longer stay. The Citadines aparthotel on La Rambla has well-appointed studios and small apartments with amenities, such as a kitchen (with oven and microwave), iron and a CD stereo. The rooftop solarium, equipped with beach chairs and showers, is just the spot to unwind. Ⓢ *La Rambla 122 • Map L2 • 93 270 11 11 • www. citadines.com • €€€*

8 Aparthotel Bertran

This aparthotel has ample studios and apartments (many with balconies), a rooftop terrace with swimming pool, a small gym and 24-hour laundry service. Breakfast is served in your apartment. Ⓢ *C/Bertran 150 • 93 212 75 50 • www.bertran-hotel. com • €€€*

9 Atenea Aparthotel

Designed with business travellers in mind, this top-notch aparthotel sits near Barcelona's business and financial district around upper Diagonal. Rooms are ample and well-equipped, and there are several conference rooms and a 24-hour laundry service. Ⓢ *C/Joan Güell 207–211 • 93 490 66 40 • www. city-hotels.es • €€€*

10 Habit Servei

This agency finds furnished apartments and flat-shares for short- and long-term stays. The average cost is around €900 a month. Ⓢ *C/Muntaner 200 • Map D2 • 93 240 50 23 • www.habitservei.com*

Unless otherwise stated, all campsites are open all year round, though many open only at weekends October–March.

Price Categories

For a standard, double room per night (with breakfast if included), taxes and extra charges.

€	under €60
€€	€60–120
€€€	€120–180
€€€€	€180–240
€€€€€	over €240

Coastline, Costa Brava

🔟 Getaways Beyond Barcelona

1 La Torre del Remei
Close to the Pyrenean town of Puigcerdà, this restored 1910 *Modernista* palace, with its series of sumptuous rooms, has an outdoor heated pool and a renowned restaurant. Take your pick of views: impressive mountain peaks or the lush garden.
Ⓢ *Camí Reial, Bolvir, 3 km SW of Puigcerdà* • *97 214 01 82* • *www.torredel remei.com* • *€€€€€*

2 El Hostal de la Gavina
This elegant mansion, set in peaceful grounds, is just 200 m (656 ft) from the beach. The rooms have antique furniture and fixtures, and there's a salt-water pool. The first-rate restaurant serves divine Mediterranean fare.
Ⓢ *Pl de la Rosaleda, 3km S of S'Agaró* • *97 232 11 00* • *Closed mid-Oct–Easter (except New Year)* • *€€€€€*

3 Hotel Aiguablava
This coastal institution is perched atop rugged cliffs overlooking the Mediterranean. It is run by the fourth generation of the same family. Many of the rooms – each individually decorated – have splendid vistas of the sea. There's a large outdoor pool and breakfast is included.
Ⓢ *Platja de Fornells, Begur* • *97 262 45 62* • *www. aiguablava.com* • *Closed mid-Oct–mid-Mar* • *€€€*

4 Fonda Biayna
The Fonda Biayna has been in operation since the 1820s. Wood-beamed ceilings and antique furniture imbue it with rustic flair. The inn's most famous guest was Picasso, who arrived here by mule en route to Paris (with paintings in tow). Ⓢ *C/de Sant Roc 11, Bellver de Cerdanya* • *97 351 04 75* • *www.fondabiayna.com* • *€€*

5 Hostal Sa Tuna
Take in the sea views from your terrace at this five-room, family-run hotel on the pretty Platja Sa Tuna. The restaurant serves excellent Catalan cuisine and breakfast is included. Ⓢ *Pg de Ancora 6, Platja Sa Tuna, 5 km N of Begur* • *97 262 21 98* • *www.hostalsatuna. com* • *Closed Oct–Mar* • *€€€*

6 Mas de Torrent
This beautifully restored 18th-century farmhouse near Pals has antique decor offset by museum-worthy contemporary art. There is an outdoor pool and spa facilities. Ⓢ *Finca Mas de Torrent, Torrent, 5 km NW of Palafrugell* • *972 30 32 92* • *www. mastorrent.com* • *DA* • *€€€€€*

7 Parador de Tortosa
Looming over the town of Tortosa is the ancient Arab Castillo de la Zuda, within which this parador is housed. Decor is suitably old-world, with dark-wood furniture and antique fixtures, and the view of countryside and mountains is superb.
Ⓢ *Castillo de la Zuda, Tortosa* • *97 744 44 50* • *www.parador.es* • *€€€*

8 Ca L'Aliu
This restored, cosy *casa rural* is in the tiny medieval town of Peratallada. Comfortable rooms all have antique furniture. The amiable owners will lend you bikes. Ⓢ *C/Roca 6, Peratallada, 12 km NW of Palafrugell* • *97 263 40 61* • *www.calaliu. com* • *€€*

9 Royal Tanau
This luxury hotel has chair lifts direct to the slopes of the ski resort Baqueira-Beret *(see p120)*. Cosy cabin-style rooms offer a view of the peaks.
Ⓢ *Ctra/de Beret, Baqueira-Beret, 120 km N of Lleida* • *97 364 44 46* • *www. solmelia.com* • *Closed mid-Apr–Nov* • *DA* • *€€€€€*

10 Hotel Historic
A good base for visiting Girona, this hotel is located in the heart of the old quarter. Choose from rooms or self-catering apartments, just around the corner from the cathedral.
Ⓢ *C/Belmirall 4a* • *972 223 583* • *www. hotelhistoric.com* • *€€€*

General Index

1898 144

A

Àbac 117
activities 60–1
Aerobús 130
Agut 79
Agut d'Avignon 79
aigua 43
Air Europa 130
Air Shop, The 84
air travel 130
Al Limón Negro 77
Alfarràs, Marques d' 113
Alfons I, King 30
Alfons XIII, King 31
Alt Penedès 120
Amargós, Josep 17
ambulances 136
American football 61
Àntic Hospital de la Santa Creu 83
Antinous Llibreria-Cafè 48
Antiquari, L' 73
antiques 139
Antoni de Padua, Sant 39
Aparthotel Bertran 148
aparthotels 148
Aquàrium, L' 62, 97
Arc de Triomf 16
Arca de l'Avia, L' 75
architecture, *Modernista* 32–3
Arena Madre 46
Arnau, Eusebi 27, 32, 33, 104
Arola 100
Aroma 115
Arribas, Alfred 46
art festivals 65
art galleries, El Raval 84
Arts Santa Mònica 12, 13
Asador d'Aranda, El 44, 113, 117
Atalanta Manufactura 75
Atenea Aparthotel 148
ATMs (cash machines) 137
Auditori de Barcelona 66
August, avoiding 141
Aventura del Nautilus, L' 132
Avinguda Diagonal 51
Avis 132

B

Bacon, Francis 21
Bagotti, Domenico 113
ballooning 126
Balsa, La 117
banking 137
Bar Almirall 86
Bar Elèctric 116
Bar L'Ascensor 76
Bar Jai Ca 100
Bar Kasparo 42
Bar Lobo 42
Bar Ra 44, 87
Bar Resolis 86
Bar-Restaurante Can Tomàs 45, 117
Bar Seco 95
Barceló, Miquel 91
Barcelona Airport 130
Barcelona by Bike 133
Barcelona Cathedral 6, **14–15**, 38, 55, 71147

Barcelona Dream
Barcelona Open 61
61Barcelona Marató
Barceloneta 98, 99 *see also Port Vell, Barcelona & Port Olímpic*
Barri Gòtic & La Ribera 58, 70–9
   best of the rest 74
   cafés & light eats 78
   clubs & music venues 77
   cocktail & conversation spots 76
   map 70
   restaurants & tapas bars 79
   shops 75
   sights & attractions 70–73
   walks 73
Barri Xinès 82–3
bars 46–7
   budget travel 131
   Gràcia, Tibidabo & Zona Alta 116
   Montjuïc 95
   Port Vell, Barceloneta & Port Olímpic 100
   El Raval 86
Báscula, La 78
Base Nàutica 133
basketball 61
Bassa, Ferrer 38
Bauma 108
beach clubs
   Port Vell, Barceloneta & Port Olímpic 100
beaches
   for children 63
   Port Vell, Barceloneta & Port Olímpic 49, 57, 97
   Sitges 49
   sunbathing & swimming 60
Beethoven, Ludwig van 27
Begur 120
Betty Ford's 86
Beyond Barcelona
   churches & monasteries 124
   national parks & nature reserves 125
   outdoor activities 126
   places to eat 127
   sights & attractions 118–121
Bernat Picornell Olympic pool 60
Biblioteca 87
bicycles 131
   bike rides 58–9
   mountain biking 132
   tours 133
Biking 61
Bikini 116
Biosca & Botey 106
bird stalls 13
Blay, Miquel 32
Blow by Le Swing 85
Blues Cafè 115
Boadas Cocktail Bar 86
boat trips
   beyond Barcelona 126
   les golondrines 54, 63, 133
   Port Vell, Barceloneta & Port Olímpic 98
   sea cruises 132
Boix 120
Boliche 67
Bonic 146
Book & Coin Market at Mercat de Sant Antoni 52

Borgonya, Joan de 14
Born, El 51, 72
Bornet Internet Café 135
Botafumeiro 117
Bravo, Arranz 28
British Airways 130
British Institute 134
Bruno Quadras Building 13
Budget (car hire) 132
Budget Bikes 131
budget travel 140
Buigas, Carles 89
Bulevard dels Antiquaris 50
Bulevard Rosa 50
bureaux de change 137, 141
buses 131
   in Catalonia 132
   getting to Barcelona 130
   nightbuses 131
   tours 132, 133
Bus Montjuïc Turístic 135

C

Ca L'Aliu 149
Ca L'Isidre 87
Caballé, Montserrat 12, 66, 89
cable cars 54, 63, 98, 133
cacaolat 43
Cacao Sampaka 108
Cactus Bar 76
Cadaqués 121
Cafè de l'Acadèmia 79
cafè amb llet 43
Cafè-Bar L'Antiquari 78
Cafè Bliss 42, 78
Café del Born 78
Café del Born Nou 76
Cafè del Centre 108
Cafè d'Estiu 78
Cafè de l'Òpera 42
Cafè Salambó 43, 115
Cafè sol 43
Cafè del Sol 115
Cafè del Teatre 115
cafés 42–3
   Barri Gòtic & La Ribera 78
   Eixample 108
   Gràcia 115
   Montjuïc 95
Cafetera, La 115
Cal Pep 44, 79
calamars 45
Calder, Alexander
   Font de Mercuri 23
Call, El 74
Cambó Bequest19
Cambó, Francesc 19
Camiseria Pons 114
Camp Nou Stadium 111
Camping Barcelona 148
Camping Masnou 148
Camping Roca-Grossa 148
Camping Sitges 148
Camping Tamariu 148
campsites 148
Can Ganassa 101
Can Manel la Puda 101
canya 43
Cap de Creus 121, 125
Capella de Sant Jordi 39
Capella de Sant Miquel 38
Capella de Santa Àgata 38
Carme Ruscalleda Sant Pau 127

→

Acknowledgements

The Authors

Travel writer, reporter and editor AnneLise Sorensen is half-Catalan and has lived and worked in Barcelona. She has penned (and wine tasted) her way across four continents, contributing to guidebooks, magazines, newspapers, TV and radio.

Ryan Chandler is a writer and journalist who has been working in Barcelona for over ten years. He currently works as Barcelona correspondent for the Spanish magazine *The Broadsheet*.

Produced by Departure Lounge, London

Editorial Director Ella Milroy
Art Editor Lee Redmond
Editor Clare Tomlinson
Designer Lisa Kosky
DTP Designer Ingrid Vienings
Picture Researcher Monica Allende
Research Assistance Amaia Allende, Ana Virginia Aranha, Diveen Henry
Consultant Brian Catlos
Proofreader Catherine Day
Indexer Hilary Bird
Fact Checkers Paula Canal, Brian Catlos, Mary-Ann Gallagher, AnneLise Sorensen

Photographers Joan Farré, Manuel Huguet

Additional photography Ian Aitken, Max Alexander, Mike Dunning, Steve Gorton, Heidi Grassley, Alan Keohane, Ella Milroy, Naomi Peck, Paul Young

Illustrators Chris Orr & Associates, Lee Redmond
Maps Martin Darlison, Tom Coulson,

Encompass Graphics Ltd

AT DORLING KINDERSLEY
Senior Publishing Manager Louise Bostock Lang
Publishing Manager Kate Poole
Senior Art Editor Marisa Renzullo
Art Director Gillian Allan
Publisher Douglas Amrine
Cartography Co-ordinator Casper Morris
DTP Jason Little, Conrad van Dyk
Production Joanna Bull
Design and Editorial Assistance Marta Bescos, Sonal Bhatt, Mariana Evmolpidou, Anna Freiberger, Mary-Ann Gallagher, Lydia Halliday, Integrated Publishing Solutions, Claire Jones, Juliet Kenny, Jude Ledger, Nicola Malone, Alison McGill, Caroline Mead, Pete Quinlan, Quadrum Solutions, Mani Ramaswamy, Julie Thompson, Sylvia Tombesi-Walton, Hugo Wilkinson, Word On Spain

Picture Credits

Placement Key; t-top; tc-top centre; tr-top right; cla-centre left above; ca-centre above; cra-centre right above; cl-centre left; c-centre; cr-centre right; clb-centre left below; cb-cent-re below; crb-centre right below; bl-below left; bc below centre; br below right.

Works of art have been reproduced with permission of the following copyright holders: *Homea* 1974 Eduardo Arranz Bravo © ADAGP, Paris and DACS, London 2006 28br; *Rainy Taxi* Salvador Dalí © Kingdom of Spain, Gala–Salvador Dalí Foundation, DACS–London 2006 119b.

The publishers would like to thank the following individuals, companies and picture libraries for permission to reproduce their photographs: AGUA RESTAURANT: 101tl; AISA, Barcelona: 1c, 11c, 30tl, 30tr, 30c, 31bl, 31tr, 31cr, 31br, 118c; ALAMY IMAGES: ICSDB 131tr; Melvyn Longhurst 61bl; John Ferro Sims 78tr; BARCELONA TURISME: 61tr; 110c; Espai d'Imatge 64c; 65b; Jordi Trullas 64t; CA L'ISIDRE: 87tl; CAL PEP: 79t; CASA ALFONSO: 108tr; CASA CALVET: 109tl; CINC SENTITS: 44tl; CLUB CATWALK: 100tl; COMERÇ 24: 44tr. DANIEL CAMPI: 146tl. EGO GALLERY: 84tl; EL PIANO: 114tr; ELEPHANT CLUB: 46ca, 46tc; FUNDACIÓN FRANCISCO GODIA: 104tl; FUNDACIÓN JOAN MIRO: Pagès Catalá al cla de Luna Joan Miró © Sucession Miró/ADAGP, Paris and DACS, London 2006 22bl; Tapis de al Fundacio Joan Miró © Sucession Miró/ADAGP, Paris and DACS, London 2006 22–3c; Home i Dona Davant un Munt d'Excrement Joan Miró © Succession Miró/ADAGP, Paris and DACS, London 2006 23tr; GAI FRIA DELS ANGELS: 84tl; GETTY IMAGES: Tony Stone/Luc Beziat 48c; GRUPO TRAGALUZ: 42bl, 107tr, 143tl; GUANTERIA Y COMPLEMENTOS ALONSO: 75tr. MANUEL HUGUET: 128–9. IMAGE-STATE: AGE Fotostock 141tr;

Courtesy of CAIXA CATALUNYA: 137tl; JAMBOREE: 47tr, 77tr; LA MANUAL ALPARGAT-ERA: 75tc; MON DE MONES: 114tl; MUSEU NACIONAL d'ART DE CATALUNYA: 18b; 19tl; 19tr; 19ca; 19b; 92–93; MUSEU d'ART CONTEMPORANI (MACBA): 28tl; 28cl; 29tl; 28–29c MUSEU PICA-SSO: Hombre con Boina Pablo Picasso © Sucession Picasso/DACS, London 2006 24b; La Espera Pablo Picasso © Sucession Picasso/DACS, London 2006 24–5; El Loco Pablo Picasso © Sucession Picasso/DACS, London 2006 25t; Sketch for Guernica Pablo Picasso © Sucession Picasso/DACS, London 2006 25cr; Las Meninas Pablo Picasso © Sucession Picasso/ DACS, London 2006 25b; MIRIAM NEGRE: 44tr; 46bl; 58bl; 114l; 144r; 112b; 113t; 117; 139r; OTTOZUTZ GROUP: 107tl; PARC ZOO-LOGIC: 16bl; FRANCISCO FERN-ANDEZ PRIFTO: 76tl; 76tr; PRISMA, Barcelona: 66b; 125t; 126t; RAZZMATAZZ: Albert Uriach 47cl; 100tr; RENFE: 132tr; SALA BECOOL: 46bl; SIDECAR FACTORY CLUB: Moises Torne (motobi@terra.es) 77tl; ZELIG: 86tl; ZENTRAUS: 86tr.

All other images are © Dorling Kindersley. For further information see www.dkimages.com.

English-Catalan Phrase Book

In an Emergency

Help!	**Auxili!**	ow-**gzee**-lee
Stop!	**Pareu!**	**pah**-reh-oo
Call a doctor!	**Telefoneu un metge!**	teh-leh-fon-**eh**-oo oon **meh**-djuh
Call an ambulance!	**Telefoneu una ambulància!**	teh-leh-fon-**eh**-oo oo-nah ahm-boo-**lahn**-see-ah
Call the police!	**Telefoneu la policía**	teh-leh-fon-**eh**-oo lah poh-lee-**see**-ah
Call the fire brigade!	**Telefoneu els bombers!**	teh-leh-fon-eh-oo uhlz boom-**behs**
Where is the nearest telephone?	**On és el telèfon més proper?**	on-ehs uhl tuh-leh-fon mehs proo-**peh**
Where is the nearest hospital?	**On és l'hospital més proper?**	on-ehs looss-pee-tahl mehs proo-**peh**

Communication Essentials

Yes	**Sí**	see
No	**No**	noh
Please	**Sí us plau**	sees plah-oo
Thank you	**Gràcies**	**grah**-see-uhs
Excuse me	**Perdoni**	puhr-**thoh**-nee
Hello	**Hola**	**oh**-lah
Goodbye	**Adéu**	ah-they-**oo**
Good night	**Bona nit**	bo-nah **neet**
Morning	**El matí**	uhl muh-**tee**
Afternoon	**La tarda**	lah **tahr**-thuh
Evening	**El vespre**	uhl **vehs**-pruh
Yesterday	**Ahir**	ah-**ee**
Today	**Avui**	uh-voo-ee
Tomorrow	**Demà**	duh-**mah**
Here	**Aquí**	uh-**kee**
There	**Allà**	uh-**lyah**
What?	**Què?**	keh
When?	**Quan?**	kwahn
Why?	**Per què?**	puhr keh
Where?	**On?**	ohn

Useful Phrases

How are you?	**Com està?**	kom uhs-**tah**
Very well, thank you.	**Molt bé, gràcies.**	mol beh **grah**-see-uhs
Pleased to meet you.	**Molt de gust.**	mol duh **goost**
See you soon.	**Fins aviat.**	feenz uhv-**yat**
That's fine.	**Està bé.**	uhs-**tah** beh
Where is/are . ?	**On és/són?**	ohn ehs/sohn
How far is it to?	**Quants metres/ kilòmetres hi ha d'aquí a ...?**	kwahnz meh-truhs/kee-**loh**-meh-truhs yah dah-**kee** uh
Which way to ...?	**Per on es va a ...?**	puhr **on** uhs **bah** ah
Do you speak English?	**Parla anglès?**	**par**-luh an-**glehs**
I don't understand	**No l'entenc.**	noh luhn-**teng**

Useful Words

Could you speak more slowly, please?	**Pot parlar més a poc a poc, si us plau?**	pot par-**lah** mehs pok uh pok sees plah-oo
I'm sorry.	**Ho sento.**	oo **sehn**-too

big	**gran**	gran
small	**petit**	puh-**teet**
hot	**calent**	kah-**len**
cold	**fred**	fred
good	**bo**	boh
bad	**dolent**	doo-**len**
enough	**bastant**	bahs-**tan**
well	**bé**	beh
open	**obert**	oo-**behr**
closed	**tancat**	tan-**kat**
left	**esquerra**	uhs-**kehr**-ruh
right	**dreta**	**dreh**-tuh
straight on	**recte**	**rehk**-tuh
near	**a prop**	uh prop
far	**lluny**	**lyoon**yuh
up/over	**a dalt**	uh **dahl**
down/under	**a baix**	uh **bah**-eeshh
early	**aviat**	uhv-**yat**
late	**tard**	tahrt
entrance	**entrada**	uhn-**trah**-thuh
exit	**sortida**	soor-**tee**-thuh
toilet	**lavabos/ serveis**	luh-**vah**-boos sehr-**beh**-ees
more	**més**	mess
less	**menys**	**men**yees

Shopping

How much does this cost?	**Quant costa això?**	kwahn kost ehs-**shoh**
I would like ...	**M'agradaria ...**	muh-**grah-thuh-ree**-ah
Do you have?	**Tenen?**	**tehn**-un
I'm just looking, thank you	**Només estic mirant, gràcies.**	noo-mess ehs-teek mee-**rahn grah**-see-uhs
Do you take credit cards?	**Accepten targes de crèdit?**	ak-**sehp**-tuhn tahr-**zhuhs** duh **kreh**-deet
What time do you open?	**A quina hora obren?**	ah **keen**-uh **oh**-ruh **oh**-bruhn
What time do you close?	**A quina hora tanquen?**	ah **keen**-uh oh -ruh **tan**-kuhn
This one.	**Aquest**	ah-**ket**
That one.	**Aquell**	ah-**kehl**
expensive	**car**	kahr
cheap	**bé de preu/ barat**	beh thuh preh-oo/bah-**rat**
size (clothes)	**talla/mida**	tah-lyah/**mee**-dah
size (shoes)	**número**	noo-mehr-oo
white	**blanc**	blang
black	**negre**	**neh**-gruh
red	**vermell**	vuhr-**mel**
yellow	**groc**	grok

English	Catalan	Pronunciation
green	verd	behrt
blue	blau	blah-oo
antique store	antiquari/ botiga d'antiguitats	an-tee-kwah-ree/ boo-tee-gah/dan-tee-ghee-tats
bakery	el forn	uhl forn
bank	el banc	uhl bang
book store	la llibreria	lah lyee-bruh-ree-ah
butcher's	la carnisseria	lah kahr-nee-suh-ree-uh
pastry shop	la pastisseria	lah pahs-tee-suh-ree-uh
chemist's	la farmàcia	lah fuhr-mah-see-ah
fishmonger's	la peixateria	lah peh-shuh-tuh-ree-uh
greengrocer's	la fruiteria	lah froo-ee-tuh-ree-uh
grocer's	la botiga de queviures	lah boo-tee-guh duh keh-vee-oo-ruhs
hairdresser's	la perruqueria	lah peh-roo-kuh-ree-uh
market	el mercat	uhl muhr-kat
newsagent's	el quiosc de premsa	uhl kee-ohsk duh prem-suh
post office	l'oficina de correus	loo-fee-see-nuh duh koo-reh-oos
shoe store	la sabateria	lah sah-bah-tuh-ree-uh
supermarket	el supermercat	uhl soo-puhr-muhr-kat
tobacconist's	l'estanc	luhs-tang
travel agency	l'agència de viatges	la jen-see-uh duh vee-ad-juhs

Sightseeing

art gallery	la galeria d' art	lah gah-luh-ree-yuh dart
cathedral	la catedral	lah kuh-tuh-thrahl
church	l'església	luhz-gleh-zee-uh
	la basílica	lah buh-zee-lee-kuh
garden	el jardí	uhl zhahr-dee
library	la biblioteca	lah bee-blee-oo-teh-kuh
museum	el museu	uhl moo-seh-oo
tourist information office	l'oficina de turisme	loo-fee-see-nuh thuh too-reez-muh
town hall	l'ajuntament	luh-djoon-tuh-men
closed for holiday	tancat per vacances	tan-kat puhr bah-kan-suhs
bus station	l'estació d'autobusos	luhs-tah-see-oh dow-toh-boo-zoos
railway station	l'estació de tren	luhs-tah-see-oh thuh tren

Staying in a Hotel

Do you have a vacant room?	¿Tenen una habitació lliure?	teh-nuhn oo-nuh ah-bee-tuh-see-oh lyuh-ruh
double room with double bed	habitació doble amb llit de matrimoni	ah-bee-tuh-see-oh doh-bluh am lyeet duh mah-tree-moh-nee
twin room	habitació amb dos llits/ amb llits individual	ah-bee-tuh-see-oh am dohs lyeets/ s am lyeets in-thee-vee-thoo-ahls
single room	habitació individual	ah-bee-tuh-see-oh een-dee-vee-thoo-ahl
room with a bath	habitació amb bany	ah-bee-tuh-see-oh am bahnyuh
shower	dutxa	doo-chuh
porter	el grum	uhl groom
key	la clau	lah klah-oo
I have a reservation	Tinc una habitació reservada	ting oo-nuh ah-bee-tuh-see-oh reh-sehr-vah-thah

Eating Out

Have you got a table for...	Tenen taula per...?	teh-nuhn tow-luh puhr
I would like to reserve a table.	Voldria reservar una taula.	vool-dree-uh reh-sehr-vahr oo-nuh tow-luh
The bill please	El compte, si us plau,	uhl kohm-tuh seus plah oo
I am a vegetarian	Sóc vegetarià/ vegetariana	sok buh-zhuh-tuh-ree-ah buh-zhuh-tuh-ree-ah-nah
waitress	cambrera	kam-breh ruh
waiter	cambrer	kam-breh
menu	la carta	lah kahr-tuh
fixed-price menu	menú del dia	muh-noo thuhl dee-uh
wine list	la carta de vins	ah kahr-tuh thuh veens
glass of water	un got d'aigua	oon got dah-ee-gwah
glass of wine	una copa de vi	oo-nuh ko-pah thuh vee
bottle	una ampolla	oo-nuh am-pol-yuh
knife	un ganivet	oon gun-ee-veht
fork	una forquilla	oo-nuh foor-keel-yuh
spoon	una cullera	oo-nuh kool-yeh-ruh
breakfast	l'esmorzar	les-moor-sah
lunch	el dinar	uhl dee-nah
dinner	el sopar	uhl soo-pah
main course	el primer plat	uhl pree-meh plat
starters	els entrants	uhlz ehn-tranz
dish of the day	el plat del dia	uhl plat duhl dee-uh
coffee	el cafè	uhl kah-feh
rare	poc fet	pok fet
medium	al punt	ahl poon
well done	molt fet	mol fet

Menu Decoder

Catalan	Pronunciation	English
l'aigua mineral	lah-ee-gwuh mee-nuh-**rahl**	mineral water
sense gas/ amb gas	sen-zuh gas/ am gas	still/sparkling
al forn	ahl **forn**	baked
l'all	lahl_yuh	garlic
l'arròs	lahr-**roz**	rice
les botifarres	lahs **boo**-tee-fah-rahs	sausages
la carn	lah **karn**	meat
la ceba	lah **seh**-buh	onion
la cervesa	lah-sehr-**ve**-sah	beer
l'embotit	lum-boo-**teet**	cold meat
el filet	uhl fee-**let**	sirloin
el formatge	uhl for-**mah**-djuh	cheese
fregit	freh-**zheet**	fried
la fruita	lah froo-**ee**-tah	fruit
els fruits secs	uhlz froo-**eets** seks	nuts
les gambes	lahs **gam**-bus	prawns
el gelat	uhl djuh-**lat**	ice cream
la llagosta	lah lyah-**gos**-tah	lobster
la llet	lah **lyet**	milk
la llimona	lah lyee-**moh**-nah	lemon
la llimonada	lah lyee-moh-**nah**-tuh	lemonade
la mantega	lah mahn-**teh**-gah	butter
el marisc	uhl muh-**reesk**	seafood
la menestra	lah muh-**nehs**-truh	vegetable stew
l'oli	**loll**-ee	oil
les olives	luhs oo-**lee**-vuhs	olives
l'ou	**loh**-oo	egg
el pa	uhl **pah**	bread
el pastís	uhl pahs-**tees**	pie/cake
les patates	lahs pah-**tah**-tuhs	potatoes
el pebre	uhl **peh**-bruh	pepper
el peix	uhl **pehsh**	fish
el pernil	uhl puhr-**neel**	cured ham
salat serrà	suh-**lat** sehr-**rah**	
el plàtan	uhl **plah**-tun	banana
el pollastre	uhl poo-**lyah**-struh	chicken
la poma	la **poh**-mah	apple
el porc	uhl **pohr**	pork
les postres	lahs **pohs**-truhs	dessert
rostit	rohs-**teet**	roast
la sal	lah **sahl**	salt
la salsa	lah **sahl**-suh	sauce
les salsitxes	lahs sahl-**see**-chuhs	sausages
sec	**sehk**	dry
la sopa	lah **soh**-puh	soup
el sucre	uhl-**soo**-kruh	sugar
la taronja	lah tuh-**rohn**-djuh	orange
el te	uhl teh	tea
les torrades	lahs too-**rah**-thuhs	toast
la vedella	lah veh-**theh**-lyuh	beef
el vi blanc	uhl **bee** blang	white wine
el vi negre	uhl bee **neh**-gruh	red wine
el vi rosat	uhl bee roo-**zaht**	rosé wine
el vinagre	uhl bee-**nah**-gruh	vinegar
el xai/el be	uhl **shah**ee/uhl beh	lamb
la xocolata	lah shoo-koo-**lah**-tuh	chocolate
el xoriç	uhl shoo-**rees**	red sausage

Numbers

	Catalan	Pronunciation
0	zero	**seh**-roo
1	un (masc)	oon
	una (fem)	**oon**-uh
2	dos (masc)	dohs
	dues (fem)	**doo**-uhs
3	tres	trehs
4	quatre	**kwa**-truh
5	cinc	seeng
6	sis	sees
7	set	set
8	vuit	**voo**-eet
9	nou	**noh**-oo
10	deu	**deh**-oo
11	onze	**on**-zuh
12	dotze	**doh**-dzuh
13	tretze	**treh**-dzuh
14	catorze	kah-**tohr**-dzuh
15	quinze	**keen**-zuh
16	setze	**set**-zuh
17	disset	dee-**set**
18	divuit	dee-voo-**eet**
19	dinou	dee-**noh**-oo
20	vint	been
21	vint-i-un	been-tee-**oon**
22	vint-i-dos	been-tee-**dohs**
30	trenta	**tren**-tah
31	trenta-un	**tren**-tah oon
40	quaranta	kwuh-**ran**-tah
50	cinquanta	seen-**kwahn**-tah
60	seixanta	seh-ee-**shan**-tah
70	setanta	seh-**tan**-tah
80	vuitanta	voo-ee-**tan**-tah
90	noranta	noh-**ran**-tah
100	cent	sen
101	cent un	sent oon
102	cent dos	sen dohs
200	dos-cents (masc)	dohs-**sens**
	dues-centes (fem)	doo-uhs sen-tuhs
300	tres-cents	trehs-**senz**
400	quatre-cents	kwah-truh-**senz**
500	cinc-cents	seeng-**senz**
600	sis-cents	sees-**senz**
700	set-cents	set-**senz**
800	vuit-cents	voo-eet-**senz**
900	nou-cents	noh-oo-**cenz**
1,000	mil	meel
1,001	mil un	meel oon

Time

	Catalan	Pronunciation
one minute	un minut	oon mee-**noot**
one hour	una hora	oo-nuh **oh**-ruh
half an hour	mitja hora	**mee**-juh **oh**-ruh
Monday	dilluns	dee-**lyoonz**
Tuesday	dimarts	dee-**marts**
Wednesday	dimecres	dee-**meh**-kruhs
Thursday	dijous	dee-**zhoh**-oos
Friday	divendres	dee-**ven**-druhs
Saturday	dissabte	dee-**sab**-tuh
Sunday	diumenge	dee-oo-**men**-juh